NMTA 13 Reading
Teacher Certification Exam

By: Sharon Wynne, M.S
Southern Connecticut State University

XAMonline, INC.
Boston

Copyright © 2007 XAMonline, Inc.
All rights reserved. No part of the material protected by this copyright notice may be reproduced or utilized in any form or by any means, electronic or mechanical, including photocopying, recording or by any information storage and retrievable system, without written permission from the copyright holder.

To obtain permission(s) to use the material from this work for any purpose including workshops or seminars, please submit a written request to:

XAMonline, Inc.
21 Orient Ave.
Melrose, MA 02176
Toll Free 1-800-509-4128
Email: info@xamonline.com
Web www.xamonline.com
Fax: 1-781-662-9268

Library of Congress Cataloging-in-Publication Data

Wynne, Sharon A.
    Reading 13: Teacher Certification / Sharon A. Wynne. -2nd ed. ISBN 978-1-58197-760-8
    1. Reading 13.   2. Study Guides.   3. NMTA
    4. Teachers' Certification & Licensure.   5. Careers

Disclaimer:

The opinions expressed in this publication are the sole works of XAMonline and were created independently from the National Education Association, Educational Testing Service, or any State Department of Education, National Evaluation Systems or other testing affiliates.

Between the time of publication and printing, state specific standards as well as testing formats and website information may change that is not included in part or in whole within this product. Sample test questions are developed by XAMonline and reflect similar content as on real tests; however, they are not former tests. XAMonline assembles content that aligns with state standards but makes no claims nor guarantees teacher candidates a passing score. Numerical scores are determined by testing companies such as NES or ETS and then are compared with individual state standards. A passing score varies from state to state.

Printed in the United States of America   œ-1

NMTA: Reading 13
ISBN: 978-1-58197-760-8

TEACHER CERTIFICATION STUDY GUIDE

TABLE OF CONTENTS

SUBAREA I.   **PLANNING, MANAGING, AND ORGANIZING READING INSTRUCTION BASED ON ONGOING ASSESSMENT**

COMPETENCY 1.0 THE TEACHER UNDERSTANDS TECHNIQUES OF READING ASSESSMENT 1

SKILL 1.1   Demonstrating knowledge of how to collect and use reading assessment data from multiple measures on an ongoing basis 1

SKILL 1.2   Recognizing how to select and administer informal reading assessments in all areas of reading 3

SKILL 1.3   Recognizing how to analyze the results of informal and formal reading assessments to plan and improve curriculum and instruction for all students, including students who are learning English as a second language 9

SKILL 1.4   Demonstrating knowledge of formal and informal methods for determining students' independent, instructional, and frustration levels of reading 13

COMPETENCY 2.0 THE TEACHER UNDERSTANDS HOW TO USE AND COMMUNICATE THE RESULTS OF READING ASSESSMENTS 14

SKILL 2.1   Analyzing evidence to determine whether a student is performing below, at, or above expected levels of performance based on grade-appropriate reading standards 14

SKILL 2.2   Recognizing when a student needs additional help within the classroom in one or more areas of reading 17

SKILL 2.3   Recognizing when a student needs additional help from other school services 18

SKILL 2.4   Applying knowledge of reading assessments to analyze and support the reading development of students who are learning English as a second language 18

SKILL 2.5   Demonstrating knowledge of effective methods for communicating assessment results and reading progress to students, parents, teachers, and support personnel 19

READING

COMPETENCY 3.0 THE TEACHER UNDERSTANDS FACTORS INVOLVED IN PLANNING, ORGANIZING, AND MANAGING READING INSTRUCTION 20

SKILL 3.1 Demonstrating knowledge of the components of a balanced, comprehensive reading program and the interrelationships among these components 20

SKILL 3.2 Identifying methods for planning instruction based on grade appropriate standards of reading performance 21

SKILL 3.3 Identifying strategies for addressing individual differences among readers 22

SKILL 3.4 Recognizing how to select appropriate instructional materials, including current technology, to promote the reading development of all students, including students who are learning English as a second language 25

SKILL 3.5 Demonstrating knowledge of strategies for creating a positive and supportive environment for literacy learning 29

SKILL 3.6 Recognizing the importance of using a wide variety of high quality literature for children and young adults 31

COMPETENCY 4.0 THE TEACHER UNDERSTANDS THE ROLES OF REFLECTION, SELF-EVALUATION, COLLABORATION, AND PROFESSIONAL DEVELOPMENT IN READING INSTRUCTION 33

SKILL 4.1 Recognizing the importance of engaging in an ongoing program of personal professional development related to reading instruction 33

SKILL 4.2 Demonstrating familiarity with professional organizations and resources that provide opportunities and support for professional development related to reading instruction 34

SKILL 4.3 Demonstrating knowledge of self-assessment techniques to help reading professionals evaluate and adjust their own performance as classroom teachers 35

SKILL 4.4 Identifying ways to collaborate effectively with colleagues to promote professional growth and to meet the reading needs of all students 36

TEACHER CERTIFICATION STUDY GUIDE

SKILL 4.5　Recognizing current reading policy and legislation that affect reading instruction in New Mexico 37

SUBAREA II.　DEVELOPING PHONOLOGICAL AND OTHER LINGUISTIC PROCESSES RELATED TO READING

COMPETENCY 5.0　THE TEACHER UNDERSTANDS THE ROLE OF PHONEMIC AWARENESS IN EMERGENT LITERACY AND DEMONSTRATES KNOWLEDGE OF STRATEGIES FOR PROMOTING PHONEMIC AWARENESS 38

SKILL 5.1　Analyzing the role of phonemic awareness in reading development 38

SKILL 5.2　Recognizing how to promote students' awareness of different levels of spoken language 39

SKILL 5.3　Demonstrating knowledge of various phonemic awareness skills 40

SKILL 5.4　Identifying explicit and implicit strategies for promoting and assessing the phonemic awareness skills of all students, including students who are learning English as a second language 44

SKILL 5.5　Identifying appropriate materials and activities to promote phonemic awareness 45

COMPETENCY 6.0 THE TEACHER UNDERSTANDS THE DEVELOPMENT OF CONCEPTS ABOUT PRINT 46

SKILL 6.1　Demonstrating knowledge of concepts about print 46

SKILL 6.2　Recognizing how concepts about print relate to other aspects of reading development 54

SKILL 6.3　Identifying appropriate materials and activities to provide effective instruction relating to concepts about print 55

SKILL 6.4　Demonstrating knowledge of strategies for selecting, designing, and using engaging materials and activities to help students recognize letter shapes and learn letter names 55

SKILL 6.5　Identifying strategies for assessing students' development of print concepts 57

COMPETENCY 7.0 THE TEACHER UNDERSTANDS PHONICS AND OTHER WORD IDENTIFICATION STRATEGIES 58

SKILL 7.1 Recognizing how to plan the sequence of phonics instruction to reflect increasing complexity of linguistic units 58

SKILL 7.2 Identifying instructional strategies, activities, and materials to teach students letter-sound correspondence, phonics generalizations, and the use of graphophonic cues to decode words in connected text 58

SKILL 7.3 Demonstrating knowledge of word identification strategies in addition to phonics, including structural analysis, morphemes, and use of semantic, syntactic, and contextual cues 62

SKILL 7.4 Recognizing the importance of rapid, automatic decoding in reading fluency and comprehension 78

SKILL 7.5 Demonstrating knowledge of strategies for helping students master sight words through multiple and varied reading and writing experiences 79

TEACHER CERTIFICATION STUDY GUIDE

SUBAREA III.	DEVELOPING READING COMPREHENSION AND PROMOTING INDEPENDENT READING

COMPETENCY 8.0 THE TEACHER UNDERSTANDS FACTORS AFFECTING READING COMPREHENSION AND STRATEGIES FOR PROMOTING READING COMPREHENSION 85

SKILL 8.1 Demonstrating knowledge of factors affecting reading comprehension 85

SKILL 8.2 Recognizing ways to activate and develop students' prior knowledge and experience related to reading 90

SKILL 8.3 Identifying techniques to help readers self-monitor their comprehension 91

SKILL 8.4 Identifying appropriate prereading and postreading strategies to help students construct meaning 92

SKILL 8.5 Identifying techniques to promote the reading comprehension skills and strategies of students who are learning English as a second language 92

COMPETENCY 9.0 THE TEACHER UNDERSTANDS STRATEGIES FOR PROMOTING LITERARY RESPONSE AND ANALYSIS 93

SKILL 9.1 Recognizing a variety of instructional approaches and activities for helping students apply comprehension strategies when reading literary texts 93

SKILL 9.2 Identifying strategies for developing and assessing students' responses to literature 102

SKILL 9.3 Demonstrating knowledge of the elements of literary analysis and criticism 103

SKILL 9.4 Identifying appropriate literature and related activities to meet the reading needs of all students, including students who are learning English as a second language 103

TEACHER CERTIFICATION STUDY GUIDE

COMPETENCY 10.0 THE TEACHER UNDERSTANDS STRATEGIES FOR PROMOTING CONTENT-AREA LITERACY 105

SKILL 10.1 Identifying strategies for improving students' comprehension of content-area texts 105

SKILL 10.2 Recognizing different types and functions of texts and different purposes for reading 106

SKILL 10.3 Demonstrating knowledge of strategies for helping students identify and analyze common text structures 107

SKILL 10.4 Recognizing how to apply reading strategies for different reading purposes 110

SKILL 10.5 Demonstrating knowledge of study skills to help readers locate, analyze, and recall information from reference materials, content-area texts, graphs, charts, and maps 117

COMPETENCY 11.0 THE TEACHER UNDERSTANDS STRATEGIES FOR PROMOTING STUDENTS' INDEPENDENT READING 118

SKILL 11.1 Recognizing ways to motivate all students to read independently at school and at home 118

SKILL 11.2 Identifying appropriate methods for determining students' reading interests and helping students develop selection criteria for independent reading 119

SKILL 11.3 Demonstrating knowledge of strategies for encouraging students who are learning English as a second language to read independently 120

SKILL 11.4 Identifying strategies for selecting and organizing a range of reading materials at various levels of difficulty 120

SUBAREA IV. SUPPORTING READING THROUGH ORAL AND WRITTEN LANGUAGE DEVELOPMENT

COMPETENCY 12.0 THE TEACHER UNDERSTANDS THE RELATIONSHIPS AMONG READING, WRITING, AND ORAL LANGUAGE, AND USES INTERRELATED INSTRUCTION IN THESE AREAS TO PROMOTE READING PROFICIENCY 121

SKILL 12.1 Applying knowledge of the relationships among reading, writing, listening, and speaking to reinforce learning across the curriculum for all students, including students who are learning English as a second language 121

SKILL 12.2 Identifying oral language activities to enhance students' reading development 121

SKILL 12.3 Recognizing how to provide authentic, relevant writing opportunities that enhance students' development as readers 122

SKILL 12.4 Recognizing ways in which oral language skills can be transferred to written language 123

COMPETENCY 13.0 THE TEACHER UNDERSTANDS STRATEGIES FOR PROMOTING VOCABULARY DEVELOPMENT 125

SKILL 13.1 Recognizing how to help students expand their vocabulary knowledge and skills by listening to and reading a wide variety of texts 125

SKILL 13.2 Demonstrating knowledge of criteria for selecting appropriate vocabulary words 130

SKILL 13.3 Demonstrating knowledge of instructional activities and materials to promote vocabulary development 132

SKILL 13.4 Applying knowledge of strategies for gaining and extending meaning from unfamiliar words in connected text 133

COMPETENCY 14.0 THE TEACHER UNDERSTANDS HOW KNOWLEDGE OF ENGLISH LANGUAGE STRUCTURES AND CONVENTIONS RELATES TO THE DEVELOPMENT OF READING PROFICIENCY 136

SKILL 14.1   Identifying strategies for helping students understand the similarities and differences between language structures used in spoken and written English.. 136

SKILL 14.2   Applying knowledge of strategies for promoting students' understanding of basic syntax and semantics 137

SKILL 14.3   Identifying strategies for helping students apply knowledge of English grammar, spelling, and other language conventions in reading, writing, listening, and speaking contexts 138

SKILL 14.4   Identifying methods for assessing students' understanding of English language structures and conventions 139

COMPETENCY 15.0 THE TEACHER UNDERSTANDS STRATEGIES FOR SUPPORTING AND PROMOTING THE READING DEVELOPMENT OF STUDENTS WHO ARE LEARNING ENGLISH AS A SECOND LANGUAGE 140

SKILL 15.1   Recognizing how to interrelate elements of language arts instruction to support the reading development of students who are learning English as a second language 140

SKILL 15.2   Demonstrating familiarity with and cultural sensitivity to the ways in which languages differ 141

SKILL 15.3   Demonstrating an understanding of the factors and processes involved in transferring literacy competencies from one language to another 142

SKILL 15.4   Demonstrating familiarity with strategies for promoting the transfer of language skills from one language to another 142

TEACHER CERTIFICATION STUDY GUIDE

Glossary 143

Directory of Theorists and Researchers 153

Bibliography of Print Resources 159

Tools for teaching and testing 172

Sample Test 176

Answer Key 208

Rationales for Sample Questions 209

Constructed Response Questions 218

Tips and Reflections 222

Additional Citations 223

TEACHER CERTIFICATION STUDY GUIDE

Great Study and Testing Tips!

What to study in order to prepare for the subject assessments is the focus of this study guide but equally important is *how* you study.

You can increase your chances of truly mastering the information by taking some simple, but effective steps.

Study Tips:

1. Some foods aid the learning process. Foods such as milk, nuts, seeds, rice, and oats help your study efforts by releasing natural memory enhancers called CCKs (*cholecystokinin*) composed of *tryptophan*, *choline*, and *phenylalanine*. All of these chemicals enhance the neurotransmitters associated with memory. Before studying, try a light, protein-rich meal of eggs, turkey, and fish. All of these foods release the memory enhancing chemicals. The better the connections, the more you comprehend.

Likewise, before you take a test, stick to a light snack of energy boosting and relaxing foods. A glass of milk, a piece of fruit, or some peanuts all release various memory-boosting chemicals and help you to relax and focus on the subject at hand.

2. Learn to take great notes. A by-product of our modern culture is that we have grown accustomed to getting our information in short doses (i.e. TV news sound bites or USA Today style newspaper articles.)

Consequently, we've subconsciously trained ourselves to assimilate information better in neat little packages. If your notes are scrawled all over the paper, it fragments the flow of the information. Strive for clarity. Newspapers use a standard format to achieve clarity. Your notes can be much clearer through use of proper formatting. A very effective format is called the *"Cornell Method."*

> Take a sheet of loose-leaf lined notebook paper and draw a line all the way down the paper about 1-2" from the left-hand edge.
>
> Draw another line across the width of the paper about 1-2" up from the bottom. Repeat this process on the reverse side of the page.

Look at the highly effective result. You have ample room for notes, a left hand margin for special emphasis items or inserting supplementary data from the textbook, a large area at the bottom for a brief summary, and a little rectangular space for just about anything you want.

READING

3. Get the concept then the details. Too often we focus on the details and don't gather an understanding of the concept. However, if you simply memorize only dates, places, or names, you may well miss the whole point of the subject.

A key way to understand things is to put them in your own words. If you are working from a textbook, automatically summarize each paragraph in your mind. If you are outlining text, don't simply copy the author's words.

Rephrase them in your own words. You remember your own thoughts and words much better than someone else's, and subconsciously tend to associate the important details to the core concepts.

4. Ask Why? Pull apart written material paragraph by paragraph and don't forget the captions under the illustrations.

Example: If the heading is "Stream Erosion", flip it around to read "Why do streams erode?" Then answer the questions.

If you train your mind to think in a series of questions and answers, not only will you learn more, but it also helps to lessen the test anxiety because you are used to answering questions.

5. Read for reinforcement and future needs. Even if you only have 10 minutes, put your notes or a book in your hand. Your mind is similar to a computer; you have to input data in order to have it processed. *By reading, you are creating the neural connections for future retrieval.* The more times you read something, the more you reinforce the learning of ideas.

Even if you don't fully understand something on the first pass, *your mind stores much of the material for later recall.*

6. Relax to learn so go into exile. Our bodies respond to an inner clock called biorhythms. Burning the midnight oil works well for some people, but not everyone.

If possible, set aside a particular place to study that is free of distractions. Shut off the television, cell phone, and pager and exile your friends and family during your study period.

If you really are bothered by silence, try background music. Light classical music at a low volume has been shown to aid in concentration over other types. Music that evokes pleasant emotions without lyrics is highly suggested. Try just about anything by Mozart. It relaxes you.

7. **Use arrows not highlighters.** At best, it's difficult to read a page full of yellow, pink, blue, and green streaks. Try staring at a neon sign for a while and you'll soon see that the horde of colors obscure the message.

A quick note, a brief dash of color, an underline, and an arrow pointing to a particular passage is much clearer than a horde of highlighted words.

8. **Budget your study time.** Although you shouldn't ignore any of the material, *allocate your available study time in the same ratio that topics may appear on the test.*

TEACHER CERTIFICATION STUDY GUIDE

Testing Tips:

1. <u>Get smart, play dumb</u>. Don't read anything into the question. Don't make an assumption that the test writer is looking for something else than what is asked. Stick to the question as written and don't read extra things into it.

2. <u>Read the question and all the choices *twice* before answering the question</u>. You may miss something by not carefully reading, and then re-reading both the question and the answers.

If you really don't have a clue as to the right answer, leave it blank on the first time through. Go on to the other questions, as they may provide a clue as to how to answer the skipped questions.

If later on, you still can't answer the skipped ones . . . *Guess.* The only penalty for guessing is that you *might* get it wrong. Only one thing is certain; if you don't put anything down, you will get it wrong!

3. <u>Turn the question into a statement</u>. Look at the way the questions are worded. The syntax of the question usually provides a clue. Does it seem more familiar as a statement rather than as a question? Does it sound strange?

By turning a question into a statement, you may be able to spot if an answer sounds right, and it may also trigger memories of material you have read.

4. <u>Look for hidden clues</u>. It's actually very difficult to compose multiple-foil (choice) questions without giving away part of the answer in the options presented.

In most multiple-choice questions you can often readily eliminate one or two of the potential answers. This leaves you with only two real possibilities and automatically your odds go to Fifty-Fifty for very little work.

5. <u>Trust your instincts</u>. For every fact that you have read, you subconsciously retain something of that knowledge. On questions that you aren't really certain about, go with your basic instincts. **Your first impression on how to answer a question is usually correct.**

6. <u>Mark your answers directly on the test booklet</u>. Don't bother trying to fill in the optical scan sheet on the first pass through the test.

Just be very careful not to miss-mark your answers when you eventually transcribe them to the scan sheet.

7. <u>Watch the clock</u>! You have a set amount of time to answer the questions. Don't get bogged down trying to answer a single question at the expense of 10 questions you can more readily answer.

READING

TEACHER CERTIFICATION STUDY GUIDE

Foundations of Reading

"Any child, who doesn't learn how to read early and well, will not easily master other skills and knowledge and is unlikely to ever flourish in school or in life."
Reading is Rocket Science, American Federation of Teachers

"If our teaching of reading is to be an art, we need to draw from all we know, think and believe in order to create something beautiful."
Lucy Calkins

This guide was developed to serve the needs of test takers on the PreK-6 level who are preparing for the Foundations of Reading certification test. The quotes which introduce this work point to the crucial nature and significance of effective teaching of reading for our children and our nation's future.

The competencies and skills shared in this guide are also intended to support the educator new to reading certification, in ongoing teaching and learning in Reading. Therefore, sample strategies, web resources, student trade books, picture book citations, and explanations of ready-to-use practices are included.

This guide had a specified page limit and is designed for immediate use. The web resources and bibliographies provided will allow the reader to keep up with new research or investigate a particular strategy, referenced theorist, or term in a deeper, more detailed fashion. In addition, there is in the Appendix, a dictionary of words and terms essential to one's knowledge base as a reading teacher. Yet another study guide is a directory of key reading theorists included for your use as well.

It is my hope that this study guide will merit placement in your home or on your classroom professional library shelf for use as you begin your teaching career. Enjoy and share with your colleagues and parents, as we work together to nurture lifelong readers and writers.

Please let XAMonline know how you are able to use this guide to help you in your teacher certification experience and in your ongoing or future teaching and learning.

TEACHER CERTIFICATION STUDY GUIDE

SUBAREA I. PLANNING, MANAGING, AND ORGANIZING READING INSTRUCTION BASED ON ONGOING ASSESSMENT

COMPETENCY 1.0 THE TEACHER UNDERSTANDS TECHNIQUES OF READING ASSESSMENT.

SKILL 1.1 Demonstrating knowledge of how to collect and use reading assessment data from multiple measures on an ongoing basis

The Use of Data and Ongoing Reading Assessment to Adjust Instruction to Meet Students' Reading Needs

Assessment is the practice of collecting information about children's progress, and evaluation is the process of judging the children's responses to determine how well they are achieving particular goals or demonstrating reading skills.

Assessment and evaluation are intricately connected in the literacy classroom. Assessment is necessary because teachers need ways to determine what students are learning and how they are progressing. In addition, assessment can be a tool which can also help students take ownership of their own learning and become partners in their ongoing development as readers and writers. In this day of public accountability, clear, definite and reliable assessment creates confidence in public education.

There are two broad categories of assessment. **Informal** assessment utilizes observations and other non-standardized procedures to compile anecdotal and observation data/evidence of children's progress. It includes but is not limited to checklists, observations, and performance tasks. **Formal** assessment is composed of standardized tests and procedures carried out under circumscribed conditions. Formal Assessments include: state tests, standardized achievement tests, NAEP tests, and the like. To be effective, assessment should have the following characteristics:

I. It should be an ongoing process with the teacher making informal or formal assessments on an ongoing basis. The assessment should be a natural part of the instruction and not intrusive.

2. The most effective assessment is integrated into ongoing instruction. Throughout the teaching and learning day, the child's written, spoken and reading contributions to the class or lack thereof, need to and can be continually noted.

3. Assessment should reflect the child's actual reading and writing experiences. The child should be able to show that he or she can read and explain or react to a similar literary or expository work.

4. Assessment needs to be a collaborative and reflective process. Teachers can learn from what the children reveal about their own individual assessments. Children, even as early as grade two, should be supported by their teacher to continually and routinely ask themselves questions assessing their reading. They might ask: "Am I understanding what the author wanted to say?," " What can I do to improve my reading?" and "How can I use what I have read to learn more about this topic?"

Teachers need to be informed by their own professional observation AND by children's comments as they assess and customize instruction for children.

5. Quality assessment is multidimensional and may include but not be limited to samples of writings, student retellings, running records, anecdotal teacher observations, self-evaluations, and records of independent reading. From this multidimensional data, the teacher can derive a consistent level of performance and design additional instruction that will enhance the child's reading performance.

6. Assessment must take into account children's age and ethnic/cultural patterns of learning.

7. Assess to teach children from their strengths, not their weaknesses. Find out what reading behaviors children demonstrate well and then design instruction to support those behaviors.

8. Assessment should be part of children's learning process and not done TO them, but rather done WITH them.

TEACHER CERTIFICATION STUDY GUIDE

SKILL 1.2 Recognizing how to select and administer informal reading assessments in all areas of reading

Characteristics and Uses of Criterion-referenced and Norm-referenced Tests to Assess Reading Development and Identify Reading Difficulties

Criterion-referenced – tests where the children are measured against criteria or guidelines which are uniform for all the test takers. Therefore by definition, no special questions, formats or considerations are made for the test taker who is either from a different linguistic/cultural background or is already identified as a struggling reader/writer. On a criterion-referenced test, it is possible that a child test taker can score 100% because the child may have actually been exposed to all of the concepts taught and mastered them. A child's score on such a test would indicate which of the concepts have already been taught and what he or she needs additional review or support to master.

Two criterion-referenced tests that are commonly used to assess children's reading achievement are the Diagnostic Indicators of Basic Early Literacy Skills (DIBELS) and the Stanford Achievement Test. DIBELS measures progress in literacy from kindergarten to grade three. It can be downloaded from the Internet free at dibels.uoregon.edu. The Stanford is designed to measure individual children's achievement in key school subjects. Subtests covering various reading skills are part of this test. Both DIBELS and the Stanford Achievement Test are group-administered.

DEGREES OF READING POWER (DRP) –This test is targeted to assess how well children understand the meaning of written text in real life situations. This test is supposed to measure the process of children's reading, not the products of reading such as identifying the main idea and author's purpose.

CTPIII- This is a criterion-referenced test which measures verbal and quantitative ability in grades 3-12. It is targeted to help differentiate among the most capable students, i.e., those who rank above the 80th percentile on other standardized tests. This is a test that emphasizes higher order thinking skills and process-related reading comprehension questions.

Norm-referenced –test in which the children are measured against one another. Scores on this test are reported in percentiles. Each percentile indicates the percent of the testing population whose scores were lower than or the same as a particular child's score. Percentile is defined as a score on a scale of 100 showing the percentage of a distribution that is equal to it or below it. This type of state standardized norm-referenced test is being used in most districts today in response to the No Child Left Behind Act. While this type of test does not help tract the individual reader's progress in his/her ongoing reading development, it does permit comparisons across groups.

READING

There are many more standardized norm-referenced tests to assess children's reading than there are criterion-referenced. In these tests, scores are based on how well a child does compared to others, usually on the local, state and national level. IF the norming groups on the tests are reflective of the children being tested (e.g. same spread of minority, low income, gifted students), the results are more trustworthy.

One of the best known norm-referenced test is the Iowa Test of Basic Skills. It assesses student achievement in various school subjects and has several subtests in reading. Other examples of norm-referenced tests used around the country are the Metropolitan Achievement Tests, the Terra Nova-2, and the Stanford Diagnostic Reading Test-4. These are all group tests. An individual test that reading specialists use with students is the Woodcock Reading Mastery Test.

Concepts of Validity, Reliability, and Bias in Testing

Validity is how well a test measures what it is supposed to measure. Teacher made tests are therefore not generally extremely valid, although they may be an appropriate measure for the validity of the concept the teacher wants to assess for his/her own children's achievement.

Reliability is the consistency of the test. This is measured by whether the test will indicate the same score for the child who takes it more than once.

Bias in testing occurs when the information within the test or the information required to respond to a multiple choice question or constructed response (essay question on the test) is information that is not available to some test takers who come from a different cultural, ethnic, linguistic or socio-economic background than do the majority of the test takers. Since they have not had the same prior linguistic, social or cultural experiences that the majority of test takers have had, these test takers are at a disadvantage in taking the test and no matter what their actual mastery of the material taught by the teacher, can not address the "biased" questions. Generally other "non-biased" questions are given to them and eventually the biased questions are removed from the examination.

To solidify what might be abstract to the reader, on a recent reading test in my school system, the grade four reading comprehension multiple choice had some questions about the well known fairy tale of the gingerbread boy. These questions were simple and accessible for most of the children in the class. But two children who were recent new arrivals from the Dominican Republic had learned English there. They were reading on grade four level, but in their Dominican grade school, the story of the Gingerbread Boy was not a major one. Therefore a question about this story on the standardized reading test did demonstrate examiner bias and was not fair to these test takers.

The Characteristics and Uses of Formal and Informal Assessments

Informal Assessments

A running record of children's oral reading progress in the early grades K-3 is a pivotal informal assessment. It supports the teacher in deciding whether a book a child is reading is matched to his/her stage of reading development. In addition this assessment allows the teacher to analyze a child's miscues to see which cueing systems and strategies the child uses and to determine which other systems the child might use more effectively. Finally the running record offers a graphic account of a child's oral reading.

Generally, a teacher should maintain an annotated class notebook with pages set aside for all the children or individual notebooks for each child. One of the benefits of using running records as an informal assessment is that they can be used with any text and can serve as a tool for teaching, rather than an instrument to report on children's status in class.

Another good point about using running records is that they can be taken repeatedly and frequently by the teacher, so that the educator can truly observe a pattern of errors. This in turn provides the educator with sufficient information to analyze the child's reading over time. As any mathematician or scientist knows, the more samples of a process you gather over time, the more likely the teacher is to get an accurate picture of the child's reading needs.

Using the notations which Marie Clay developed and shared in her *An Observation Study of Early Literacy Achievement*, Sharon Taberski offers in her book, *On Solid Ground*, a lengthy walk through keeping a running record of children's reading. She writes in the child's miscue on the top line of her running record above the text word. Indeed she records all of the child's miscue attempts on the line above the text word. Sharon advises the teacher to make all the miscue notations as the child reads, since this allows the teacher to get additional information about how and why the child makes miscue choices. Additionally, the teacher should note, self corrections (coded SC) when the child is monitoring his/her own reading, crosschecks information, and uses additional information.

As part of the informal assessment of primary grade reading, it is important to record the child's word insertions, omissions, requests for help, and attempts to get the word. In informal assessment the rate of accuracy can be estimated by dividing the child's errors by the total words read.

READING

Results of a running record assessment can be used to select the best setting for the child's reading. If a child reads from 95%-100% correct, the child is ready for independent reading. If the child reads from 92% to 97% right, the child is ready for guided reading. Below 92% the child needs a read-aloud or shared reading activity. Note that these percentages are slightly different from those one would use to match books to readers.

One of the increasingly popular and meaningful forms of informal assessment is the compilation of the literacy portfolio. What is particularly compelling about this type of informal portfolio is that artists, television directors, authors, architects and photographers use portfolios in their careers and jobs. This is a most authentic format for documenting children's literacy growth over time. The portfolio is not only a significant professional informal assessment tool for the teacher, but a vehicle and format for the child reader to take ownership of his or her progress over time. It models a way of compiling one's reading and writing products as a lifelong learner, which is the ultimate goal of reading instruction.

Portfolios can include the following six categories of materials:

Work samples: These can include children's story maps, webs, K-W-L charts, pictures, illustrations, storyboards, and writings about the stories which they have read.

Records of independent Reading and Writing: These can include the children's journals, notebooks or logs of books read with the names of the authors, titles of the books, date completed, and pieces related to books completed or in progress.

Checklists and Surveys: These include checklists designed by the teacher for reading development, writing development, ownership checklists, and general interest surveys.

Self Evaluation Forms: These are the children's own evaluations of their reading and writing process framed in their own words. They can be simple templates with starting sentences such as: "I am really proud of the way I ...

I feel one of my strengths as a reader is _____

To improve the way I read aloud I need to _____

To improve my reading I should _____

Generally at the beginning of a child's portfolio in grade 3 or above there is a letter to the reader explaining the work that will be found in the portfolio and from fourth grade level up, children write a brief reflection detailing their feelings and judgments about their growth as readers and writers.

When teachers are maintaining the portfolios for mandated school administrative review, district review, or even for their own research, they often prepare portfolio summary sheets. These provide identifying data on the children and then a timeline of their review of the portfolio contents plus professional comments on the extent to which the portfolio documents satisfactory and ongoing growth in reading.

Portfolios can be used beneficially for child-teacher and of course, parent/teacher conversations to review the child's progress, discuss areas of strength, set future goals, make plans for future learning activities and evaluate what should remain in the portfolio and what needs to be cleared out for new materials.

Rubrics

Holistic scoring involves assessing a child's ability to construct meaning through writing. It uses a scale called a RUBRIC which can range from 0 to 4.

0- This indicates the piece can not be scored. It does not respond to the topic or is illegible.

1- The writing does respond to the topic, but does not cover it accurately.

2- This piece of writing does respond to the topic but lacks sufficient details or elaboration.

3- This piece fulfills the purpose of the writing assignment and has sufficient development (which refers to details, examples, and elaboration of ideas).

4- This response has the most details, best organization, and presents a well expressed reaction to the original writer's piece.

MISCUE ANALYSIS

This is a procedure that allows the teacher a look at the reading process. By definition, the miscue is an oral response different from the text being read. Sometimes miscues are also called unexpected responses or errors. By studying a student's miscues from an oral reading sample, the teacher can determine which cues and strategies the student is correctly using or not using in constructing meaning. Of course, the teacher can customize instruction to meet the needs of this particular student.

INFORMAL READING INVENTORIES (IRI)

These are a series of samples of texts prearranged in stages of increasing difficulty. Listening to children read through these inventories, the teacher can pinpoint their skill level and the additional concepts they need to work on.

Characteristics and uses of Group versus Individual Reading Assessments

In assessment, tests are used for different purposes. They have different dimensions or characteristics whether they are given individually or in a group and whether they are standardized or teacher-made. The chart below shows the relationships of these elements.

	Standardized	**Teacher-made**
Individual	*Characteristics* • is uniformly administered *Uses* • is best for younger children • helps with placement for special services	*Characteristics* • has more flexibility *Uses* • assists teaching decisions • used for diagnostic purposes
Group	*Characteristics* • is uniformly administered • is time efficient *Uses* • permits comparisons across groups • used for policy decisions by administrators	*Characteristics* • has high face validity • is time efficient *Uses* • informs teach-reteach & enrichment decisions • documents students' learning

TEACHER CERTIFICATION STUDY GUIDE

SKILL 1.3 Recognizing how to analyze the results of informal and formal reading assessments to plan and improve curriculum and instruction for all students, including students who are learning English as a second language

Techniques for Assessing Particular Reading Skills

Sharon Taberski recommends that the teacher build in one-on-one time for supporting individual children as needed in considering what makes sense, sounds right and matches the letters.

She has noted that emergent and early readers tend to focus on meaning without adequate attention to graphophonic cues. She suggests using the following prompts for children who are having problems with graphophonic cues:

Does what you said match the letters?

If the word were what you said ___, what would it have to start with?
Look carefully at the first letters... then look at the middle letters. . then look at the last letters. What could it be?

If it were ____, what would it end with?
Oral retellings can be used to test children's comprehension.

Children who are retelling a story to be tested for comprehension should be told that that is the purpose when they sit down with the teacher.
It is a good idea to let the child start the retelling on his or her own, because then the teacher can see whether he or she needs prompts to retell the story. Many times more experienced readers summarize what they have read. This summary usually flows out along with the characters, the problem of the story and other details.

Other signs that children understand what they are reading when they give an oral retelling include their use of illustrations to support the retelling, references to the exact text in the retelling, emotional reaction to the text, making connections between the text and other stories or experiences they the readers have had, and giving information about the text without the teacher's asking for it.

Awareness of Text Leveling

The classroom library in the context of the balanced literacy approach to reading instruction is focused on leveled books. These are books which have been leveled with the support of Fountas and Pinnell's Guided Reading: *Good First Teaching for All Children* and *Matching Books to Readers: Using Leveled Reading in Guided Reading*, K-3.

The books which are leveled according to the designations in these reference books need to be stored in bins or crates with front covers facing out. This makes them much easier for the children to identify. In that way the children can go through the appropriate levels and find those books that they are particularly interested in which are also at the right level for them to read. These are those books which the children can read with the right degree of reading accuracy. When young children can see the cover of a book, they are more likely to flip through the book until they can independently identify an appealing book. Then they will read a little bit of the book to see if it's "just right."

"Just right" leveled books, that children can read on their own, need to be available for them to read during independent reading. The goal is for the more fluent readers to select books on their own. Ultimately the use of leveled books helps the children, in addition to the teacher, decide which books are "good" or "just right" for them.

Levels are indicated by means of blue, yellow, red, and green dot stickers at their right upper corners which parallel emergent, early, transitional, and fluent reading stages. They are then kept in containers with other "blue," "yellow," "red," and "green" books.

Other lists and resources other than Fountas and Pinnell which can be used to match children with "just right" books include the Reading Recovery level list. Ultimately, the teacher has to individualize whatever leveling is used in the library to address the individual child learners' needs.

Awareness of the Challenges and Supports in a Text

Illustrations can be key supports for emergent and early readers. Teachers should not only use wordless stories (books which tell their narratives through pictures alone), but can also make targeted use of Big Books for read-alouds, so that young children become habituated to the use of illustrations as an important component for constructing meaning. The teacher should model for the child how to reference an illustration for help in identifying a word in the text the child does not recognize. Of course, children can also go on a picture walk with the teacher as part of a mini-lesson or guided reading and anticipate the story (narrative) using the pictures alone to construct meaning.

Decodability: Use literature which contains examples of letter sound correspondences you wish to teach. First, read the literature with the children or read it aloud to them. Then take a specific example from the text and have the children reread it as the teacher points out the letter-sound correspondence to the children. Then ask the children to go through the now familiar literature to find other letter-sound correspondences. Once the children have correctly made the letter-sound correspondences, have them share similar correspondences they find in other works of literature.

Cooper (2004) suggests that children can become word detectives so that they can independently and fluently decode on their own. The child should learn the following word detective routines so that he or she can function as an independent fluent reader who can decode words on his/her own. First the child should read to the end of a sentence. Then the child should search for word parts which he or she knows. The child should also try to decode the word from the letter sounds. As a last resort, the child should ask someone for help or look up the word in the dictionary.

Techniques for Determining Students' Independent, Instructional and Frustration Reading Levels

Instructional reading is generally judged to be at the 95 percent accuracy level, although, Taberski places it at between 92 and 97 percent. Taberski tries to enhance the independent reading levels by making sure that readers on the instructional reading levels read a variety of genres, and have a range of available and interesting books within a particular genre to read.

Taberski's availability for reading conferences helps her to both assess first hand her children's frustration levels and to model ongoing teacher/reader book conversations by scheduling child-initiated reading conferences when she personally replenishes their book bags.

In order to allay children's frustration levels in their reading and to foster their independent reading, it is important to some children that the teacher personally take time out to hear them read aloud and to check for fluency and expression. Children's frustration level can be immeasurably lessened if they are explicitly told by the teacher after they have read aloud that they need to read without pointing and that they should try chunking words into phrases which mimic their natural speech.

Assessment of the Reading Development of Individual Students

For young readers who are from ELL backgrounds, even if they have been born in the United States, the use of pictures validates their story authoring and story telling skills and provides them with access and equity to the literary discussion and book talk of their native English speaking peers. These children can also demonstrate their storytelling abilities by drawing sequels or prequels to the story detailed in the illustrations alone. They might even be given the opportunity to share the story aloud in their native language or to comment on the illustrations in their native language.

Since many stories today are recorded in two or even three languages at once, discussing story events or analyzing pictures in a different native language is a beneficial practice which can be accomplished in the 21st century marketplace.

Use of pictures and illustrations can also help the K-3 educator assess the capabilities of children who are struggling readers if the children's learning strength is spatial. Through targeted questions about how the pictures would change if different plot twists occurred or how the child might transform the story through changing the illustrations, the teacher can begin to assess struggling reader's deficits and strengths.

Children from ELL backgrounds can benefit from listening to a recorded version of a particular story which they can read along with the tape. This gives them another opportunity to "hear" the story correctly pronounced and presented and to begin to internalize its language structures. In the absence of taped versions of some key stories or texts, the teacher may want to make sound recordings her or himself.

Highly proficient readers can also be involved in creating these literature recordings for use with ELL peers or younger peers. This of course develops oral language proficiency and also introduces these skilled readers into the intricacies of supporting ELL reading instruction. When they actually see their tapes being used by children, they will be tremendously gratified.

SKILL 1.4 Demonstrating knowledge of formal and informal methods for determining students' independent, instructional, and frustration levels of reading

When considering both formal and informal assessment data gathered on students, it is important to quantify the information into terms easily recognized by other teachers, administrators and parents. In reading, general practice is to categorize the information into levels of reading. These levels go across both kinds of assessments. They are compromised of a combination of a word accuracy percentage and a comprehension percentage.

Independent. This level is the level at which the child can read text totally on their own. When reading books at the independent level, students will be able to decode between 95 and 100% of the words and comprehend the text with 90% or better. Many bodies of research indicate that about 98% accuracy makes for a good independent reader; however, there is other research that goes as low as 95% accuracy.

Instructional. This is the level at which the student should be taught because it provides enough difficulty to increase their reading skills without providing so much that it becomes to cumbersome to finish the selection. Typically, the acceptable range for accuracy is between 85-94% with 75% or greater comprehension. Some standards rely on the number of errors made instead of the accuracy percentage with no more than one error out of twenty words read being the acceptable standard.

Frustrational. Books at a student's frustrational level are too difficult for that child and should not be used. The frustrational level is any text with less than 85% word accuracy and/or less than 75% comprehension.

The use of independent, instructional and frustrational levels allow educators to provide children with texts of different ranges depending on the skills necessary to be completed. Typically, standardized or formal assessments test to the instructional level. Therefore, if reading a standardized assessment such as an Iowa Test of Basic Skills, the reported reading level would be the instructional level for that student.

Additionally, some formal and informal test results use alternate methods of reporting information. Some use the grade level and month equivalent, where a 3.2 reading level would indicate the child is reading at the third grade level second month or typically October. Still others use their own leveling system. The Developing Readers Assessment (DRA) has its own unique method of coding book levels based on the work of Fountas and Pinnell. Regardless of the levels listed, the work can easily be translated into independent, instructional and frustrational levels, by examining the comprehension and the word reading accuracy portions of the assessment.

COMPETENCY 2.0 THE TEACHER UNDERSTANDS HOW TO USE AND COMMUNICATE THE RESULTS OF READING ASSESSMENTS.

SKILL 2.1 Analyzing evidence to determine whether a student is performing below, at, or above expected levels of performance based on grade-appropriate reading standards

Awareness of Strategies and resources for supporting individual students (e.g. English language learners, struggling readers through highly proficient readers)

"If you teach reading with phonics, you will have no cases of non-readers."

Rudolf Flesch

Highly proficient readers can sometimes support early readers through a partner relationship. Some children, particularly the emergent and beginning early readers, benefit from reading books with partners. The partners sit side by side and each one takes turns reading the entire text.

Use of talking book and author web resources provides special needs learners with visual or auditory handicapping conditions to immediate contact with authors, and to direct sharing in the joy of their oral language story telling. In addition to the accessibility of the keyboard, their responses to literature can be shared with a broad network of other readers, including close peers and distanced peers. Technology literally enfranchises special needs learners into the circle of connected readers and writers.

In the classroom, there are numerous ways to determine which students are in need of additional assistance. The most effective methods are to examine the classroom performance, assessment data available and to work individually with the student.

Regular classroom teachers often have numerous concerns about the students they are working with in the classroom. They will seek out help from the reading specialist for additional strategies and support to help increase the reading skills. It is important that the specialist be able to determine what difficulties require additional assistance and in which specific areas of reading to provide that assistance.

As previously discussed, running records are of tremendous value in helping in this area. A fast and efficient way to examine the errors the students are making and the number of errors they are making. Also, the levels at which the students are able to read can be a warning flag. If a student is struggling with material several grade levels below their current grade it is important to determine the cause.

Once a general warning flag appears, it may be necessary for the specialist to look in depth and administer additional skill specific assessments or examine the data present in a more in depth manner. In general, it's good to keep in mind the five larger areas of reading as a method of narrowing down the problem. These include: phonemic awareness, phonics, fluency, comprehension, and vocabulary.

Identifying which of these areas is causing the problems helps the teacher and specialist to determine an appropriate plan of action to address the skill deficits. Many children will demonstrate deficits in more than one area, so it is critical to follow the appropriate skill sequence to move the students forward in the most efficient manner possible.

Even knowing the broad area of difficulty may not be enough in itself. Sometimes very skill specific assessment or identification will need to occur before the instruction can begin. Other times, a more global approach would be prudent. An example of a time that a global approach becomes more beneficial might include a student who has all of the phonics skills in isolation but has difficulty applying them in text. In this case, spending more time teaching the phonics skills will not benefit the child, but rather spending the time helping the child to use other cueing systems beyond phonics in a broader sense through many passages and texts would be a more suitable use of time.

One of the first things that a teacher learns is how to obtain resources and help for his/her students. All schools have guidelines for receiving this assistance especially since the implementation of the Americans with Disabilities Act. The first step in securing help is for the teacher to approach the school's administration or exceptional education department for direction in attaining special services or resources for qualifying students. Many schools have a committee designated for addressing these needs such as a Child Study Team or Core Team. These teams are made up of both regular and exceptional education teachers, school psychologists, guidance counselors, and administrators. The particular student's classroom teacher usually has to complete some initial paper work and will need to do some behavioral observations.

The teacher will take this information to the appropriate committee for discussion and consideration. The committee will recommend the next step to be taken. Often subsequent steps include a complete psychological evaluation along with certain physical examinations such as vision and hearing screening and a complete medical examination by a doctor.

The referral of students for this process is usually relatively simple for the classroom teacher and requires little more than some initial paper work and discussion. The services and resources the student receives as a result of the process typically prove to be invaluable to the student with behavioral disorders.

Collaborative teams play a crucial role in meeting the needs of all students, and they are an important step in identifying students with special needs. Under the Individuals with Disabilities Act (IDEA), which federally mandates special education services in every state, it is the responsibility of public schools to ensure consultative, evaluative and if necessary, prescriptive services to children with special needs. In most school districts, a collaborative group handles this responsibility called the Child Study Team (CST). If a teacher or parent suspects a child to have academic, social or emotional problems the teacher should refer the student to the CST where a team consisting of educational professionals (including teachers, specialists, the school psychologist, guidance, and other support staff) review the student's case and situation through meetings with the teacher and/or parents/guardians. The CST will determine what evaluations or tests are necessary, if any, and will also assess the results. Based on these results, the CST will suggest a plan of action if one is necessary.

One plan of action is an Academic Intervention Plan (AIP). An AIP consists of additional instructional services that are provided to the student in order to help them better achieve academically if the student has met certain criteria (such as scoring below the state reference point on standardized tests or performing more than two levels below grade-level).

Another plan of action is a 504 plan. A 504 plan is a legal document based on the provisions of the Rehabilitation Act of 1973 (which preceded IDEA). A 504 plan is a plan for instructional services to assist students with special needs in a regular education classroom setting.

When a student' with physical, emotional, or other impairments (such as Attention Deficit Disorder) impact his or her ability to learn in a regular education classroom setting, that student can be referred for a 504 meeting. Typically, the CST and perhaps even the student's physician or therapist will participate in the 504 meeting and review to determine if a 504 plan will be written.

Finally, a child referred to CST may qualify for an Individualized Education Plan (IEP). An IEP is a legal document, which delineates the specific, adapted services a student with disabilities will receive. An IEP differs from a 504 plan in that the child must be identified for special education services to qualify for an IEP, and ALL students who receive special education services must have an IEP. Each IEP must contain statements pertaining to the student's present performance level, annual goals, related services and supplementary aids, testing modifications, a projected date of services, and assessment methods for monitoring progress. Each year, the CST and guardians must meet to review and update a student's IEP.

At times, the teacher must go beyond the school system to meet the needs of some students. An awareness of special services and resources and how to obtain them is essential to all teachers and their students. When the school system is unable to address the needs of a student, the teacher often must take the initiative and contact agencies within the community. Frequently there is no special policy for finding resources.

It is simply up to the individual teacher to be creative and resourceful and to find whatever helps the student needs. Meeting the needs of all students is certainly a team effort that is most often spearheaded by the classroom teacher

SKILL 2.2 Recognizing when a student needs additional help within the classroom in one or more areas of reading

In the classroom, there are numerous ways to determine which students are in need of additional assistance. The most effective methods are to examine the classroom performance, the assessment data available, and to work individually with the student.

Regular classroom teachers often have numerous concerns about the students they are working with in the classroom. They will seek out help from the reading specialist for additional strategies and support to help increase the reading skills. It is important that the specialist be able to determine what difficulties require additional assistance and in which specific areas of reading to provide that assistance.

As previously discussed, running records are of tremendous value in helping in this area. A fast and efficient way to examine the errors the students are making and the number of errors they are making. Also, the levels at which the students are able to read can be a warning flag. If a student is struggling with material several grade levels below their current grade it is important to determine the cause.

Once a general warning flag appears, it may be necessary for the specialist to look in depth and administer additional skill specific assessments or examine the data present in a more in depth manner. In general, it's good to keep in mind the five larger areas of reading as a method of narrowing down the problem. These include: phonemic awareness, phonics, fluency, comprehension, and vocabulary.

Identifying which of these areas is causing the problems helps the teacher and specialist to determine an appropriate plan of action to address the skill deficits. Many children will demonstrate deficits in more than one area, so it is critical to follow the appropriate skill sequence to move the students forward in the most efficient manner possible.

Even knowing the broad area of difficulty may not be enough in itself. Sometimes very skill specific assessment or identification will need to occur before the instruction can begin. Other times, a more global approach would be prudent. An example of a time that a global approach becomes more beneficial might include a student who has all of the phonics skills in isolation but has difficulty applying them in text. In this case, spending more time teaching the phonics skills will not benefit the child, but rather spending the time helping the child to use other cueing systems beyond phonics in a broader sense through many passages and texts would be a more suitable use of time.

SKILL 2.3 Recognizing when a student needs additional help from other school services

See skill 2.1

SKILL 2.4 Applying knowledge of reading assessments to analyze and support the reading development of students who are learning English as a second language

When considering students for whom English is not the primary language, it is critical to understand the natural development of second language acquisition before applying the general knowledge of reading assessments to this subgroup of students.

In general, second language students can take up to seven years to become proficient in the second language. This development factors in the acculturation process with speaking, listening, reading and writing. Students who are fluent and able to read in their primary language before starting the second language are more likely to become fluent in the second language than those who are not fluent in the primary language.

This group of students, attempting to learn in a second language, generally tends to lag behind in vocabulary particularly. The connection between words and their meanings is essential to understand what is being read. Students who can make the transition easily between the two languages have the advantage of seeing or hearing a word, translating it in their mind to the same or a similar word in their native language, then making the connection and being able to access that information to help them understand the text. Though this is a slow and labor-intensive process in the end the students are able to understand.

However, it is the students who are unable to complete these numerous steps that will require additional support particularly in vocabulary development. Helping to build background knowledge is critical when introducing texts to these students through as concrete a process as is possible. The more concrete examples a teacher can provide the better for the students.

In looking at the other areas of reading; phonics and phonemic awareness skills can also pose problems. Students will sometimes substitute the sounds from their native language in the middle of the process or at other times. Additionally, they may have no connection within their native language because there may be no letters/combinations that make those sounds.

In the end, good reading assessment and instruction is essential when working with students acquiring a second language. However, it must be married well with the body of research into how one learns a second language. Remembering that oral language will develop first (receptive before expressive) and after oral language reaches a conversational level, one can begin the reading instruction.

SKILL 2.5 **Demonstrating knowledge of effective methods for communicating assessment results and reading progress to students, parents, teachers, and support personnel**

As previously discussed, communicating general information about reading and appropriate reading instruction is important. It is just as important to share more specific information about students with parents, other school personnel and the community.

Developing a variety of reporting procedures is essential. However, once you have the reports and have gathered the information, the next step involves finding appropriate methods to share this information with the people that need the data. Again, depending on the audience the amount and type of information may change.

Some ways to share information with parents/guardians include:

- Individual parent meetings
- Small group meetings
- Regular parent updates through phone calls
- Charts and graphs of progress sent home
- Notes home

Some ways to share information with school personnel include:

- Faculty meetings
- Power point or other presentations
- Email
- Conferences
- School board presentation
- Graphs and charts

COMPETENCY 3.0 THE TEACHER UNDERSTANDS FACTORS INVOLVED IN PLANNING, ORGANIZING, AND MANAGING READING INSTRUCTION.

SKILL 3.1 Demonstrating knowledge of the components of a balanced, comprehensive reading program and the interrelationships among these components

The balanced reading approach is taking on new meaning after the now well-known report from the National Reading Panel. A comprehensive and well-balanced reading program is becoming more and more complex and difficult to define.

In general, it should include instruction in phonemic awareness, phonics, fluency, comprehension and vocabulary. There also needs to be time where the teacher reads to the children, where the teacher reads with the children, and where the children read for themselves. The catch phrase To, With and By, has often been used to remind teachers of the types of reading that must occur within the classroom.

In reading to students, generally teachers use a read aloud approach. The read aloud helps build vocabulary and listening comprehension. It allows modeling of fluent reading and builds a love of reading.

When reading with students, teachers use two different approaches: shared reading and guided reading. Shared reading allows the teacher to share more difficult texts with the students than they might be able to read on their own. The teacher generally focuses on comprehension skills and will often complete think alouds or use other comprehension strategies to increase the development of these skills. Vocabulary development and modeling appropriate fluency are also key factors in shared reading. In guided reading, the students are reading texts on their instructional levels. In these small groups, skill development occurs regularly. This is where the phonics skills and phonemic awareness skills can be focused on specifically for a small group of students.

Finally, independent reading or the by students, provides each child the opportunity to practice all of the parts of reading. They are able to get multiple repetitions of the same skills taught otherwise to build the automatic nature with which they read.

No one part of the reading program as described above would be sufficient to help the students develop and become proficient readers. It is the inter-relationship of them all that makes it work. It is the combination and reliance on each other, which makes for success. If one part is removed, not only are skills missed, but also the practice opportunities and modeling opportunities are lost.

While all of the components of good reading instruction can be taught or practiced in each section individually it is when they are combined that the most economical use of the time occurs.

SKILL 3.2 Identifying methods for planning instruction based on grade appropriate standards of reading performance

Consideration for the planning of reading can be a complex set of skills to undertake. It is important to base the information you are relaying to the students on the appropriate grade level standards and grade level curriculum for the students with which you are working.

The dilemma comes into play when the students are not functioning at grade level or demonstrating grade level skills. The reading specialist must find yet another balance in her planning and then later in her instructional methodologies. Finding the right combination of skills to teach requires much planning.

Since the teacher will be working with students across grade levels or with skills at various grade levels, it is necessary to be familiar with the appropriate standards/curriculum at various grade levels. In this manner, one can sit down and look at the standards, curriculum and needs of the students and find the correct blend and match.

However, it is important that all students no matter how far behind be exposed to grade level standards/curriculum. The question for the teacher then becomes how to deliver that piece of information. When planning instruction the reading specialist must think carefully about what strategies will allow the student to receive this exposure while gaining the most from it.

From here it is simply determining the techniques or modifications that will need to be made to deliver this instruction. Will the vocabulary work well if you introduce some synonyms the students have already learned successfully? Would this story work better if taught in smaller chunks so the students can better manage the information? Is there a piece of information, which needs to be taught first in order for the students to be successful with the material?

In the end, it is these types of questions that must be thought of prior to the teaching in order for the information to be presented to the students. Sometimes this planning phase requires tremendous thought and effort to determine the appropriate method to help the students be successful.

General expectations for grade levels include phonemic awareness to be the focus in kindergarten and grade one. Phonics the emphasis through grade one and grade two. The remainder of the skills, fluency, comprehension, and vocabulary then become the focus as reading shifts from learning to read in the early primary grades to reading to learn from the late elementary grades through life. Keep in mind however, that all general areas can certainly be worked outside of these general guidelines.

SKILL 3.3 Identifying strategies for addressing individual differences among readers (e.g., using flexible grouping, individualizing reading instruction, planning and implementing timely interventions for students with reading difficulties)

Adjustment of Reading Instruction Based on Ongoing Assessment

The running records taken of children help the teacher learn about the cueing systems that children use. It is important for the teacher to adjust reading instruction based on the pattern of miscues gathered from several successive reading records. When the teacher carefully reviews a given student's substitutions and self corrections, certain patterns begin to surface. A child may use visual cues as he or she reads and adds meaning to self correct. To the alert teacher, the reliance on visual miscues indicates that the reader doesn't make sense of what she is reading. This means that the teacher needs to check to see what cueing system the child uses when he or she is reading "just right" books. Children, who use meaning and structure but not visual/graphophonic cues, need to be reminded and facilitated to understand the importance of getting and reconstructing the author's message. They have to be able to share the author's story, not their own.

Not only can and should the teacher use the material in the children's ongoing assessment notebook to adjust the child's current instruction but the material also serves to document for the child his/her growth as a successful reader over time. In addition, if the same concerns surface over the use of a particular cueing system or high frequency word, the teacher can adjust the class wall chart and even devote a whole class lesson to the particular element.

Instructional Reading Strategies for Promoting the Development of Particular Reading Skills

Phonemic awareness can be developed through using leveled books that deal with rhyming words and segmenting phonemes into words. Children can also work with word or letter strips to continue the poems from the books and create their own "sequels" to the phoneme-filled story. They can also create an in-style rhyming story using some of the same phonemes from the leveled story they have heard.

Word Identification- Selective Cue Stage. Sometimes children have not yet experienced an awareness of the conventions of print and labeling in their own home environments. The teacher or an aide may have to go on a label adventure and support children in recognizing or affixing labels to parts of the classroom, halls and school building. A neighborhood walk with a digital or hand held camera may be required to help children identify uses and functions of print in society. A classroom photo essay or bulletin board could be the outgrowth of such an activity.

Sight Vocabulary- Beginning readers may enjoy outdoing Dolch (1936), who compiled the best known sight vocabulary word list. They can create their own class version of this list with illustrations and even some comments about why they have nominated certain words for the list.

Uses of Large Group, Small Group, and Individualized Reading Instruction

The framework for organizing the balanced literacy classroom is referred to as the one book-whole class mode. What this means is that everyone in the class has experiences with the same book. Everyone in the class discusses the literature. The teacher starts by activating prior knowledge and developing the context or background for the piece of literature. Some of the children within the class may have less prior knowledge or context with which to frame the book. The teacher will need to provide a preview of the book or develop key concepts to provide a stronger base for what the class will read together.

Some children will have to work with a paraprofessional or with a reading tutor before the class studies the book. Different modes of reading are accommodated within the class, by the books being read as a read-aloud, as part of shared reading or as guided reading. Student reader choices can also include: cooperative reading, reading with a partner, or independent reading.

Following the reading, the children respond to it which can be done through a literature circle and/or the whole class or in writing.

Strategies for Selecting and Using Meaningful Reading Materials at Appropriate Levels of Difficulty

Matching young children with "just right" books fosters their reading independently, no matter how young they are. The teacher needs to have an extensive classroom library of books. Books that emergent readers and early readers can be matched with should have fairly large print, appropriate spacing, so that the reader can easily see where word begins and ends, and few words on each page so that the young reader can focus on all important concerns of top-to-bottom, left-to-right, directionality, and the one-to-one match of word to print.

Illustrations for young children should support the meaning of the text and language patterns and predictable text structures should make these texts appealing to young readers. Most important of all the content of the story should relate to the children's interests and experiences as the teacher knows them.

Only after all these considerations have been addressed, can the teacher select "just right" books from an already leveled bin or list. In a similar fashion, when the teacher is selecting books for transitional and fluent readers, the following ideas need to be taken into account:

The book should take at least two sittings to read, so children can get used to reading longer books. The fluent and transitional reader needs to deal with more complex characters and more intricate plotting. Look for books that set the stage for plot development with a compelling beginning. Age appropriateness of the concepts, plot and themes is important so that the child will sustain interest in the book. Look for book features such as a list of chapters to help children navigate through the book.

Series books are wonderful to introduce at this point in the children's development.

Awareness of Strategies and Resources for Supporting Individual Students

Children who come from family backgrounds where English is not spoken lack a solid understanding of its syntactic structure. Therefore as they are being assessed using the oral running record, they may need additional support from their teacher in examining the structure and meaning of English. A child from a non-native English Language speaking background may often pronounce words that make no sense to him or her and just go on reading. They have to learn to stop to construct meaning. This child may have to be prompted to self-correct.

Children from non-native English Language speaking backgrounds can benefit from independent reading opportunities to listen to a familiar story on tape and read along. This also gives them practice in listening to Standard English oral reading. Often these children can begin to internalize the language structures by listening to the book on tape several times.

Highly proficient readers can sometimes support early readers through a partner relationship. Some children, particularly the emergent and beginning early readers, benefit from reading books with partners. The partners sit side by side and each one takes turns reading the entire text.

Use of talking book and author web resources provides special needs learners with visual or auditory handicapping conditions immediate contact with authors. This can lead to direct sharing in the joy of oral language story telling. In addition to the accessibility of the keyboard, children's responses to literature can be shared with a broad network of other readers, including close and distance peers. Technology literally invites special needs learners into the circle of connected readers and writers.

SKILL 3.4 Recognizing how to select appropriate instructional materials, including current technology, to promote the reading development of all students, including students who are learning English as a second language

Strategies for Planning, Organizing, Managing, and Differentiating Reading Instruction to Support the Reading Development of All Students

The physical set up of your classroom is exceedingly important to support the effective development of all children.

The homey look of the classroom belies its deliberate design as a space where children can experience, practice, share and learn. Some teachers have done away with the large desk and use smaller tables instead. Sharon Taberski advocates for young children K-3 adjusting the height of the table legs so the children can use the tables as writing spaces and sit on the floor. Sharon gives each of her children a personal 12"x 9"x 2" tray on which they place their home possessions, books, homework, folder, etc. This is kept in a small storage unit near the coat closet during the day.

Children put their completed homework in a wire basket and notes from parents or the office in a second wire basket. Supplies such as pencils, markers, crayons, scissors, and erasers are not brought from home, but rather available for all in the class from "community" containers at the center of each of the children's tables.

All the children's reading, writing, and individual math folders are stored together in plastic bins in the meeting area. Every child has an individual book bag which is kept in one of two large wicker baskets set in different areas of the room.

This storing of materials away from children decreases their "fiddling with" their belongings during class, makes the room look much neater, and frees the children to focus on their learning experiences, rather than where their belongings are at any given time of day.

As you can see on the accompanying diagram the 10'x10' meeting area is the center of classroom learning. This is where the whole class is gathered at the beginning of the reading and the writing workshop and for sharing sessions. It is also the demonstration and modeling center for both the teacher and for children.

Generally, the presenter sits on the adult chair (in some balanced literacy classrooms, this is a rocking chair) near the easel with the chart. Generally, this chair and the easel are strategically positioned so that the teacher can see the door and any visitors or urgent messages from the office. Rearranging furniture during the day takes away from instruction time and is disruptive. Have a designated comfortable section of the room that can be a gathering place for a literacy community and then organize the rest of the classroom activities around that center.

The conference table which is at the back of the room (see diagram) is another key piece of classroom space furniture. It is the place where the four or five children and the teacher confer, wait and do their work. Having children come to a set conference table, rather than the teacher's going to them (although some teachers do advocate going to the children) saves time as far as Taberski is concerned. It serves to keep her and the children on task.

Taberski keeps two separate trays of supplies: a small magnetic board, letters, chalkboard, chalk, sentence strips, index cards, and blank books for her demonstrations during her conferences. She believes that teachers should store materials close to where they are used, so the teacher does not have to take time from the child to get up and get the materials.

The Classroom Library

On the tables, Taberski generally has book crates with books that are not leveled. Children choose from these books during the first independent reading session of her day which is from 8:40-9:00. During the second reading session from 9:30-10:20 the children select books from the leveled reading bins which are stored on the bookcase shelves.

Beyond the leveled books, which have already been discussed, Taberski also maintains a non-leveled, non fiction library which includes dictionaries, atlases, almanacs and informational books related to the themes, projects and investigations that the children will undertake throughout the year.

Beyond the leveled books and non-fiction books in the classroom, Taberski and other balanced literacy advocates generally include at least 10-15 big books which they routinely use to engage children with the text.

Since Guided Reading with groups of 6 children is a major part of the balanced literacy approach, Taberski and other disciplined and dedicated teacher educators "bundle" up six copies of selected books so that they can distribute them to their guided reading groups whenever they choose to do them. Taberski models the concept of a home library collection for the children by keeping books which she particularly likes in a bookcase behind her chair. She sometimes places "her" books on the easel so that they can be shared by the children and returned to her.

Wall Works

Much of creating a family atmosphere lies in the use of the room walls to document the children's learning experiences, skills work, and readings.

Generally at least one wall in a reading classroom is the Chart Wall. Charts with various spelling patterns discussed in class can be posted. If a child later has issues or concerns with that particular pattern, he or she should be directed to look at and to review the chart.

One of the centerpieces of the K-2 classroom is the High Frequency Word Chart. This is a growing list of commonly used words which the teacher tapes under the appropriate beginning letter according to the children's directions. At the end of each month, the newest high frequency words go into the children's folders and become part of their spelling words. Therefore reading, writing, and spelling are all intricately connected.

Supplies for children K-3 and beyond can include:

A red plastic double pocket reading folder
A blue plastic double pocket reading folder
A four sectioned pressed board spelling/poetry folder
A 4" x 6" assessment notebook for reading
A 4" x 6" assessment notebook for writing
A reading response notebook (loose-leaf- 60 pages)
A handwriting notebook

The Reading Folder contains the assessment notebooks, the reading response notebooks, a Weekly Reading Log, and the strategy sheets the child may be using that particular week.

The Assessment Notebook is a key evaluative tool and a recording document for the conscientious balanced literacy specialist. The teacher uses the notebook to record the child's running record, the retellings of stories shared by the child, and summarizing talks about leveled books read. Within the assessment books, the teacher also has notes about the child's progress, the strategies the child has learned to use well, the books he or she has read and those strategies the child still needs to practice. These assessment notebooks must be kept accessible so that the teacher can use them to confer with the child, parents, and administrator as needed.

The reading response notebook becomes a compilation of reading strategy sheets and children's writings and art in response to literature.

The Weekly Reading Log allows the child to maintain for himself or herself the titles of books they have read and written a bit about the narrative, style, and genre of that given book.

Book Bags: These are 10" x 12" heavy duty freezer bags which keep 3-10 books a child is "working on" during his/her free time. The teacher generally matches the children to the books and changes these books as needed by the children.

Writing Folders

Children keep several pieces of writing in their folders at a time. Within the writing folder is also a handwriting notebook and a beginning word book as well. The Spelling/Poetry Folder is one which helps children focus on the sequence of letters in words and learn more how words work.

The balanced literacy advocates have a definite schedule for the teaching of reading and writing workshop from which they generally do not deviate. A sample follows.

8:40-9:00- FIRST INDEPENDENT READING/WORD STUDY GROUP

9:00-9:30- MEETING-WHOLE GROUP SESSION in the meeting area
Read Aloud, Shared Reading, or Shared Writing

9:30-10:30- READING WORKSHOP
Reading Conferences or Guided Reading
Second Independent Reading
Reading Share 10:20-10:30

10:30-10:40- Writing Mini Lesson or Writing Share

10:40-11:20- Writing Workshop Writing Conferences, Guided Writing, Modeled Writing, Independent Writing

(11:10-11:20)-Writing Share

Uses of Instructional Technology to Promote Reading Development

One of the most interesting ways in which the web complements the Reading and Writing Workshop involves the proliferation of author specific websites. If used judiciously, these web resources allow authors to come into the classroom and allow children to write, question, discuss and share their literacy experiences with the authors themselves. Children can also readily become part of a distanced community of peers who are also reading works by a given author.

For instance, children who have been introduced to the work of Faith Ringgold, the author of *Tar Beach*, can easily visit her online site, www.faithringgold.com. Here they will not only find extensive biographic data on Ringgold, but they will also be able to learn a song inspired by her main character Cassie. They will be able to help illustrate a new story Ringgold has put up on the website, and also see if any of the questions they may have generated in their shared or independent reading of her books, has already been answered in the "frequently asked questions" section of her web resource. A few of the author websites respond online to individual children's questions.

There are even some reader response web resources such as the spaghetti review web site where young readers can post their response to different books they are reading. http://www.book-club-review.com/view.php?cid=1

SKILL 3.5 Demonstrating knowledge of strategies for creating a positive and supportive environment for literacy learning

Creation of an Environment that Promotes Love of Reading

The aforementioned creation of the meeting area and the reading chair (sometimes a rocking chair) with throw pillows around it promotes a love of reading. Beyond that, some classrooms have adopted an author's hat, decorated with the pictures of famous authors and book characters which children wear when they read from their own works.

Many classrooms also have children's storyboards, artwork, story maps, pop-up books, and "in the style of" writing inspired by specific authors. Some teachers buy calendars for the daily schedule which celebrate children's authors or types of literature. Children are also encouraged to bring in public library books and special books from their home libraries. The teacher can model this habit of sharing beautiful books and inviting stories from his or her home library.

In addition, news stories about children's authors, series books, television versions of books, theatrical film versions of books, stuffed toy book character decorations and other memorabilia related to books can be used to decorate the room.

Various chain book stores including Barnes and Nobles and Borders give out free book marks and promotional display materials related to children's books which can be available in the room for children to use as they read independently or in their guided groups. They might even use these artistic models to inspire their own book themed artifacts.

Strategies for Promoting Independent Reading in the Classroom and at Home

Pre-select books for the children that are just right for them. Provide the children with a quiet, relaxing space within the classroom where they can go to read these books. Don't get upset if they seem to take a break or wander around the room after fifteen minutes. Adults take breaks as well.

Make certain that the children who are reading independently fill in their weekly logs. Beyond telling what books they were reading and how many pages they have read, have the children respond to prompts like "This week I was successful at ..." or, "Next week I plan to..." A response can also be an illustration or a sentence or two about the book.

Deliberately assign a child or a pair of children to read big books. These are a guaranteed success for the children because they have already been shared in class. Some children enjoy reading these independently using big rulers to point at words. This provides them with a sense of mastery over the words and ownership of their independent reading.

Some children enjoy working on their own strategy sheet such as a story map, character map, or storyboard panel, to demonstrate how they can apply a strategy to their own independent learning.

SKILL 3.6 **Recognizing the importance of using a wide variety of high quality literature for children and young adults**

As the reading specialist, it is important to familiarize yourself with carious genres of literature, including those which specifically appeal to the students with which you work. In addition, it is important to be able to locate appropriate resources which can support content area learning for students.

There are numerous fictional genres which can apply to students in kindergarten through twelfth grade. They include: '

- Mystery
- Fantasy
- Drama
- Historical Fiction
- Fable
- Mythology
- Fairy tale
- Poetry
- Folklore
- Legends
- Realistic Fiction
- Tall Tales
- Science Fiction

When reading any genre of fiction students need to have well developed phonemic awareness, phonics, and fluency skills. Vocabulary and comprehension development will continue to occur throughout schooling, and should be an integral part of the reading process. Texts for teaching reading specifically, should include many of the various genres, both nonfiction and fiction, and provide some authentic works of literature even if in a condensed format. It is imperative to expose students to various types of authentic literature. In the nonfiction realm, it is important for students to have access to materials which will support their learning in content areas as well as books which match their interests and learning desires. Some nonfiction genres include:

- Essays
- Narrative Nonfiction
- Biography
- Speech
- Autobiographies

Understanding and using these different types of nonfiction text will provide the students with the opportunity to explore various topics or support their learning in content specific classes. In addition to books, it may be necessary to utilize reference materials including:

- Dictionaries
- Thesauruses
- Encyclopedias
- Almanacs

COMPETENCY 4.0 THE TEACHER UNDERSTANDS THE ROLES OF REFLECTION, SELF-EVALUATION, COLLABORATION, AND PROFESSIONAL DEVELOPMENT IN READING INSTRUCTION.

SKILL 4.1 Recognizing the importance of engaging in an ongoing program of personal professional development related to reading instruction

As a reading specialist, one job duty you will be asked to participate in may be updating and correlating the district reading curriculum. Curriculum writing is a skill unto itself and requires an understanding of developmentally appropriate practices, state standards and materials and resources available.

It is important to under that curriculum is not the same thing as a program. Many districts have what are called Core Curriculum programs. These commercially developed products are meant to reach the majority of students and provide them with the necessary skills to be successful readers. Companies work hard to look at the state standards and have their products meet these standards. The problem occurs usually due to this all encompassing nature. The products have so many pieces and parts that certain specific areas are not taught to the level some students need.

Each district across the country has its own reading curriculum. While they are aligned with the state standards, they are not exactly the same. Generally, the state provides its guidelines, in the form of standards, for the basic information felt it is important for students to have to be productive members of society. Therefore, state standards do not necessarily cover all aspects of reading that a district may feel are important to be taught. In this way, curriculums can be more involved and cover more details than the state requires. However, they should at a minimum address all of the identified state standards at a particular grade level.

Periodically, state departments of education will update and change the standards. This would be a time to revise the district curriculum and incorporate the changes. Additionally, new information may arise through research or through an analysis of testing scores, which would further indicate a revision might be necessary. Curriculums should be living changing almost continuous works in progress. Keeping them current and filled with relevant information is important for the students and teachers to continue to provide adequate education.

As curriculum changes are made, it's important to update and inservice all teachers. After all, the teachers are the direct personnel responsible for implementing the curriculum on a day-to-day basis. Sometimes, it may be necessary to model or provide professional development activities to the teachers to allow them to be able to properly implement the new curricular changes.

SKILL 4.2 Demonstrating familiarity with professional organizations and resources that provide opportunities and support for professional development related to reading instruction

It is imperative one keeps up on the current research validated methods for working in the field of reading. This can be best done through membership to professional organizations such as International Reading Association (IRA) or the National Reading Conference (NRC). Joining these or other similar organizations will help the professional stay current with methodologies and provide appropriate literature and other publications for review.

Technology and the availability of the Internet also provide staff with materials and strategies to help keep abreast of the issues and current literature in the field of reading. Online journals, search engines, study groups and chat groups can be integral to ongoing professional development. Coursework at the graduate level will also help educators continue to build their understandings, as does mentoring and collaborative teaching. In fact, finding an experienced mentor in the same field can provide more information as to roles, issues and current topics in the field of reading than a variety of other sources.

Other specific skills in reading, such as Reading Recovery©, require additional training specifically in their program. These types of programs usually have a rigorous ongoing professional development plan that require numerous hours over years.

It is important to seek out conferences and workshops specifically designed for reading specialists because districts typically provide inservice to the majority of their populations, which would be regular education teachers, they often overlook the lower incidence employees. Sometimes therefore the standard professional development of the district will not pertain to this area of expertise. Other times, reading specialists may be asked to provide inserivce to groups of teachers.

Having a professional development plan can be an integral component of staying current. In this plan, the reading teacher looks ahead down the road at what skills she would like to attain and then develops a plan over the years to help achieve these goals. Looking into the future as an educator and having a set plan for what goals and objectives the teacher hopes to achieve herself helps tremendously in implementing the current research.

As with any educational profession thinking of yourself as an appropriate role model for your students is paramount. Appropriate ethics and demonstration regularly of those ethics is a key component to professionalism.

SKILL 4.3 Demonstrating knowledge of self-assessment techniques to help reading professionals evaluate and adjust their own performance as classroom teachers

As a teacher of any sort you will experience many forms of evaluations. Through student teaching to formal evaluations completed by supervisors, ongoing critical looks at your performance will be a part of the regular process. One area that is often under utilized but perhaps more valuable than outside evaluations is the self-assessment.

Examining with a critical eye one's own performance is the highest level of reflection. There are several forms that self-assessments can undertake. One format is to videotape yourself completing a lesson with the students. Then replaying the tape for yourself at a later time. Before watching the tape, you should have specific questions or areas in mind. Simply watching the tape itself is much less valuable than when you watch it with a purpose. The questions might include things like: Did I keep the students engaged throughout the lesson? Was I clear in explaining the content I wanted them to understand? What could I do to improve the understanding of this concept for the students?

Another method of self-assessment might include providing your students with surveys to complete. When compiling the data from the questions, you will have a better understanding of how you are perceived by your students and what skills you can work on to improve the weak areas. Carefully written questions focused on the items you are interested in learning about is necessary.

Sometimes a self-assessment could be as simple as keeping a reflection journal. With this strategy, the teacher simply keeps a regular notebook and after each day or week or even lesson takes a few minutes to write down her thoughts and feelings. Writing down what went well, what did not go well, what could have been done differently, or what was a surprise can provide valuable insight into teaching style and improvement. The drawback to this strategy is finding the time to use this method. Self reflection has been found to provide the most immediate and effective changes to instructional practice. If used authentically and kept confidential, it can be one of the best tools for improvement available to an educator.

Regular use of self-evaluation tools allows the teacher to understand what goals and objectives to include in the personal improvement plan. These ideas then become a part of the professional development plan. Remembering to review the state standards and using them, as a guide for the self-evaluation will provide further guidance and a place to start for the development of such plans.

SKILL 4.4 Identifying ways to collaborate effectively with colleagues to promote professional growth and to meet the reading needs of all students

As a specialist of any kind within a school building, it is imperative that collaboration among all staff be of top priority. It is not enough to simply service the students who are assigned through whatever means the district or building uses. Current educational trends have collaboration of the utmost priority.

In some cases reading specialists are becoming literacy coaches and then become responsible for working closely with regular educators to increase the reading skills of the students across the building. This collaborative model has the reading specialist working in the classroom beside the teacher in a team teaching model. At times, lessons may be modeled to demonstrate new or innovative ideas or different ways to structure lessons. Still other times, the two professionals would work together to provide instruction to groups of students.

This coaching model also provides out of the classroom time where professional development activities may occur. These may take the form of study groups, individual discussion sessions, or workshop offerings for different strategies. For this to be a successful implementation, it is important for all parties to realize this is a learning session for everyone and one party is not evaluating another.

Another less formal collaboration model simply involves regular meetings where children and their needs are discussed. These meetings may be formal or informal. Usually they revolve around the assessment data gathered on the students, but may not. As the data and needs of the students are reviewed, the teachers present will discuss items indicating various needs. This allows for the most appropriate professional development to occur.

As it is directly related to an immediate need for the teacher with his current students, the skills learned are more likely to be implemented. In an informal setting, anyone with knowledge can share his or her ideas, suggestions, strategies or skills. It is in this format that all parties feel less threatened and comfortable sharing.

As the reading specialist, it is vital to collaborate with other reading specialists as much as possible. Today's use of technology and the availability of email can make this a much less cumbersome task. Collaboration is a vital part of growth for all teachers and should not be seen as a negative. It should instead be viewed as a team of professionals working together to ensure that all students receive the most appropriate educational experience possible.

SKILL 4.5 Recognizing current reading policy and legislation that affect reading instruction in New Mexico (e.g., standards and benchmarks, the EPSS, reading programs)

The implication of the No Child Left Behind Act brought education back to the forefront, making headlines and led to a round of new legislation. Followed with the publication of the now infamous National Reading Panel report, reading instruction took center stage. Terms like research based, response to intervention, standards, benchmarks, improvement, annual yearly progress and many others became buzzwords across the nation.

The federal mandates and educational legislation sparked lawmakers in each state to make further interpretations and changes to the laws within their states. In New Mexico, the bodies enacted the Educational Plan for Student Success (EPSS) program. As with many other states, New Mexico has made the shift to using assessment data as the basis for educational planning for all students. The EPSS is a thought out plan where school information, community resources are utilized, data is interpreted and reviewed, plans for improving the school is developed, and all school based programs and serves are brought together to meet the needs of the students. EPSS shifts the focus from specific students to the academic achievement of all New Mexico students.

Furthermore, the New Mexico state department of education has launched a reading initiative. The website for this initiative http://reta.nmsu.edu/reading/reading.html provides suggested readings, articles, additional contact information, discussion forums and additional resources to help New Mexico teachers improve their knowledge of reading instruction.

The reading initiative has teaching and assessment components as well affecting all of New Mexico's students. The assessment component consists of statewide testing at grades kindergarten through third grade in reading and writing to document progress and areas of deficit, which need to be addressed. Specifically, this assessment focuses on phonemic awareness, phonics and comprehension skills. The teaching component is aimed at providing appropriate professional development activities in reading. The goal is to improve the skills of all certified teachers reading knowledge thereby, reaching all of New Mexico's students.

As with any legislation, it is important to keep track of changes as new information is learned. Staying current with the changes requires the teacher to not only focus on state initiatives but to also watch federal trends. This occurred with Reading First, which began as a federal program, but one which all states adopted, including New Mexico, in some format.

New Mexico also has a listing of the standards approved by the legislature regarding all content areas. The reading standards can be found at http://www.nmstandards.org/standards/language_arts/.

SUBAREA II. DEVELOPING PHONOLOGICAL AND OTHER LINGUISTIC PROCESSES RELATED TO READING

COMPETENCY 5.0 THE TEACHER UNDERSTANDS THE ROLE OF PHONEMIC AWARENESS IN EMERGENT LITERACY AND DEMONSTRATES KNOWLEDGE OF STRATEGIES FOR PROMOTING PHONEMIC AWARENESS.

SKILL 5.1 Analyzing the role of phonemic awareness in reading development

"The two best predictors of early reading success are alphabetic recognition and phonemic awareness."
    Marilyn Jager Adams

"In order to benefit from formal reading instruction, children must have a certain level of phonemic awareness. . . phonemic awareness is both a prerequisite for and a consequence of learning to read."
    Hallie Kay Yopp

Phonemic awareness is a specific skill within the broader category of phonological awareness. Probably developing fairly late, it is the knowledge that words are comprised of individual phonemes that can be blended.
Theorist Marilyn Jager Adams who researches early reading has outlined five basic types of phonemic awareness tasks.

Task 1- Ability to hear rhymes and alliteration.
For example, the children would listen to a poem, rhyming picture book or song and identify the rhyming words heard which the teacher might then record or list on chart.

Task 2- Ability to do oddity tasks (recognize the member of a set that is different [odd} among the group.
For example, the children would look at the pictures of grass, a garden and a rose, answering, Which one starts with a different sound?

Task 3 –The ability to orally blend words and split syllables.
For example, the children can say the first sound of a word and then the rest of the word and put it together as a single word.

Task 4 –The ability to orally segment words.
For example, the ability to count sounds. The child would be asked to count or clap the sounds in "hamburger."
Task 5- The ability to do phonics manipulation tasks.
For example, replace the "r" sound in rose with a "p" sound.

SKILL 5.2 Recognizing how to promote students' awareness of different levels of spoken language (e.g., spoken words, spoken syllables, phonemes)

The Role of Phonemic Awareness in Reading Development

Children who have problems with phonics generally have not acquired or been exposed to phonemic awareness activities at home or in preschool-2. This includes extensive songs, rhymes and read–alouds.

Instructional Methods

Since the ability to distinguish between individual sounds, or phonemes, within words is a prerequisite to association of sounds with letters and manipulating sounds to blend words—a fancy way of saying "reading," the teaching of phonemic awareness is crucial to emergent literacy (early childhood K-2 reading instruction). Children need a strong background in phonemic awareness in order for phonics instruction (sound –spelling relationship-printed materials) to be effective.

Instructional methods that may be effective for teaching phonemic awareness can include:

- Clapping syllables in words

- Distinguishing between a word and a sound

- Using visual cues and movements to help children understand when the speaker goes from one sound to another

- Incorporating oral segmentation activities which focus on easily distinguished syllables rather than sounds

- Singing familiar songs (e.g. Happy Birthday, Knick Knack Paddy Wack) and replacing key words those of a different ending

- Dealing children a deck of picture cards and having them sound out the words for the pictures on their cards or calling for a picture by asking for its first and last sound.

SKILL 5.3 Demonstrating knowledge of various phonemic awareness skills (e.g., discrimination of onsets/rimes, segmentation of a word into phonemes, blending of phonemes to form a word, substitution of phonemes in a word)

Teachers can maintain ongoing logs and rubrics for assessment throughout the year of phonemic awareness for individual children. Such assessments would identify particular stated reading behaviors or performance standards, the date of observation of the child's behavior (in this context-phonemic activity or exercise), and comments.

The rubric or legend for assessing these behaviors might include the following descriptors:
- demonstrates or exhibits reading behavior consistently,
- makes progress/strides toward this reading behavior, and
- has not yet demonstrated or exhibited this behavior.

Depending on the particular phonemic task the teacher models, the performance task might include:

- Saying rhyming words in response to an oral prompt
- Segmenting a word spoken by the teacher into its beginning, middle and ending sounds
- Counting correctly the number of syllables in a spoken word

Phonological awareness involves the recognition that spoken words are composed of a set of smaller units such as onsets and rimes, syllables, and sounds.

Phonemic awareness is a specific type of phonological awareness which focuses on the ability to distinguish, manipulate and blend specific sounds or phonemes within an individual word.

Think of phonological awareness as an umbrella and phonemic awareness as a specific spoke under this umbrella.

Phonics deals with printed words and the learning of sound-spelling correlations, while phonemic awareness activities are oral.

In reviewing reading research and theory, new distinctions and definitions appear often. The body of reading knowledge changes over time. The information and definitions in this guide are those accepted in the year of its publication and the time of its authoring and updating. As changes occur in accepted theories, they will be made in the guides and in the certification exams.

"If you believe that you learn to read by reading, you must learn to want to read. Reading to children, therefore models both the "how" and "why" of reading."

Helen Depree and Sandra Iversen-Early Literacy in the Classroom
"The long talk that parents have put off about the ways of the world might need to be an introduction to the facts about the English alphabet."
Terrence Moore-Ashbrook Center Fellow-Principal of Ridgeview Classical Schools in Fort Collins, Colorado

Phonological Awareness

Phonological awareness means the ability of the reader to recognize the sounds or phonemes of spoken language. This recognition includes how these sounds can be blended together, segmented (divided up), and manipulated (switched around). This awareness eventually leads to phonics, a method for decoding language by unlocking letter-sound or grapheme-phoneme relationships.

Development of phonological skills for most children begins during the pre-K years. Indeed by the age of 5, a child who has been exposed to fingerplays and poetry can recognize a rhyme. Such a child can demonstrate phonological awareness by filling in the missing rhyming word in a familiar rhyme or rhymed picture book. The procedure of filling in a missing word is called the cloze procedure. It can be used in oral or print literacy activities.

One teaches children phonological awareness by directly pointing out the sounds made by letters singly (as in /b/) or in combination (as in /bl/), and to recognize individual sounds in words.

Phonological awareness skills include but are not limited to the following:

l. Rhyming and syllabification
2. Blending sounds into words—such as pic-tur-bo-k
3. Identifying beginning or initial phonemes and ending or final phonemes in short, one-syllable words
4. Breaking words down into sounds- which is also called "segmenting" words
5. Removing initial sounds, and substituting others. An example is /bat/ minus the /b/ with an /m/ substituted becomes /mat/.

The Role of Phonological Awareness in Reading Development

Instructional methods to teach phonological awareness may include any or all of the following:

1. Auditory games, during which children recognize and manipulate the sounds of words, separate or segment the sounds of words, take out sounds, blend sounds, add in new sounds, or take apart sounds to recombine them in new formations.

2. Snap game- the teacher says two words. The children snap their fingers if the two words share a sound, which might be at the beginning, or end of the word. Children hear initial phonemes most easily, followed by final ones. Medial or middle sounds are most difficult for young children to discriminate. One sees this in their oral responses as well as in their invented spelling. Silence occurs if the words share no sounds. Children love this simple game and it also helps with classroom management.

3. Language games model for children identification of rhyming words. These games help inspire children to create their own rhymes.

4. Read books that rhyme such as *Sheep in A Jeep* by Nancy Shaw or *The Fox on a Box* by Barbara Gregorich.

5. Share books with children that use alliteration (words that begin with the same sound) such as *Avalanche, A to Z*.

Assessment of Phonological Awareness

These skills can be assessed by having the child listen to the teacher say two words. Then ask the child to decide if these two words are the same word repeated twice or two different words.

When making this assessment, when using two different words, make certain that they only differ by only one phoneme, such as /d/ and /g/.

Children can be assessed on words which are not real words that are familiar to them. Words used can be make-believe words.

The Role of Phonological Processing in the Development of Individual Students

Children who are raised in homes where English is not the first language and or where standard English is not spoken, may have difficulty with hearing the difference between similar sounding words like "send" and "sent." Any child who is not in a home, day care, or preschool environment where English phonology operates, may have difficulty perceiving and demonstrating the differences between English language phonemes. If children can not hear the difference between words that "sound the same" like "grow" and "glow," they will be confused when these words appear in a print context. This confusion will of course, sadly, impact their comprehension.

Considerations for teaching phonological processing to ELL children include recognition by the teacher that what works for the English language speaking child from an English language speaking family, does not necessarily work in other languages.

Research recommends that ELL children learn to read initially in their first language. It is critical for ELL learn to speak English before being taught to read English. Research supports that oral language development lays the foundation for phonological awareness.

All phonological instruction programs must be tailored to the children's learning backgrounds. Rhymes and alliteration introduced to ELL children should be read or shared with them in their first language, if at all possible.

Struggling Readers

"Students who cannot read by age 9 are unlikely to become fluent readers and have a greater tendency to drop out"
Beth Antunez

Among the causes of reading difficulties for some children (and adults) are auditory trauma or ear infections that affect their ability to hear speech. Such children need one-on-one support with articulation and perception of different sounds. When a child says a word such as "parrot" incorrectly, repeat it back as a question with the correct. If the child "gets" the sound correctly after your question, all is well. Extra support was needed. If the child still has difficulty with pronunciation after repeated instances, then consult with a speech therapist or audiologist. Early identification of medical conditions that affect hearing is crucial to reading development.

Points to Ponder

Phonological awareness is auditory.
It does not involve print.
It begins before children have learned letter-sound relationships.
It is the basis for the successful teaching of phonics and spelling.
It can and must be taught and nurtured.
It precedes and must be in place before the alphabetic principle can be taught.

SKILL 5.4   Identifying explicit and implicit strategies for promoting and assessing the phonemic awareness skills of all students, including students who are learning English as a second language

Consideration for ELL Students

Given the demographics of our country with its influx of New Americans, the likelihood it is likely that you will be teaching at least some children who are from a non-native English speaking background. Therefore, as a conscientious educator, it is important that you understand the special factors involved in supporting children's second language literacy development.

Not all English phonemes are present in various ELL native languages; for example, the sound of /th/ does not appear in Spanish. Some native language phonemes may and do conflict with English phonemes.

It is recommended that all teachers of reading and particularly those who are working with ELL students use meaningful, student centered, and culturally customized activities. These activities may include: language games, word walls, and poems. Some of these activities might, if possible, be initiated in the child's first language and then reiterated in English.

Reading and the ELL Learner

Research has shown that there is a positive and strong correlation between a child's literacy in his/her native language and his/her learning of English. The degree of native language proficiency and literacy is a strong predictor of English language development. Children who are literate and engaged readers in their native language can easily transfer their skills to a second language (i.e. English).

What this means is that teacher educators should not approach the needs of ELL learners in reading the same as they do native speakers. Those children whose families are not from a focused oral literacy and reading culture in the native language will need additional oral language rhymes, read-alouds, and singing as supports for reading skills development in both their native and the English language.

SKILL 5.5 Identifying appropriate materials and activities to promote phonemic awareness

Since phonemic awareness is a mostly auditory skill, it can often be completed with little to no materials necessary. It can also be integrated into almost any activity you are completing during the day in any subject. The other nice thing about phonemic awareness instruction is that it is best delivered in short segments several times throughout the day. Usually, it is best worked on in less than five-minute intervals a few times during the school day.

As stated before, phonemic awareness skills are auditory skills. Some of these skills later will be combined with print as the child transitions to phonics, but in a true phonemic awareness activity, there is no print involved. Phonemic awareness skills include: rhyming, beginning sound identification, ending sound identification, syllabication, insertion of sounds, deletion of sounds, and segmentation of sounds.

In order to promote phonemic awareness in students a teacher can complete many different types of activities. One of the most powerful methods can be found in texts that contain rhyming and alliteration patterns. Using nursery rhymes or songs is an excellent way to help children begin to hear the patterns of sounds in words. Books with repetitive language also help students begin to apply these concepts. Many students also enjoy tongue twisters or the old fashion jump rope songs.

As you progress to more complex levels of phonemic awareness, introducing pictures and game formats are fun ways for the students to the move into the next level. Anytime a teacher can add some form of manipulatives to a normally auditory only skill, the students have a better chance at obtaining the skill. An example of this might be when counting syllables or sounds in a word, providing the students with blocks or cubes to connect to represent the number of sounds. The game format allows the students to receive numerous repetitions in a friendly format that they enjoy and will want to continue.

Other activities can be integrated throughout the day as opportunities arise. While waiting in the hall for a special class or students to finish at the bathroom, the teacher could ask one or several students for words that rhyme with a certain word or to name words that begin with a given sound. In math class, the teacher could test a counting skill and a phonemic awareness skill by asking students to count out the same number of blocks as a given word has syllables. In science class, clues could be given for the key concept by using phonemic awareness skills. For example, the teacher could state that he is thinking of a word that rhymes with ant and begins like please. The children would then respond with plant and a unit on plants has been introduced. These easy to implement, quick activities are indeed the most effective method for teaching phonemic awareness.

COMPETENCY 6.0 THE TEACHER UNDERSTANDS THE DEVELOPMENT OF CONCEPTS ABOUT PRINT.

SKILL 6.1 Demonstrating knowledge of concepts about print (e.g., letter, word, and sentence representation; directionality; tracking of print; understanding that print carries meaning; one-to-one voice-print correspondence)

The Alphabetic principle is sometimes called graphophonemic awareness. This term means that written words are composed of letter (graphemes) which represent the sounds (phonemes) of written words.

Development of the Understanding that Print Carries Meaning

This understanding is demonstrated every day in the elementary classroom as the teacher holds up a selected book to read aloud to the class. The teacher explicitly and deliberately talks aloud about how to hold the book, focuses the class on looking at its cover, points to where to start reading, and sweeps her hands in the direction to begin, left to right.

When writing the morning message on the board, the teacher reminds the children that the message begins in the upper left hand corner at the top of the board to be followed by additional activities and a schedule for the rest of the day.

When the teacher invites children to make posters of a single letter such as *b* and list items in the classroom, their home, or outside which start with that letter, the children are concretely demonstrating that print carries meaning.

Strategies for Promoting Awareness of the Relationship between Spoken and Written Language

- Writing down what the children say on a language chart.
- Highlighting the uses of print products found in the classroom such as labels, yellow sticky pad notes, labels on shelves and lockers, calendars, signs, and directions.
- Reading together big-print and oversized books to teach print conventions such as directionality.
- Practicing how to handle a book: How to turn pages, to find the top and bottom of pages, and how to tell the difference between the front and back covers.
- Discussing and comparing with children the length, appearance and boundaries of specific words. For example, children can see that
- the names Dan and Dora share certain letters and a similar shape.
- Having children match oral words to printed words by forming an echo chorus as the teacher reads poetry or rhymes aloud and they echo the reading.

- Having the children combine, manipulate, switch and move letters to change words.
- Working with letter cards to create messages and respond to the messages that they create.

The Role of Environmental Print in Developing Print Awareness

An environmental print book can be created by the children, which contains collaged symbols of their favorite lunch or breakfast foods. The children cut and clip symbols from the packaging of these foods and then place them in alphabetical order in their class-made book. Magazines and catalogues are another source of environmental print that is accessible with ads for child centered products. Supermarket circulars and coupons from the newspaper are also excellent for engaging children in using environmental print as reading, especially when combined with dramatic play centers or prop boxes.

What is particularly effective in using environmental print is that it immediately invites the child from ELL background into print awareness, through the familiarity of commercial logos and packaging symbols used.

Development of Book Handling Skills

Understanding the value and importance of the concepts of print for beginning readers developed out of the work of Marie Clay in New Zealand. Assessment of these skills typically occurs in kindergarten and into first grade as necessary. The following skills are part of the assessment process:

- Print carries a message – The students can demonstrate this skill even if unable to read the text by pretending to read. This may be demonstrated even if the child does not demonstrate any of the other concepts.
- Book organization – Students demonstrate an understanding of the organization of books by being able to identify the title, cover, author, left to right progression, top to bottom order, and one to one correspondence. Students may learn these skills individually as they become more familiar with books.
- Print Consistencies- This is the understanding that text is made up of letters, which then form words, which then are combined to form sentences. As the beginning reader makes these connections, they will next develop the concept of capital letters at the beginning and basic punctuation marks.
- Letter Identification- The final stage of the concepts of print assessment involves the identification of both upper- and lower- case letters. More advanced students may begin to recognize some of the most common spelling patterns in beginning texts.

Have the children identify the front cover, back cover, and title page of a specific book.

Model storytelling with the book held so that the audience can see the illustrations shown to them. Then have children demonstrate the skills for their peers.

Have children search through the class libraries for special features on the fronts or backs of books as they help return the books to their bins. Have the children display and talk about the special symbols they have found.

Review with the children, in an age and grade appropriate format, additional parts of the book as appropriate during mini lessons and read alouds. These additional parts of the book can include: title pages, dedication page, table of contents, and copyright date and glossary.

Strategies for Promoting an Understanding of the Directionality of Print

In order to become proficient readers, young students need to develop a complete understanding that all print is read from left to right and top to bottom. Modeling is one of the most important strategies a teacher can use to develop this understanding in children. The use of big books, poems, and charts are strategies teachers can use in both large and small group instruction. Simple questions can engage the students to pay closer attention to these skills (i.e. "We are going to read this passage, where should I put my pointer to start reading?").

Directionality of print should also be taught during the writing process. In language experience stories, interactive writing, and Kidwriting©, the teacher can incorporate explicit modeling and instruction in these skills. Sometimes it may be necessary to provide children with a dot at the top left corner of the paper in order to provide a visual reminder of where to begin.

Techniques for Promoting the Ability to Track Print in Connected Texts

Model directionality and one-to-one word matching by pointing to words, while using a big book, pocket chart, or poem written out on a chart. As you repeatedly lead the children in this reading, they can follow along and eventually track the print and make one to one matches on the connected text independently. They can also practice by using a pointer (all children love to use the pointer because then pleasure becomes associated with the reading) or their fingers to follow the words. Children happily volunteer to be the point person. Even before Vanna White, the joy of "signifying letters" existed and has tremendous appeal for children.

Copy down a brief, familiar rhyme (perhaps from a favorite book or song) and post it in the room at child's eye level, so the children can independently walk around and read it.

Copy down a brief or familiar rhyme or poem on individual word cards. Then challenge the children in small groups or independently to reassemble and display them on a pocket chart. As children "play" with constructing and reconstructing this pocket chart, they will develop an awareness of directionality, one on one matching of print to spoken words, spacing, and punctuation.

Model interactive emergent writing with the class. While the teacher is noting down the weather, deliberately ask and have the children suggest where the first word in that report should go, top or bottom of the board? Will the first letter be upper case or lower case? What goes at the end of the sentence?

Create with the children sing-song repetitions/rules for using capitals, periods, commas, etc. Encourage the children to begin reciting these sing-songs as soon as they identify specific concepts of print in connected texts.

Model for children how, when pointing at words, they can start at the top and move from left to right. Tell the children that if there are more words to the sentence they are reading under the first line of print, they must go back to the left and under the previous line. Young children enjoy practicing this kinesthetic "return sweep." You might want to teach them to identify the need to do this by saying "Don't fall asleep at the page" or "Time to get to the "return sweep" stage!!" Post this saying and encourage them to singsong as they joyously take ownership of their reading.

Have even beginning readers "read" through the text to find letters they recognize in the story and then share some of the text that includes these specific letters to whet their appetite for reading.

Strategies for Promoting Letter Knowledge and Letter Formation

Engage the children in a Tale Trail game. Use a story they have already heard or read. Ask the children to circle certain letters and then reread the story, sharing the letters they have circled.

Give the children lots of opportunities to do letter sorts. Pass out word cards which have the targeted letter on them. Ask the children to come up and display their answers to questions like these about the letter, say *R*.

*R as the first letter--rose, rise, ran,
*R as the last letter--car, star, far,
*R with a t after it--start, heart, part, smart
*R, two r's in the middle of a word-- carry, sorry, starry

Play "What's in a Name?"- Select a student's name "William." Copy it down on a sentence strip. Have the children count the number of letters in the name and how many of them appear twice. Allow them to talk about which letter is upper case and which letters are lower case. Have the students chant the name. Then rewrite the name on another sentence strip. Have the strip cut into separate letters and see if some one from the class can put the name back correctly.
As you read a book with or to children, ask that they show you specific letters or lower case or upper case letters. Read the text first and encourage as many children to come up and identify the letters as possible. Use a big book and have felt and sandpaper letters available for display as well. If grade, age and developmentally appropriate, have children then write the letter they identified themselves or even more fun, construct it using pipe cleaners, play dough or coded colored markers (different colors for upper and lower case letters).

Play "letter leap" with the children and have them look carefully at the room to identify labeled items that begin with a specific letter by "leaping" over to them and placing a large lettered placard next to them. Children who are advanced in letter formation can then be challenged to "leap" through the classroom when called upon to literally "letter" unlabeled objects.

Recognition that Phonemes are Represented by Letters and Letter Pairs

As young children begin to learn to read, connections are made between the printed letters on the page and the sounds they have heard in language. Phonemic awareness activities are crucial for building this bridge. Students have engaged in many auditory activities. At this time, it is important the teacher use explicit and systematic methods to demonstrate to the students how these auditory sounds are represented on a page by letters or sometimes letter pairs. As this occurs, students can begin to decode text and move toward becoming proficient readers.

Assessment Throughout the Year of Graphophonemic Awareness

The teacher will want to maintain individual records of children's reading behaviors demonstrating alphabetic principle/graphophonemic awareness.

The following performance standards should be part of a record template form for each child in grades K-1 and beyond as needed (depending on ELL or special needs):
- Match all consonant and short vowel sounds.
- Read one's own name.
- Read one syllable words and high frequency words.
- Demonstrate ability to read and understand that as letters in words change, so do the sounds.
- Generate the sounds from all letters including consonant blends and long vowel patterns. Blend those different sounds into recognizable words.
- Read common sight words.
- Read common word families.
- Recognize and use knowledge of spelling patterns when reading: run/running, hop/hopping.

Any record kept of an individual child's progress should include each date of observation and some legend or rubric detailing the level of performance, standard acquisition, or mastery.

The following template can be used by teachers to record student progress for each child in grades K-1 and beyond as needed (depending on ELL or special needs):

Reading Progress

Skill Area	Mastered	Making Progress	Not Yet	Comments
Matches all consonant and short vowel sounds				
Reads one's own name				
Reads one syllable words and high frequency words				
Demonstrates ability to read and understand that as letters in words change, so do the sounds				
Generates the sounds from all letters including consonant blends and long vowel patterns. Blend those different sounds into recognizable words				
Reads common sight words				
Reads common word families				
Recognizes and uses knowledge of spelling patterns when reading: run/running, hop/hopping				

Any record kept of an individual child's progress should include each date of observation and some legend or rubric detailing the level of performance, standard acquisition, or mastery.

Development of Alphabetic Knowledge in Individual Students

Researchers Laura M. Justice and Helen K. Ezell (2002) evaluated alphabetic knowledge and print awareness in pre-school children from low income households. In their post-tests, children who had participated in shared reading sessions that emphasized a print focus outperformed their control group peers (other Head Start children) on three measures of print awareness: words in print, print recognition, and alphabetic knowledge.

Other researchers including Chaney (1994) have demonstrated a statistically significant and inverse relationship between household income and children's performance on measures of print awareness and the alphabetic principle. Lonigan (l999) found that substantial group differences existed on a variety of pre literacy tasks administered to 85 preschool children from lower and middle income households. The researchers looked at environmental print, print and book reading conventions, and alphabet knowledge. Results showed that preschool children from middle income households showed significantly higher levels of skill across all print awareness tasks in comparison with preschoolers from low income households.

Obviously this data highlights the importance of extensive alphabetic knowledge activities and print awareness opportunities for some children from low income households in grades K-1 and even beyond if necessary.

Two other studies undertaken by Ezell and Justice (in the year 2000) suggested that structuring adult-child shared book reading interactions to include an explicit print awareness and alphabetic principle focus resulted in a substantial increase in children's verbal interactions with print.

This work highlights the importance of not only classroom and preschool emphasis on print awareness and alphabetic principle routines, but also the need for teachers to reach out to parents and to model for them these shared reading experiences so that family life can parallel the classroom experiences. Many schools currently have parent volunteers and reading buddy programs. Training of these volunteers, particularly in high need, low economic income status communities is certainly warranted.

David J. Chard and Jean Osborn (l999) have reflected on the guidelines necessary for teachers to use in selecting supplemental phonics and word-recognition materials for addressing students with learning disabilities. They note that an important way to help children with reading disabilities figure out the system underlying the printed word is leading them to understand the alphabetic principle. Children with learning disabilities (LD) in particular, benefit from organized instruction that centers on letters, sounds, and the relations between sounds and letters. They also benefit from word-recognition patterns instruction that offers practice with word families that share similar letter patterns.

Children who are LD also benefit from opportunities to apply what they are learning to the reading and re-reading of stories and other texts. Such texts contain a high portion of words which reflect the letters, sounds, and spelling patterns the children are learning.

For special needs children, a beginning reading program should include the following elements of alphabetic knowledge instruction:

1. A variety of alphabetic knowledge activities in which the children learn to identify and name both upper and lower case letters.
2. Games, songs, and other activities that help children to learn to name the letters quickly.
3. Writing activities that encourage children to practice the letters which they are writing.
4. A sensible sequence of letter introduction that can be adjusted to the needs of the children.

SKILL 6.2 Recognizing how concepts about print relate to other aspects of reading development

As we examine the concepts of print and learn how to teach them, it is important to understand how they represent the underlying principles to other aspects of reading development.

The concepts of print provide the foundation to all other reading skills. In order for students to develop phonemic awareness skills, they must understand the difference between a word and a letter. They must understand that words are made up of smaller parts of language: phonemes (sounds). Making the transition to the written word, students need to realize that letters or letter combinations represent those smaller sounds.

Once they realize that letters and words are different, they can then begin to see how putting letters together make different sound combinations and then putting more and more letters together make words and finally sentences. Without this basic level of understanding, the child has no hook with which to tie the information, which will later be the root of comprehension.

Since the English language is written in a left to right format, it is essential that this concept of print be taught to the students from the very beginning. If not learned, the child will not understand how to look at a page of print and even begin. Imagine a student could have advanced skills in phonemic awareness and phonics but still be unable to read a text if they did not understand left to right progression.

Another concept of print that would directly impact a student's ability to progress is the idea of a return sweep. The child could begin to read and come to the end of the first line and without efficiently knowing to return back to the left and begin again, he would become confused by the words on the page.

TEACHER CERTIFICATION STUDY GUIDE

Book handling skills should begin at such a young age so they will seem almost automatic by the time the child is in kindergarten. However, for some children this is not the case. The inability to master these simple concepts of print will hinder any and all further reading progress until they can be mastered. As fluent readers, we take for granted the ease with which these skills were obtained, but for some students they were quite a struggle. The key to mastery is more time spent with print, looking at books and the written word, and interacting with books.

SKILL 6.3 Identifying appropriate materials and activities to provide effective instruction relating to concepts about print (e.g., environmental print, trade books, big books, patterned language, newspapers)

See skill 6.1

SKILL 6.4 Demonstrating knowledge of strategies for selecting, designing, and using engaging materials and activities to help students recognize letter shapes and learn letter names

Use of Reading and Writing Strategies for Teaching Letter-sound Correspondence

Provide children with a sample of a single letter book (or create one from environmental sources, newspapers, coupons, circulars, magazines or your own text ideas). Make sure that your already published or created sample includes a printed version of the letter in both upper and lower case forms. Make certain that each page contains a picture of something that starts with that specific letter and also has the word for the picture. The book you select or create should be a predictable one in that when the picture is identified, the word can be read.

Once the children have been provided with your sample and have listened to it being read, challenge them to each make a one letter book. Often it is best to focus on familiar consonants for the single letter book or the first letter of the child's first name. Using the first letter of the child's first name invites the child to develop a book which tells about him or her and the words that he or she finds. This is an excellent way to have the reading and writing workshop enhance the teaching of the alphabetic principle. Encourage children to be active writers and readers by finding words for their book on the classroom word wall, in alphabet books in the special alphabet book bin and in grade and age appropriate pictionaries, (dictionaries for younger children which are filled with pictures).

READING

Of course, the richest resource within the reading and writing workshop classroom for teaching and fostering the alphabetic principle lies in the use of alphabet books as anchor books for inspiring students writing. While young children in grades K-1 will do better with the one letter book authoring activity, children in grades 2 and beyond can truly be inspired and motivated by alphabet books to enhance their own reading, writing and alphabetic skills. Furthermore, use of these books which have and are being produced in a variety of formats to enhance social studies, science and mathematical themes, provide an opportunity for even young children to create a meaningful product that authenticates their content study as it enhances alphabetic skills and, of course, print awareness

An annotated bibliography of selected alphabet books has been provided in the bibliography section of this guide. It was limited by space considerations, but the teacher can with no expense and with much pleasure catch up on the latest titles and identify those most appropriate for the grade taught, by visiting a bookstore. Hold the print book in hand and then consider selecting an alphabet book that has a particularly inviting concept, art style, or adaptable format within the children's capacity to use as a model.

For instance, Tina Hoban uses actual color photographs of letters in her *26 Letters and 99 Cents.* Children may want to make clay letters or create letter sculptures that develop their own alphabet book similar to Hoban's. If nutrition is the science topic, children might want to examine Ehlert's very accessible *Eating the Alphabet: Fruits and Vegetables from A to Z.* This, combined with an examination of the fruits and vegetables in a local store (perhaps a pleasant walk from the school and a quick break from the routine) can yield a wonderful alphabet book on fruits and vegetables which can also include those fruits and vegetables eaten in various cultures (i.e. mangos, plantains, pomegranates, etc).

The alphabet book can also offer the class a chance to work collaboratively using a template page created by the teacher. Completion of this collaborative work can be shared with peers in another class and parents and be kept in the classroom library as a model for the following year's class with their recognition and acceptance of the authors!

SKILL 6.5 Identifying strategies for assessing students' development of print concepts

Assessment of the development of the concepts of print for students is a generally simple procedure. This can be handled in an informal basis with any book available. The easiest method for keeping track is to keep dated notes on a card or folder as to the progress students make through all of the concepts of print to report to parents or other pertinent personnel.

Simply asking the student to show you one letter on a given page will provide the teacher with the knowledge as to whether or not a student can isolate a letter and truly understands what one letter is. The same strategy works for a word and a sentence. Just asking the student to identify where one word is or where a sentence can be located on a page.

An easy method to assess left to right progression and the concept of a return sweep is to ask the students to pretend they are reading a page that they may be unable to read. Asking them to pretend to be the teacher and show you with their finger how they would read that page. Watching how the child moves his finger across the page tells the teacher whether or not the child is progressing through or has mastered these skills.

Some assessments of print concepts include a word identification portion. In this part, there are two words printed on a line for the student to see. One word is two or three letters long and the other word starts with the same letter but is significantly longer, usually eight or more letters. The teacher then says one of the two words and the child points to the word the teacher states. In this assessment, the teacher gathers some insight into whether the child has the understanding that a multisyllabic word will be longer than a single syllable word.

Concepts of print are almost always completed through informal assessment methods. It is an easy assessment to complete, but should be completed on an individual basis to ensure valuable results. For the most part, concepts of print are mastered during the kindergarten year of schooling.

COMPETENCY 7.0 THE TEACHER UNDERSTANDS PHONICS AND OTHER WORD IDENTIFICATION STRATEGIES.

SKILL 7.1 Recognizing how to plan the sequence of phonics instruction to reflect increasing complexity of linguistic units (e.g., letters, letter combinations, syllables)

Sequence of Phonics Skills

- Letter Naming
    - Lower Case Letters
    - Upper Case Letters
- Letter Sounds
    - Continuous Sounds
    - Stop Sounds
    - Both Consonant and Vowel Sounds
- Short Vowels in CVC Words
- Short Vowels with Digraphs and –tch Trigraph
- Short Vowels and Consonant Blends
- Long Vowels
- Variant Vowels and Diphthongs
- R- and L- Controlled Vowels
- Multisyllabic Words

SKILL 7.2 Identifying instructional strategies, activities, and materials to teach students letter-sound correspondence, phonics generalizations, and the use of graphophonic cues to decode words in connected text

Explicit and Implicit Strategies for Teaching Phonics

Uta Frith has identified three phases which describe the progression of children's phonic learning from ages four through eight. These are:

Logographic Phase
Children recognize whole words that have significance for them such as their own names or the names of stores they frequent or products that their parents buy. Examples are McDonald's, SuperValu, and the like. Strategies which nurture development in this phase include explicit labeling of class room objects, components, furniture and materials and showing the children's names in print as often as possible. Toward the end of this phase children start to notice initial letters in words and the sounds that they represent.

Analytic Phase
During this phase the children begin to make associations between the spelling patterns in the words they know and new words they encounter. Children in this phase of reading development are able to generalize that hat and cat are going to be read in a similar manner because they recognize that the /at/ portions of the words are the same. This is helpful with word families and can be transferred to encoding words through many activities. Some teachers find it helpful to add word families or family houses to their word walls around the room. In this way, students can begin to make these generalizations more rapidly. As the students find more complex words that fall into the family/house, they add them.

Orthographic Phase
In this phase, children recognize words almost automatically. They can rapidly identify an increasing number of words. Students are able to apply many different strategies in a seamless manner to help them decode unknown words. This may include: phonics, structural analysis, syntax, semantics, and contextual clues. Students at this level are fluent readers with good prosody. They are reading to make the shift from learning to read to reading to learn. It is a critical shift for children.

To best support these phases and the development of emergent and early readers, teachers should focus on elements of phonics learning which help children analyze words for their letters, spelling patterns, and structural components. The children need to be involved in activities in which they use what they know about words to learn new ones.

The teacher needs to build on what the children know to introduce new spelling patterns, vowel combinations, and short and long vowel investigations. The teacher must do this and be aware that these will be reintroduced again and again as needed.

Keep in mind that children's learning of phonics and other key components of reading is not linear, but rather falls back to review and then flows forward to build new understandings.

Among suggested activities to support phonics instruction to address the needs of these three phases of phonics learning are:

(These activities have specifically been provided in detail so that the educator can study them and use them in the sample constructed response questions which have been provided at the end of the guide. Since the role of phonics in promoting reading development is so crucial, it is highly likely that a constructed response question on the certification test will focus on the use of such strategies. Therefore it is a good idea for the certification candidate to study them closely. As a bonus, the detail with which these strategies are set forth also makes them readily useful with classes the teacher is currently teaching).

Sorting Words

This activity allows children to focus closely on the specific features of words and to begin to understand the basic elements of letter sound relationships. Start with one syllable (monosyllabic) words. Have the children group them by their length, common letters, sound, and/or spelling pattern.

Prepare for the activity by writing ten to fifteen words on oaktag strips and place them randomly on the sentence strip holder. These words should come from a book previously shared in the classroom or a language experience chart.

Next begin to sort out the words with the children, perhaps by where a particular letter appears in a word. While the children sort the place of a particular letter in a given word, they should also be coached (or facilitated) by the teacher to recognize that sometimes a letter in the middle of the word can still be the last sound that we hear and that some letters at the end of a word are silent (such as "e").

Children should be encouraged to make their own categories for word sorts and to share their own discoveries as they do the word sorts. The children's discoveries should be recorded and posted in the rooms with their names so they have ownership of their phonics learning.

Spelling Pattern Word Wall

One of the understandings emergent readers come to about a word is that if they know how to read, write, and spell one word, they can write, read, and spell many other words as well.

Create in your classroom a spelling pattern word wall. The spelling word wall can be created by stapling a piece of 3" x 5" butcher block paper to the bulletin board. Then attach spelling pattern cards around the border with thumbtacks, so that the cards can be easily removed to use at the meeting area.

Once you decide on a spelling pattern for instruction, remove the corresponding card from the word wall. Then take a 1"x 3" piece of a contrasting color of butcher block paper and tape the card to the top end of a sheet the children will use for their investigation.

After the pattern is identified the children can try to come up with other words that have the same spelling pattern. The teacher can write these on the spelling pattern sheet, using a different color marker to highlight the spelling pattern within the word. The children have to add to the list until the sheet is full, which might take two days or more.

After the sheet is full, the completed spelling pattern is attached to the wall.

Letter Holder Making Words

Use a 2" x 3" piece of foam board to make a letter holder. On the front of the board, attach 16 library pockets –one for each letter from A to P. Use the back of the board to attach another 10 pockets for the rest of the alphabet.

Write the letter name on each pocket and use clear bookbinding tape to secure each row of cards with clear tape. Make twelve cards for each letter. On the front of each 2"x 6" strip, make a capital letter and on its back write that letter in lower case. Write consonants in, say, black marker and vowels in red marker.

Through use of this letter holder, children can experience how letters can be rearranged, added, or removed to make new words. They can use these cards also to focus as needed on letter sequences and to support them in recognizing spelling patterns in words.

The words you choose to use for this activity can be selected from Patricia Cunningham and Dorothy P. Hall's, *Making Words* (1994). Select a word that is called the "secret word." Build up toward the creation of that word through a focus on the smaller words within it. Words should be chosen which reflect the spelling patterns being studied by the class.

You can create letter holders for the children by folding up the bottom third of a used manila file folder and taping the ends to form a shallow pocket. Give them letter cards which are made of 2"x 6" oaktag. So, for example, if the secret word is bicycle, the children would be given the separate letter cards which would make up that word. The children keep the letters on the floor in front of them and only place them in the holder when they are actually making a word.
Making words should begin with making two letter words and then progress as the individual child is ready to make larger words. The teacher provides the instruction of which two letters the child is to use to make a word. After the instruction is given the children select the correct letters and make the word in their folder. The teacher then writes the word down and the children check their letter holder word against it. The teacher goes around checking through and reviewing the letter holders to see which children are "getting it" and then continues to build up words with more letters if the children are ready.

Word Splits

Splitting compound words. Through working with compound words, children can actually experience bigger words that are often made up of smaller words. By working with five to ten compound words on oaktag cards, children can analyze letter-sound relationships and meaning.

Before children meet in a group, write five to ten words on oaktag cards and arrange them on the sentence strip holder. After the words have been read, cut each of the words into its two smaller words and randomly arrange them on the sentence strip holder. Allow the children to randomly take turns arranging the small words back into the original compound words. Also, encourage them to form new compound words. For example, if one of two original compound words is "rainbow" and the other is "dropping," the children should be able to come with "raindrop." The new words the children come up with should be written on blank oaktag cards with the names of the children who came up with them attached. In this way the children can add to their growing bank of new words and have ownership in the words that they have added.

SKILL 7.3   Demonstrating knowledge of word identification strategies in addition to phonics, including structural analysis (e.g., recognition of word roots and affixes), morphemes, and use of semantic, syntactic, and contextual cues

Use of Semantic and Syntactic Cues to Help Decode Words

Semantic Cues

Students will need use their base knowledge of word meanings, semantics, to help them decipher unknown words or text as well as to clarify reading when it does not seem to make sense. Some prompts the teacher can use which will alert the children to semantic cues include:
- Does that sentence make sense?
- Which word in that sentence does not seem to fit?
- Why doesn't it fit?
- What word might make sense in that sentence?

Syntactic Cues

The first strategy good readers use from their own knowledge base to help determine misreading, is syntactic cues. Syntactic cues use the order of words and the student's knowledge of the oral English language to help determine if what was read could be accurate. Some prompts the teacher can use to encourage and develop syntactic cues in reading include:
- You read (child's incorrect attempt). Does that sound right?
- You read (child's incorrect attempt). When we talk, do we talk that way?
- How would we say it?
- Recheck that sentence. Does it sound right the way you read it?

Specific Terminology Associated With Phonics

It is important to have a clear understanding of the terms associated with phonics. Here are some definitions, which are helpful in having a clear understanding of phonic development in children.

Phoneme – a phoneme is the smallest unit of sound in the English language. In print phonemes are represented by the letter and a slash. So, /b/ represents the sound the letter b would make.

Morpheme- a morpheme is the smallest unit of grammar in the English language. In other words, it is the smallest unit of meaning, not just sounds.

Consonant Digraph – a consonant digraph are two consonants of the English language who when placed together in a word make a unique sound, neither makes when alone. Examples: ch, th, sh, and wh.

Consonant Blend- a consonant blend is when two consonants are put together, but each retains their individual sound. The two sounds go together in a seamless manner to produce a blended sound. Examples: st, br, cl, etc.

Schwa sound- schwa sound is a vowel sound which is neutral. It typically occurs in the unaccented syllable of a word. An example would be the sound of the a at the end of the word sofa. It is represented in print by an upside down e

Development of Phonics Skills with Individual Students

In ON SOLID GROUND (2000), researcher and educator Sharon Taberski said that it is much harder for children from ELL backgrounds and children from homes where other English dialects are spoken to use syntactic cues to attempt to self-correct.

These children, through no fault of their own, do not have sufficient experience hearing Standard English spoken to use this cueing system as they read. The teacher should sensitively guide them through by modeling the use of syntactic and semantic cues.

Highly proficient readers can be paired as buddy tutors for ELL or special needs classroom members or to assist the resource room teacher during their reading time. They can use the CVC Game developed by Jacki Montrieth to support their peers and can even modify the game to meet the needs of classroom peers. Of course, this also offers the highly proficient reader the opportunity to do a service learning project, while still in elementary school. It also introduces the learner to another dimension of reading, the role of the reader as trainer and recruiter of other peers into the circle of readers and writers!.

If the highly proficient readers are so motivated or if their teachers so desire, the peer tutors can also maintain an ongoing reading progress journal for their tutees. This will be a wonderful way to realize the goals of the reading and writing workshop.

There are many different strategies to help children who are struggling with their phonics skill development. A beginning step is to identify the area of difficulty within phonics. A simple assessment to help determine the exact area of difficulty is the CORE Phonics Survey which can be downloaded free. Once the area of deficit has been identified, small group instruction can be developed around these areas to increase specific skills.

When working on specific phonics skills, it is important to utilize decodable texts. There are numerous publishers who have available a variety of different skills and texts for use within the classroom. If students continue to struggle, it may be necessary to utilize a more specific systematic and explicit phonics program. Some examples of these include: Wilson Reading, Early Intervention Reading, and Open Court.

Development of Word Analysis Skills and Strategies, Including Structural Analysis

Structural analysis is a process of examining the words in the text for meaningful word units (affixes, base words, inflected endings). There are six types of word types which are formed and therefore can be analyzed using structural analysis strategies. They include:

1. Common prefixes or suffixes added to a known word ending with a consonant
2. Adding the suffix –ed to words that end with consonants
3. Compound words
4. Adding endings to words that end with the letter e
5. Adding endings to words that end with the letter y
6. Adding affixes to multisyllabic words

When teaching and using structural analysis procedures in the primary grades, teachers should remember to make sound decisions on which to introduce and teach. Keeping in mind the number of primary words in which each affix appears and how similar they are will help the teacher make the instructional process smoother and more valuable to the students.

Adding affixes to words can be started when students are able to read a list of one-syllable words by sight at a rate of approximately twenty words correct per minute. At the primary level, there is a recommended sequence for introducing affixes. The steps in this process are:
- Start by introducing the affix in the letter-sound correspondence format
- Practice the affix in isolation for a few days
- Provide words for practice which contain the affix (word lists, flash cards, etc.)
- Move from word lists to including passage reading, which include words with the affix (and some from the word lists/flash cards).

1. Word Study Group

This involves the teacher taking time to meet with children from grades 3-6 in a small group of no more than 6 children for a word study session. Taberski (2000) suggests that this meeting take place next to the Word Wall. The children selected for this group are those who need to focus more on the relationship between spelling patterns and consonant sounds.

It is important that this not be a formalized traditional reading group that meets at a set time each week or biweekly. Rather the group should be spontaneously formed by the teacher based on the teacher's quick inventory of the selected children's needs at the start of the week. Taberski has templates in her book of *Guided Reading Planning Sheets.* These sheets are essentially targeted word and other skills sheets with her written dated observations of children who are in need of support to develop a given skill.

The teacher should try to meet with this group for at least two consecutive twenty minute periods daily. Over those two meetings, the teacher can model a Making Words Activity. Once the teacher has modeled making words the first day, the children would then make their own words. On the second day, the children would "sort" their words.

Other topics for a word study group within the framework of the Balanced Literacy Approach that Taberski advocates are: inflectional endings, prefixes and suffixes, and/or common spelling patterns. These are covered later in this chapter.

It should be noted that this activity would be classified by theorists as a structural analysis activity because the structural components (i.e. prefixes, suffixes, and spelling patterns) of the words are being studied.

2. Discussion Circles

Cooper (2004) believes that children should not be "taught" vocabulary and structural analysis skills. Flesch and E.D. Hirsch, who are key theorists of the phonics approach and advocates of Cultural Literacy (a term coined and associated with E. D. Hirsch), believe that specific vocabulary words at various grade and age levels need to be mastered and must be explicitly taught in schools. As far as J. David Cooper is concerned, all the necessary and meaningful (for the child and ultimately adult reader) vocabulary can't possibly be taught in schools (no apologies to Hirsch). To Cooper it is far more important that the children be made aware of and become interested in learning words by themselves. Cooper feels that through the child's reading and writing, he or she develops a love for and a sense of "ownership" of words. All of Cooper's suggested structural analysis word strategies are therefore designed to foster the child's love of words and a desire to "own" more of them through reading and writing.

Discussion Circles is an activity which fits nicely into the balanced literacy lesson format. After the children conclude a particular text, Cooper suggests that respond to the book in discussion circles. Among the prompts, the teacher-coach might suggest that the children focus on words of interest they encountered in the text. These can also be words that they heard if the text was read aloud. Children can be asked to share something funny or upsetting or unusual about the words they have read. Through this focus on children's response to words as the center of the discussion circle, peers become more interested in word study.

3. Banking, Booking, and Filing It: Making Words My Own

Children can literally realize the goal of making words their own and exploring word structures through creating concrete objects or displays that demonstrate the words they own. Children can create and maintain their own files of words they have learned or are interested in learning.

The files can be categorized by the children according to their own interests. They should be encouraged to develop files using science, history, physical education, fine arts, dance, and technology content. Newspapers and web resources, which the teacher has approved, are excellent sources for such words. In addition, this provides the teacher with the opportunity to instruct the child in appropriate age and grade-level research skills. Even children in grades 2 and 3 can begin simplified bibliographies and webliographies for their "found" words. Children can learn how to annotate and note the page of a newspaper, book, or URL for a particular word.

They can also copy down the word as it appears in the text (print or electronic). If appropriate the child can place the particular words found for a given topic or content in an actual bank of the child's own making. The words can be printed on cards. This allows for differentiated word study and appeals to those children who are kinesthetic and spatial learners. Of course, children can also choose to create their own word books which include their specialized vocabulary and descriptions of how they identified or hunted down their words. Richard Scarry, watch out! Scarry books can be anchor books to inspire this structural analysis activity.

ELL learners can share their accounts in their native language first and then translate (with the help of the teacher) these accounts into English with both the native language and the English language versions of the word exploration posted.

4. Write out your Words, Write with your words

Ownership of words can be demonstrated by having the children use them as part of their writings. The children can author a procedural narrative (a step by step description) of how they went about their word searches to compile the words they found for any of the activities. If the children are in grades K-1, or if the children are struggling readers and writers, their procedural narratives can be dictated. Then they can be posted by the teacher.

ELL students can share their accounts in their native language first and then translate (with the help of the teacher) these accounts into English with both the native language and the English language versions of the word exploration posted.

Children with special needs may model a word box on a specific holiday theme, genre or science/social studies topic with the teacher. Initially this can be done as a whole class. As the children become more confident, they can work with peers or with a paraprofessional to create their own individual or small team/pair word boxes.

Special needs children can create a storyboard with the support of a paraprofessional, their teacher or a resource specialist. They can also narrate their story of how they all found the words, using a tape recorder.

5.- Word Study Museum Within the Classroom

This strategy has been presented in detail so it can be used by the teachers within their own classrooms. In addition, the way the activity is described and the mention at the end of the description of how the activity can address family literacy, ELL, and special needs children's talents, provides an example of other audiences a teacher should consider in curriculum design.
Almost every general education teacher and reading specialist will have to differentiate instruction to address the needs of special education and ELL learners. Family or shared literacy is a major component of all literacy instruction.

Children can create either a single or multiple exhibits, museum style, within their classrooms celebrating their word study. They can build actual representations of the type of study they have done including word trees (made out of cardboard or foam board), elaborate word boxes and games, word history timelines or murals, and word study maps. They can develop online animations, Kids Spiration graphic organizers, quick movies, digital photo essays, and PowerPoint presentations to share the word they have identified. The classroom or the gym or cafeteria can be transformed into a gallery space. Children can author brochure descriptions for their individual, team or class exhibits. Some children can volunteer to be tour guides or docents for the experience. Other children can work to create a banner for the Museum. The children can name the Museum themselves and send out invitations to its opening. Invitations can be sent to parents, community, staff members and peer or younger classes.

Depending on their age and grade level, children can also develop interactive games and quizzes focused on particular exhibits. An artist or a team of class artists can design a poster for the exhibit, while other children choose to build the exhibits. Another small group can work on signage and a catalogue or register of objects within the exhibit. Greeters who will welcome parents and peers to the exhibit can be trained and can develop their own scripts.

If the children are in grades 4-6, they can also develop their own visitor feedback forms and design word-themed souvenirs. The whole museum within the school or classroom can be captured digitally or with a regular camera. The record of this event can be hung near the word walls. Of course, the children can use many of their newly recognized and owned words to describe the event.

The Word Study Museum activity can be used with either a phonics-based or a balanced literacy approach. It promotes additional writing, researching, discussing, and reading about words.

It is also an excellent family literacy strategy in that families can develop their own Word Exhibits at home. This activity can also support and celebrate learners with disabilities. It can be presented in dual languages by children who are ELL learners and fluent in more than a single language.)

Relationship Between Word Analysis Skills and Reading Comprehension

The explicit teaching of word analysis requires that the teacher pre-select words from a given text for vocabulary learning. These words should be chosen based on the storyline and main ideas of the text. The educator may even want to create a story map for a narrative text or develop a graphic organizer for an expository text. Once the story mapping and/or graphic organizing have been done, the educator can compile a list of words which relate to the storyline and/or main ideas.

The number of words that require explicit teaching should only be two or three. If the number is higher than that, the children need guided reading and the text needs to be broken down into smaller sections for teaching. When broken down into smaller sections, each text section should only have two to three words which need explicit teaching.

Some researchers, including Tierney and Cunningham, believe that a few words should be taught as a means of improving comprehension.

It is up to the educator whether the vocabulary selected for teaching needs review before reading, during reading, or after reading.

Introduce vocabulary BEFORE READING if. . .

- Children are having difficulty constructing meaning on their own. Children themselves have previewed the text and indicated words they want to know.

- The teacher has seen that there are words within the text which are definitely keys necessary for reading comprehension

- The text, itself, in the judgment of the teacher, contains difficult concepts for the children to grasp.

Introduce vocabulary DURING READING if . . .

- Children are already doing guided reading.

- The text has words which are crucial to its comprehension and the children will have trouble comprehending it, if they are not helped with the text.

Introduce vocabulary AFTER READING if. . .

- The children themselves have shared words which they found difficult or interesting

- The children need to expand their vocabulary

- The text itself is one that is particularly suited for vocabulary building.

Strategies, to support word analysis and enhance reading comprehension, include:

- Use of a graphic organizer such as a word map
- Semantic mapping
- Semantic feature analysis
- Hierarchical and linear arrays
- Preview in context
- Contextual redefinition
- Vocabulary self-collection
- (Note that these terms are in the Glossary.)

Identification of Common Morphemes, Prefixes, and Suffixes

This aspect of vocabulary development is to help children look for structural elements within words which they can use independently to help them determine meaning.

Some teachers choose to directly teach structural analysis. In particular, those who teach by following the phonics-centered approach for reading do this. Other teachers, who follow the balanced literacy approach, introduce the structural components as part of mini lessons that are focused on the students' reading and writing.

Structural analysis of words as defined by J. David Cooper (2004) involves the study of significant word parts. This analysis can help the child with pronunciation and constructing meaning.

The term list below is generally recognized as the key structural analysis components.

Root Words

This is a word from which another word is developed. The second word can be said to have its "root" in the first, such as *vis, to see,* in visor or vision. This structural component can be illustrated by a tree with roots to display the meaning for children. Children may also want to literally construct root words using cardboard trees to create word family models.

ELL learners can construct these models for their native language root word families, as well for the English language words they are learning. ELL learners in the 5th and 6th grade may even appreciate analyzing the different root structures for contrasts and similarities between their native language and English.

Learners with special needs can focus in small groups or individually with a paraprofessional on building root word models.

Base Words

These are stand-alone linguistic units which cannot be deconstructed or broken down into smaller words. For example, in the word *re-tell*, the base word is "tell."

Contractions

These are shortened forms of two words in which a letter or letters have been deleted. These deleted letters have been replaced by an apostrophe.

Prefixes

These are beginning units of meaning which can be added (the vocabulary word for this type of structural adding is "affixed") to a base word or root word. They can not stand alone. They are also sometimes known as "bound morphemes" meaning that they can not stand alone as a base word. Examples are *re-, un-,* and *mis-*.

Suffixes

These are ending units of meaning which can be "affixed" or added on to the ends of root or base words. Suffixes transform the original meanings of base and root words. Like prefixes, they are also known as "bound morphemes," because they can not stand alone as words. Examples are *-less, -ful,* and *-tion*.

Compound Words

These occur when two or more base words are connected to form a new word. The meaning of the new word is in some way connected with that of the base word. Examples are *firefighter, newspaper*, and *pigtail*.

Inflectional Endings

These are types of suffixes that impart a new meaning to the base or root word. These endings in particular change the gender, number, tense, or form of the base or root words. Just like other suffixes, these are also termed "bound morphemes." Examples are *–s* or *-ed*.

Comments

Definitions are included because the structural analysis components are explicitly taught in schools which advocate the phonics-centered approach and are also incorporated into the word work component of the schools which advocate the balanced literacy approach for instruction.

Definition questions are multiple choice questions which have only a single right answer, test whether the teacher candidate has memorized the appropriate terminology. They constitute for no less than 15% of the multiple choice question on the test. Therefore by taking the time to memorize these easy definitions, scores are likely to improve.

Some of these activities are presented in detail to help answer the constructed response questions of the test.

Knowledge of Greek and Latin Roots That Form English Words

Knowledge of Greek and Latin roots which comprise English words can measurably enhance children's reading skills and can also enrich their writing.

Word Webs

Sharon Taberski (2000) does not advocate teaching Greek and Latin derivatives in the abstract to young children. However, when she comes across (as is common and natural) specific Greek and Latin roots while reading to children, she uses that opportunity to introduce children to these rich resources.

For example, during readings on rodents (a favorite of first and second graders), Taberski draws her class's attention to the fact that beavers, gnaw at things with their teeth. She then connects the "dent" root or derivative to the children's lives, other words they are familiar with or experiences. The children then volunteer "*dentist,*" "*dental,*" "*denture.*" Taberski begins to place these in a graphic organizer, or word web.

When she has tapped the extent of the children's prior knowledge of "dent" words, she shares with them the fact that *dens/dentis* is the Latin word for teeth. Then she introduces the word "indent," which she has already previewed with them as part of their conventions of print study. She helps them to see that the "indenting" of the first line of a paragraph can even be related to the "teeth" Latin root in that it looks like a "print" bite was taken out of the paragraph.

Taberski displays the word web in the Word Wall Chart section of her room. The class is encouraged throughout, say, a week's time to look for other words to add to the web. Taberski stresses that for her, as an elementary teacher of reading and writing, the key element of the Greek and Latin word root web activity is the children's coming to understand that if they know what a Greek or Latin word root means, they can use that knowledge to figure out what other words mean.

She feels the key concept is to model and demonstrate for children how fun and fascinating Greek and Latin root study can be.

Greek and Latin Roots Word Webs With an Assist From the World Wide Web

Older children in grades 3-6 can build on this initial print activity by searching online for additional words with a particular Greek or Latin root which has been introduced in class.

They can easily do this in a way that authentically ties in with their own interests and experiences by reading reviews for a book which has been a read-aloud online or by just reading the summaries of the day's news and printing out those words which appear in the stories online that share the root discussed.

The children can be encouraged to circle these instances of their Latin or Greek root and also to document the exact date and URL for the citation. These can be posted as part of their own online web in the word wall section study area. If the school or class has a website or webpage, the children can post this data there as a special Greek and Latin root word page.

Expanding the concept of the Greek and Latin word web from the printed page to the world wide web, nicely inculcates the child in the habits of lifelong reading and researching online. This beginning expository research will serve them well in intermediate level content area work and beyond.

Use of Syllabification as a Word Identification Strategy

Strategy: Clap Hands, Count those Syllables as They Come!! (Taberski, 2000)

The objective of this activity is for children to understand that there are every syllable in a polysyllabic word can be studied for its spelling patterns in the same way that monosyllabic words are studied for their spelling patterns.

The easiest way for the K-3 teacher to introduce this activity to the children is to share a familiar poem from the poetry chart (or to write out a familiar poem on a large experiential chart).

First the teacher reads the poem with the children. As they are reading it aloud, the children clap the beats of the poem and the teacher uses a colored marker to place a tic (/) above each syllable.

Next, the teacher takes letter cards and selects one of the polysyllabic words from the poem which the children have already "clapped" out.

The children use letter cards to spell that word on the sentence strip holder or it can be placed on a felt board or up against a window on display. Together the children and teacher divide the letters into syllables and place blank letter cards between the syllables. The children identify spelling patterns they know.

Finally and as part of continued small group syllabification study, the children identify other polysyllabic words they clapped out from the poem. They make up the letter combinations of these words. Then they separate them into syllables with blank letter cards between the syllables.

Children who require special support in syllabification can be encouraged to use many letter cards to create a large butcher paper syllabic (in letter cards with spaces) representation of the poem or at least a few lines of the poem. They can be told that this is for use as a teaching tool for others. In this way, they authenticate their study of syllabification with a real product that can actually be referenced by peers.

Techniques for Identifying Compound Words

The teaching of compound words should utilize structural analysis techniques. (See above section on structural analysis).
Here are some other strategies for helping students to identify and read compound words.
- Use songs and actions to help children understand the concept that compound words are two smaller words joined together to make one bigger word
- Use games like concentration, memory and go fish for students to practice reading compound words
- Use word sorts to have students distinguish between compound words and non-examples of compound words

Identification of Homographs

Homographs are words that are spelled the same but have different meanings. A subgroup within this area includes words that are spelled the same, have different meanings, and are pronounced differently. Some examples of homographs include:
- Lie
- Tear
- Bow
- Fair
- Bass

Teaching homographs can be interesting and fun for the students. Incorporating them into passages where the students can use the context clues to decipher the different meanings of the homographs. Games are also a good strategy for using to help students understand multiple meaning words. Jokes and riddles are usually based on homographs, and students love to make collections or books of these.

READING

Semantic Feature Analysis: This technique for enhancing vocabulary skills by using semantic cues is based on the research of Johnson and Pearson (1984) and Anders and Bos (1986). It involves young children in setting up a feature analysis grid of various subject content words which is an outgrowth of their discussion about these words.

For instance, Cooper (2004) includes a sample of a Semantic Features Analysis Grid for Vegetables. .

Vegetables	Green	Have Peels	Eat Raw	Seeds
Carrots	-	+	+	-
Cabbage	+	-	+	-

Note: that the use of the + for yes, - for no, and possible use for + and - if a vegetable like squash could be both green and yellow.

Teachers of children in grade one and beyond can design their own semantic analysis grids to meet their students' needs and to align with the topics the kids are learning. Select a category or class of words (could be planets, rodent family members, winter words, weather words).

Use the left side of the grid to list at least three if not more items that fit this category. The number of actual items listed will depend on the age and grade level of the children with three or four items fine for K-1 and up to 10-15 for grades 5 and 6. Brainstorm with the children or if better suited to the class, the teacher may list on his/her own features that the items have in common. As can be noted from the example excerpted from *Cooper's Literacy -Helping Children Construct Meaning (*2004), these common features such as vegetables' green color, peels, and seeds are usually fairly easy to identify.

Show the children how to insert the notations +, -, and even ?, (If they are not certain) on the grid. The teacher might also explore with the children the possibility that an item could get both a + and a -. For example, a vegetable like broccoli might be eaten cooked or raw depending on taste and squash can be green or yellow.

Whatever the length of the grid when first presented to the children (perhaps as a semantic cue lesson in and of itself tied in to a text being read in class), make certain that the grid as presented and filled out is not the end of the activity.

Children can use it as a model for developing their own semantic features grids and share them with the whole class. Child-developed grids can become part of a Word Work center in the classroom or even be published in a Word Study Games book by the class as a whole. Such a publication can be shared with parents during open school week and evening visits and with peer classes.

Contextual Redefinition

This strategy encourages children to use the context more effectively by presenting them with sufficient context BEFORE they begin reading. It models for the children the use of contextual clues to make informed guesses about word meanings.

To apply this strategy, the teacher should first select unfamiliar words for teaching. No more than two or three words should be selected for direct teaching. The teacher should then write a sentence in which there are sufficient clues supplied for the child to successfully figure out the meaning. Among the types of context clues the teacher can use are: compare/contrast, synonyms, and direct definition.

Then the teacher should present the words only on the experiential chart or as letter cards. Have the children pronounce the words. As they pronounce them, challenge them to come up with a definition for each word. After more than one definition is offered, encourage the children to decide as a whole group what the definition is. Write down their agreed upon definition with no comment as to its accurate meaning.

Then share with the children the contexts (sentences the teacher wrote with the words and explicit context clues). Ask that the children to read the sentences aloud. Then have them come up with a definition for each word. Make certain that as they present their definitions, the teacher does not comment. Ask that they justify their definitions by making specific references to the context clues in the sentences. As the discussion continues; direct the children's attention to their previously agreed upon definition of the word. Facilitate their discussing the differences between their guesses about the word when they saw only the word itself and their guesses about the word when they read it in context. Finally have the children check their use of context skills to correctly define the word by using a dictionary.

Development of Word Analysis Skills by Individual Students

This type of direct teaching of word definitions is useful when the children have dictionary skills and the teacher is aware of the fact that there are not sufficient clues about the words in the context to help the students define it. In addition, struggling readers and students from ELL backgrounds may benefit tremendously from being walked through this process that highly proficient and successful readers apply automatically

By using this strategy, the teacher can also "kid watch" and note the students' prior knowledge as they guess the word in isolation. The teacher can also actually witness and hear how various students use context skills.

Through their involvement in this strategy, struggling readers gain a feeling of community as they experience the ways in which their struggles and guesses resonate with other peers' responses to the text.

SKILL 7.4 Recognizing the importance of rapid, automatic decoding in reading fluency and comprehension

In the instruction of reading, fluent reading has often been an overlooked and under taught skill in schools. It was with the research review from the work of the National Reading Panel that fluency came to the forefront.

The research has indicated that there is a correlation that a child who reads fluently will be more likely to comprehend the text than a child who does not demonstrate fluent reading. Since the end result of all reading is comprehension, or the understanding of what one has read, this body of research cannot be ignored.

Reading fluency is a broad term that is used to describe reading that has a high degree of accuracy, appropriate phrasing, is smooth and is paced fittingly for the text. In order to achieve all of these areas, it requires the child to be able to decode words in a very automatic and rapid way.

As reading is a complex task, it requires many cognitive processes to occur simultaneously. Efficient and automatic decoding of text allows the student to free up some of these cognitive processes to better address other areas, particularly comprehension. The child who struggles with decoding spends so much mental energy attempting to decode words that there is not enough of a reserve to be able to adequately address the comprehension issues.

Fluency develops over time and with much repetition and practice. The analogy is often drawn to learning to drive a car. When an individual is first learning to drive a car, they must concentrate on every little aspect involved. Which foot is the accelerator, how much pressure to place on the pedal, how to keep the car within the lane, etc. Often distractions such as pedestrians or radio noise cause large over corrections or require additional time for the newer drivers to respond correctly. However, as the driver becomes more skilled, he spends less energy on those more rote tasks previously described. He now has more time to devote to anticipating events. In some cases, he can use his mental energy to think about things unrelated to driving completely. How many times have you driven somewhere and not remembered how you got there? This is because for you driving has become automatic and freed you up for other more complex cognitive thoughts.

This automatic nature in reading is essential as the amount of information in texts grows and students are required to comprehend more and more information in order to be successful. Imagine trying to proceed through a college level course or text if you had to spend time decoding every word presented. You would gain nothing from the work and time you devoted, thus it is vital that students develop automaticity with decoding.

SKILL 7.5 Demonstrating knowledge of strategies for helping students master sight words through multiple and varied reading and writing experiences

Role of Phonics in Developing Rapid, Automatic Word Recognition, Decoding, and Reading Comprehension

To decode means to change communication signals into messages. Reading comprehension requires that the reader learn the code within which a message is written and be able to decode it to get the message.

Although effective reading comprehension requires identifying words automatically (Adams, 1990, Perfetti, 1985), children do not have to be able to identify every single word or know the exact meaning of the every word in a text to understand it. Indeed, Nagy (1988) says that, children can read a work with a high level of comprehension even if they do not fully know as many as 15 percent of the words within a given text.

Children develop the ability to decode and recognize words automatically. They then can extend their ability to decode to multi-syllabic words.

J. David Cooper (2004) and other advocates of the Balanced Literacy Approach, feel that children become literate, effective communicators and able to comprehend, by learning phonics and other aspects of word identification through the use of engaging reading texts. Engaging text, as defined by the balanced literacy group, are those texts which contain highly predictable elements of rhyme, sound patterns, and plot. Researchers, such as Chall (1983) and Flesch (1981), support a phonics-centered foundation before the use of engaging reading texts. This is at the crux of the phonics versus whole language/ balanced literacy/ integrated language arts, teaching of reading controversy.

It is important for the new teacher to be informed about both sides of this controversy, as well as the work of theorists who attempt to reconcile these two perspectives, such as Kenneth Goodman (1994). There are powerful arguments on both sides of this controversy, and each approach works wonderfully with some students and does not succeed with others.

As far as the examinations go, all that is asked of you is the ability to demonstrate that you are familiar with these varied perspectives. If asked on a constructed response question, you need to be able to show that you can talk about teaching some aspect of reading using strategies from one or the other or a combination of both approaches.

This guide is designed to provide you with numerous strategies representing both approaches.

The working teacher can, depending on the perspective of his /her school administration and the needs of the particular children he or she serves, choose from the strategies and approaches which work best for the children concerned.

Blending Letter Sounds

Prompts for Graphophonic Cues

You said (the child's incorrect attempt). Does that match the letters you see?
If it were the word you just said, (the child's incorrect attempt), what would it have to start with?

If it were the word you just said (the child's incorrect attempt), what would it have to end with?

Look at the first letter/s . . . look at the middle letter/s
. . . the last letter. . What could it be?

If you were writing (the child's incorrect attempt) what letter would you write first? What letters would go in the middle?

What letters would go last?

A good strategy to use in working with individual children is to have them explain how they finally correctly identified a word that was troubling them. If prompted and habituated through one on one teacher/tutoring conversations, they can be quite clear about what they did to "get" the word.

If the children are already writing their own stories, the teacher might say to them: "You know when you write your own stories, you would never write any story which did not make sense. You wouldn't and probably this writer didn't either. If you read something that does make sense, but doesn't match the letters, then it's probably not what the author wrote. This is the author's story, not yours right now, so go back to the word and see if you can find out the author's story. Later on, you might write your own story."

Letter Sound Correspondence and Beginning Decoding

Use this procedure for letter-sound investigations that support beginning decoding.

First, focus on a particular letter/s which you want the child to investigate. It is good to choose one from a shared text which the children are familiar with. Make certain that the teachers' directions to the children are clear and either focuses them on looking for a specific letter or listening for sounds.

Next, begin a list of words that meet the task given to the children. Use chart paper to list the words that the children identify. This list can be continued into the next week as long as the children's focus is maintained on the list. This can be easily done by challenging the children with identifying a specific number of letters or sounds and "daring" them as a class team to go beyond those words or sounds.

Third, continue to add to the list. Focus the children at the beginning of the day on the goal of their individually adding to the list. Give them an adhesive note (sticky pad sheet) on which they can individually write down the words they find. Then they can attach their newly found words with their names on them to the chart. This provides the children with a sense of ownership and pride in their letter-sounding abilities. During shared reading, discuss the children's proposed additions and have the group decide if these meet the directed category. If all the children agree that they do meet the category, include the words on the chart.

Fourth, do a word sort from all the words generated and have the children put the words into categories that demonstrate similarities and differences. They can be prompted to see if the letter appeared at the beginning of the word, or in the end of the word. They might also be prompted to see that one sound could have two different letter representations. The children can then "box" the word differences and similarities by drawing colors established in a chart key.

Finally, before the children go off to read, ask them to look for new words in the texts which they can now recognize because of the letter sound relationships on their chart. During shared reading, make certain that they have time to share these words they were able to decode because of their explorations.

Strategies for Helping Students Decode Single Syllable Words that Follow Common Patterns and Multi-syllable Words

(This activity is presented in detail so it can actually be implemented with children in an intermediate classroom and also to provide detail for a potential constructed response question on a certification examination.)

The CVC phonics card game developed by Jackie Montierth, a computer teacher in South San Diego for use with 5th and 6th grade students, is a good one to adapt to the needs of any group with appropriate modifications for age, grade level and language needs.

The children use the vehicle of the card game to practice and enhance their use of consonants and vowels. Their fluency in this will increase their ability to decode words. Potential uses beyond whole classroom instruction include use as part of the small group word work component of the reading workshop and as part of cooperative team learning. This particular strategy also is particularly helpful for grade four and beyond English Language learners who are in a regular English Language classroom setting.

The card game works well because the practice of the content is implicit for transfer as the children continue to improve their reading skills. In addition, the card game format allows "instructional punctuation" using a student centered high interest exploration.

Card Design: The teacher can use the computer or use 5"x 8" index cards or actual card deck sized oaktag cards to create a deck. For repeated use and durability, it is recommended that the deck be laminated.

The deck should consist of the following:
44 consonant cards (including the blends)
15 vowel cards (including 3 of each vowel)
5 wild cards (which can be used as any vowel)
6 final e cards

The design of this project can also focus on particular CVC words that are part of a particular book, topic or genre format. In advance of playing the game, children can also be directed to review the words on the word wall or other words on a word map.

Procedure:

The game is best introduced first as part of a mini lesson with the teacher reading the rules, and a pair of children demonstrating step by step, when the game is played before the class for the first time. Have the children divide into pairs or small groups of no more than 4 per group. Each group needs one deck of C-V-C cards.

Have each group choose a dealer. The dealer shuffles the cards and deals 5 cards to each player. The remaining cards are placed face down for drawing during the play. One card is turned over to form the discard pile. Players may not show their cards to the other players. The first player to the left of the dealer looks at his/her cards and if possible, puts down three cards which make a consonant-vowel-consonant word. For more points, four cards forming a consonant-vowel-consonant word can be placed down. The player must then say the word and draw the number of cards he or she laid down. If he or she is unable to form a word, he/she draws either a card from either the draw or discard pile. The player then discards one card. All players must have 5 cards at all times. Play moves to the left.

The game continues until one or more of the following happens:
1. There are no more cards in the draw pile
2. All players run out of cards.
3. All players cannot form a word

The winner is the player who has laid down the most cards during the game.

Players may only lay down words at the beginning of their turn.
Proper names may not be counted as words.

Other ways the game may be played:

The game can be played with teams of individuals in a small group of four or fewer competing against one another (Excellent for special needs or resource room students). It can also be done as a whole class activity where all the students are divided into cooperative teams or small groups who compete against one another. This second approach will work well with a heterogeneous classroom that includes special needs and/or ELL children.

Teachers of ELL learners can do this game in the native language first and then transition it into English, facilitating native language reading skills and second language acquisition. They can develop their own appropriate decks to meet the vocabulary needs of their children and to complement the curricula.

Using Phonics to Decode Words in Connected Text

Identifying New Words

Some strategies to share with children during conferences or as part of shared reading include the following prompts:

- Look at the beginning letter/s... What sound do you hear?

- Stop to think about the text or story. What word with this beginning letter would make sense here?

- Look at the book's illustrations. Do they provide you with help in figuring out the new word?

- Think of what word would make sense, sound right, and match the letters that you see. Start the sentence over, making your mouth ready to say that word.

- Skip the word, read to the end of the sentence, and then come back to the word. How does what you've read help you with the word?

- Listen to whether what you are reading makes sense and matches the letters (asking the child to self-monitor). If it doesn't make sense, see if you can correct it on your own.

- Look for spelling patterns you know from the spelling pattern wall.

- Look for smaller words you might know within the larger word.

- Read on a little, and then return to the part that confused you.

SUBAREA III.	DEVELOPING READING COMPREHENSION AND PROMOTING INDEPENDENT READING

COMPETENCY 8.0 THE TEACHER UNDERSTANDS FACTORS AFFECTINGREADING COMPREHENSION AND STRATEGIES FOR PROMOTING READING COMPREHENSION.

SKILL 8.1 Demonstrating knowledge of factors affecting reading comprehension (e.g., reading rate and fluency, word recognition, prior knowledge and experiences, vocabulary)

The Relationship Between Oral and Written Vocabulary Development and Reading Comprehension

Biemiller's (2003) research documents that those children entering 4th grade with significant vocabulary deficits demonstrate increasing reading comprehension problems. Evidence shows that these children do not catch up, but rather continue to fall behind.

Strategy One: Word Map Strategy

This strategy is useful for children grades 3-6 and beyond. The target group of children for this strategy includes those who need to improve their independent vocabulary acquisition abilities. The strategy is essentially teacher-directed learning where children are "walked through" the process. They are helped by the teacher to identify the type of information that makes a definition. They are also assisted in using context clues and background understanding to construct meaning.

The word map graphic organizer is the tool teachers use to complete this strategy with children. Word map templates are available online from the Houghton Mifflin web site and from READWRITETHINK, the web site of the NCTE (see webliography section). The word map helps the children to visually represent the elements of a given concept.

The children's literal articulation of the concept can be prompted by three key questions: What is it?; What is it like? What are some examples?

For instance, the word "oatmeal" might yield a word map with "What?", and in a rectangular box a hot cereal you eat in the morning, "What is it like?"; hot, mushy, salty, "What are some examples?", instant oatmeal you make in a minute, apple-flavor oatmeal, Irish Oatmeal.

The procedure to be used in sharing this strategy with children is to select three concepts the children are familiar with. Then show them the template of a word map. Tell them that the three questions asked on the map and the boxes to fill in beneath them helps readers and writers to see what they need to know about a word. Next, help the children to complete at least two word maps for two of the three concepts that were pre-selected. Then have the children select a concept of their own to map either independently or in a small group. As the final task for this first part of the strategy, have the children, in teams or individually, write a definition for at least one of the concepts using the key things about it listed on the map. Have the children share these definitions aloud and talk about how they used the word maps to help them with the definitions.

For the next part of this strategy, the teacher should pick up an expository text or a textbook the children are already using to study mathematics, science or social studies. The teacher should either locate a short excerpt where a particular concept is defined or use the content to write model passages of definition on his/her own.

After the passages are selected or authored, the teacher should duplicate them. Then they should be distributed to the children along with blank word map templates. The children should be asked to read each passage and then to complete the word map for the concept in each passage. Finally, have the children share the word maps they have developed for each passage. Give them a chance to explain how they used the word in the passage to help them fill out their word map. End by telling them that the three components of the concept- class, description, example- are just three of the many components for any given concept.

This strategy has assessment potential because the teacher can literally see how the students understand specific concepts by looking at their maps and hearing their explanations. The maps the students develop on their own demonstrate whether they have really understood the concepts in the passages. This strategy serves to ready students for inferring word meanings on their own. By using the word map strategy, children develop concepts of what they need to know to begin to figure out an unknown word on their own. It assists the children in grades 3 and beyond to connect prior knowledge with new knowledge.

This word map strategy can be adapted by the teacher to suit the specific needs and goals of instruction. Illustrations of the concept and the comparisons to other concepts can be included in the word mapping for children grades 5 and beyond. This particular strategy is also one that can be used with a research theme in other content areas.

Strategy Two: Preview in Context

This is a direct teaching strategy which allows the teacher to guide the students as they examine words in context prior to reading a passage. Before beginning the strategy, the teacher selects only two or three key concept words. Then the teacher reads carefully to identify passages within the text that evidence strong context clues for the word.

Then the teacher presents the word and the context to the children. As the teacher reads aloud, the children follow along. Once the teacher has finished the read aloud, the children re-read the material silently. After the silent re-reading, the children will be coached by the teacher to a definition of one of the key words selected for study. This is done through a child-centered discussion. As part of the discussion, the teacher asks questions which get the children to activate their prior knowledge and to use the contextual clues to figure out the correct meaning of the selected key words. Make certain that the definition of the key concept word is finally made by the children.

Next, help the children to begin to expand the word's meaning. Do this by having them consider the following for the given key concept word: synonyms, antonyms, other contexts or other kinds of stories/texts where the word might appear. This is the time to have the children check their responses to the challenge of identifying word synonyms and antonyms by having them go to the thesaurus or the dictionary to confirm their responses. In addition, have the children place the synonyms or antonyms they find in their word boxes or word journals. The recording of their findings will guarantee them ownership of the words and deepen their capacity to use contextual clues.

The main point to remember in using this strategy is that it should only be used when the context is strong. It will not work with struggling readers who have less prior knowledge. Through listening to the children's responses as the teacher helps them to define the word and its potential synonyms and antonyms, the teacher can assess their ability to successfully use context clues. The key to this simple strategy is that it allows the teacher to draw the child out and to grasp through the child's responses the individual child's thinking process. The more talk from the child the better.

Strategies for Promoting Comprehension Across the Curriculum by Expanding Knowledge of Content Area Vocabulary

Key Words

Cooper (2004) feels that it is up to the teacher to preview the content area text to identify the main ideas. Then the teacher should compile a list of terms related to the content thrust. These terms and words become part of the key concepts list. Next, the teacher sees which of the key concept words and terms are already defined in the text. These will not require direct teaching. Words for which children have sufficient skills to determine their meaning through base, root, prefixes or suffixes, also will not require direct teaching.

Instruction in the remaining key words, which should not be more than two or three in number, can be provided before, during or after reading. If students have previewed the content area and identified those words they need support on, the instruction should be provided before reading. Instruction can also easily be provided as part of guided reading support. After reading support is indicated, the text offers the children an opportunity to enrich their own vocabularies.

Having children work as a whole class or in small groups on a content specific dictionary for a topic regularly covered in their grade level social studies, science, or mathematics, curriculum offers an excellent collaborative opportunity for children to design a dictionary/word resource that can celebrate their own vocabulary learning. Such a resource can then be used with the next year's classes as well.

Development of Vocabulary Knowledge and Skills in Individual Students

Hierarchical and linear array vocabulary development strategies lend themselves well to support the struggling learners or second language learners. The use of the arrays allows these learners to use a visual format to "see" and diagram word relationships. Furthermore the diagrams are easy to make, and they can be illustrated. With sufficient support and modeling, many special needs children can do simple linear and hierarchical arrays on their own. The arrays can also be attractively displayed in resource rooms and in regular education classrooms as a demonstration of these individual students' ownership of their words.

English Language Learners should first capably demonstrate their capacity to fill out hierarchical and linear arrays in their native language and then can work with this same format to hone their English Language vocabulary development. Their native language hierarchical relationships and arrays can be displayed in their general education classrooms. Teachers may also want to encourage children grades 3 and beyond to make connections between some of the native, other than English, words and words derived from them in English. This could be a rich "buddy" (ELL child and native English Language speaker) investigation or it could be one for ELL children alone. At any rate, use of the array with the ELL child's native language makes that child a second language vocabulary owner which immediately includes the child positively in ongoing vocabulary development.

Cooper (2004) suggests that teachers who have children from different language backgrounds use any unscheduled or "extra" time that emerges for read-alouds.

Using the Semantic Feature Analysis Grid

Highly proficient readers can be asked to help same grade peers or better yet younger peers with their word analysis skills by having them work with these struggling readers on filling out teacher developed semantic analysis grids. Some 5th and 6th grade highly proficient readers may also evidence the aptitude and desire to create their own semantic analysis grids for their peer or younger peer tutees. In this way, highly proficient readers can gain insights into the field of teaching reading at an early age and younger struggling readers can have the edge taken off their struggles by working with a peer or an older student. For both individual students the experience is one that promotes and celebrates word analysis skills and nurtures the concept of a literate and caring community of readers.

ELL students can also add in deliberate items to the categories which reflect their cultures. For instance, Latino children can add in plantains and guava to the fruits their non-Latino peers might list. This provides the ELL learners with an opportunity to enrich the knowledge base of their peer's subject category inventory and puts them in a positive spotlight. The easy notations on the grid make it accessible for even ELL children with limited English language writing and speaking capacities.

Special Needs learners can benefit from the grid. It can be developed by teachers, paraprofessionals, and tutors. It can be notated by the children themselves. They can also illustrate it. It can be posted or kept in the word center. The grid provides these learners who are often spatial learners with a concrete demonstration of their word analysis achievement.

Biemiller's research indicates that the listening vocabulary for a 6th grader who tests at the 25 percentile in reading is equivalent to that attained by the 75th percentile 3rd grader. This deficit in vocabulary presents a formidable challenge for the 6th grader to succeed, not only on reading tests, but in various content subjects in elementary school and beyond.

SKILL 8.2 Recognizing ways to activate and develop students' prior knowledge and experience related to reading

Schemata are structures which represent generic concepts stored in our memory (Rumelhart, 1980). Young children develop their schemata through experiences. Prior knowledge and the lack of experiences in some cases influence comprehension. The more closely the reader's experiences and schemata approximate those of the writer, the more likely the reader is to comprehend the text. It is obvious that for many children from non-native English language speaking backgrounds and perhaps for those from struggling socio-economic family structures schemata deficits indicate the need for intense teacher support as these children become emergent and early readers.

Often the teacher will have to model and scaffold for the child the steps to form a schemata from the information provided in a text.

Comprehension

Cooper defines comprehension as: "a strategic process by which readers construct or assign meaning to a text by using the clues in the text and their own prior knowledge. " We view comprehension as a process where the reader transacts with the text to construct or assign meaning. Reading and writing are both interconnected and mutually supportive. Comprehension is a strategic process in which readers adjust their reading to suit their reading purpose and the type or genre of text they are reading. Narrative and expository texts require different reading approaches because of their different text structures.

Strategic readers also call into play their metacognitive capacities as they analyze texts so that they are self aware of the skills needed to construct meaning from the text structure.

SKILL 8.3 Identifying techniques to help readers self-monitor their comprehension

When using running records as a form of informal assessment as to the progress a student is making with their reading skills, it is important to be sure and look at the types of errors the child is making. In this way, you can examine the strategies and errors the student makes to plan instruction, monitor progress, and assess skill levels. Even if not using a running record, teachers can use even more informal methods of using the errors a student makes to find significant ways to help the student improve in their reading.

Miscue analysis can be multi-faceted and provide both the teacher and reader with a wealth of important information. First, examining the methods a student uses to figure out unknown words, helps the teacher to understand which methods require further instruction, fine tuning or have already been mastered. Typically, students use phonics skills (letter sound correspondence), contextual clues (the other words in the sentence/passage), semantic analysis, or structural analysis techniques to solve problems in reading. It is not through one of these methods that a reader becomes more proficient, but rather using a combination of all of the approaches.

After collecting the running record, teachers can then go back and look at which of the described strategies the students are using with success. Tallying is one method to use, in this way; the educator can see the strategies used by the student and if one seems to be more dominant than others. This method will also help to point out specific strategies which are very weak for the student and would require more instruction. After this analysis, the teacher can develop an instructional plan to address weak areas and increase a more balanced problem solving approach for the student.

Additionally, the teacher can look at the student's ability to monitor their own reading and comprehension. Noting these self-monitoring attempts, allows the teacher to see if the student recognizes when they make a mistake which does not make sense. This is a very important skill for readers to develop. Once they realize something does not make sense, are they able to go back and then apply a correction strategy so as to not hinder comprehension. This becomes more important as the complexity of text increases.

Self-corrections by students begin to show a maturity of reading skills. However, students who make a tremendous amount of self-corrections lack fluency in reading and will eventually lose some comprehension. It is an important step to begin for readers, but as with any other learning process, we want students to pass through it rapidly, leaving in its place fluent, well comprehended reading.

SKILL 8.4 **Identifying appropriate prereading and postreading strategies to help students construct meaning (e.g., predicting, questioning, summarizing, discussing, writing, using graphic organizers)**

See skill 10.1

SKILL 8.5 **Identifying techniques to promote the reading comprehension skills and strategies of students who are learning English as a second language**

See competencies 9.0 and 10.0

TEACHER CERTIFICATION STUDY GUIDE

COMPETENCY 9.0 THE TEACHER UNDERSTANDS STRATEGIES FOR PROMOTING LITERARY RESPONSE AND ANALYSIS.

SKILL 9.1 Recognizing a variety of instructional approaches and activities for helping students apply comprehension strategies (e.g., retelling, graphic organizers, dramatization) when reading literary texts

Knowledge of Reading as a Process to Construct Meaning

If there were two words synonymous with reading comprehension as far as the balanced literacy approach is concerned, they would be "constructing meaning."

Cooper, Taberski, Strickland, and other key theorists and classroom teachers conceptualize the reader as interacting with the text and bringing his/her prior knowledge and experience to it. Writing is interlaced with reading and is a mutually integrative and supportive parallel process. Hence the division of literacy learning by the balanced literacy folks into reading workshop and writing workshop, with the same anchor "readings" or books being used for both.

Consider the sentence, "The test booklet was white with black print, but very scary looking."

According to the idea of constructing meaning as the reader read this sentence, the schemata (generic information stored in the mind) of tests the reader had experienced was activated by the author's notion that tests are scary. Therefore the ultimate meaning that the reader derives from the page is from the reader's own responses and experiences coupled with the ideas the author presents. The reader constructs a meaning that reflects the author's intent and also the reader's response to that intent.

It is also to be remembered that generally readings are fairly lengthy passages, composed of paragraphs which in turn are composed of more than one sentence. With each successive sentence, and every new paragraph, the reader refocuses. The schemata are reconsidered, and a new meaning is constructed.

Knowledge of levels of reading comprehension and strategies for promoting comprehension of imaginative literary texts at all levels

Sharon Taberski (2000) recommends that initially strategies for promoting comprehension of imaginative literary texts be done with the whole class.

Here are Taberski's four main strategies for promoting comprehension of imaginative literary texts. She feels that if repeated sufficiently during the K-3 years and even if introduced as late as grade 4, these strategies will even serve the adult lifelong reader in good stead.

Strategy One: "Stopping to Think" –reflecting on the text as a whole. x
As part of this strategy, the reader is challenged to come up with the answer to these three questions: What do I think is going to happen? (Inferential)
Why do I think this is going to happen? (Evaluative and inferential)
How can I prove that I am right by going back to the story? (inferential)

Taberski recommends that teachers introduce these key strategies with books that can be read in one sitting and recommends the use of picture books for these instructive strategies.

Taberski also suggests that books which are read aloud and used for this strategy also contain a strong storyline, some degree of predictability, a text that invites discussion and a narrative with obvious stopping points.

Strategy Two: story mapping, for promoting comprehension of imaginative/literary texts.

For stories to suit this strategy, they should have distinct episodes, few characters and clear-cut problems to solve. In particular, Taberski tries to use a story where a single, central problem or issue is introduced at the beginning of the story and then resolved or at least followed through by the close of the story. To make a story map of a particular story, Taberski divides the class into groups and asks one group of children to illustrate the "Characters" in the book. Another group of children are asked to draw the "Setting," while a third and fourth group of children tackle "Problem " and "Resolution." The story map may also help children hold together their ideas for writing in the writing workshop as they take their reading of an author's story to a new level.

Strategy Three: The Character Mapping strategy also used by Taberski focuses the children as readers on the ways in which the main character's personal traits can determine what will happen in the story. Character mapping works best when the character is a non-stereotypical individual, has been featured perhaps in other books by the same author, has a personality that is somewhat predictable, and is capable of changing behavior as a consequence of what happens.

Using writing to share, deepen, and expand understanding of literary texts is a cornerstone of the balanced literacy approach.

Strategy Four: Taberski advocates reading sections of stories aloud and then having the teacher pause to reflect on what's happened in the story and model writing down a response to it. The teacher can use a chart to record his/her response to the events or characters of a particular story being read and the children can contribute their comments as well. Later on, the children can start reflective reader's notebooks or journals recording their reactions to their readings independently.

The best types of texts for this type of response are those that relate to age appropriate issues for young children (i.e. homework, testing, bullies, and friendship), a plot that can be interpreted in different ways, a text that is filled with questions, and a text full of suspense or wonder.

Development of Literary Response Skills

Literary response skills are dependent on prior knowledge, schemata and background. Schemata (the plural of schema) are those structures which represent concepts stored in our memory.

Without schemata and experiences to call upon as they read, children have little ability to comprehend. Of course, the reader's schemata and prior knowledge have more influence on the comprehension of plot or character information that is implied rather than directly stated.

Prior Knowledge

Prior knowledge can be defined as all of an individual's prior experiences, learning, and development which precede his/her entering a specific learning situation or attempting to comprehend a specific text. Sometimes prior knowledge can be erroneous or incomplete. Obviously, if there are misconceptions in a child's prior knowledge, these must be corrected so that the child's overall comprehension skills can continue to progress. Prior knowledge of children includes their accumulated positive and negative experiences both in and out of school.

These might come from wonderful family travels, watching television, visiting museums and libraries, to visiting hospitals, prisons and surviving poverty.

Whatever the prior knowledge that the child brings to the school setting, the independent reading and writing the child does in school immeasurably expands his/her prior knowledge and hence broadens his/her reading comprehension capabilities.

The teacher must consider as he/she prepares to begin any imaginative/literary text the following about the students' level of prior knowledge:

1. What prior knowledge needs to be activated for the text, theme or for the writing to be done successfully?
2. How independent are the children in using strategies to activate their prior knowledge?

Holes and Roser (1987) have suggested five techniques for activating prior knowledge before starting an imaginative/literary text:
Free Recall: Tell us what you know about...

Unstructured Discussion: Let's talk about...

Structured Question: Who exactly was Jane Aviles in the life of the hero of the story?

Word Association: When you hear these words--hatch, elephant, who, think-- What author do you think of?

Recognition: Mulberry Street...What author comes to mind?

Previewing and predicting and story mapping are also excellent strategies for activating prior knowledge.

Development of Literary Analysis Skills

There are many exciting ways to sensitize and to teach children about the features and formats of different literary genres.

Strategy One: Genre Switch-Reader and Writer Transformation

This strategy should be introduced as a read aloud with young children or with children who are struggling readers. In a similar fashion, it would be introduced as a read-aloud for ELL learners. Older children in grades 3-6 might just be "started off" by a teacher prompt and do the required reading on their own.

To begin, the teacher selects a particular genre book. If it is close to Halloween, a goblin or suspense story will do well. The teacher begins to read the story with the open invitation to the students to determine as the story is being read, what type of story it is and what makes it that type of story.

Older children take notes in their reading journals, while younger children and those more in need of explicit teacher support contribute their ideas and responses as part of the discussion in class. Their responses are recorded on a chart.

As the reading continues, the story type components are listed on the chart (most of the responses are those which have been elicited from the children).

At some point in what is either an oral read aloud, guided reading or independent reading, the teacher directs the children's attention to the components which have emerged on the chart. They then use these components which are generally components of character - setting, plot, style, conflict, language – to identify the story genre.

The teacher provides the children with an opportunity to expound at length on why this story is an example of the genre which they have identified.
Once they have done so, the teacher challenges them to consider how this story with its set of given characters, plot, and setting would be changed if the genre were different. The teacher can challenge the class as a whole with the idea of changing the story to a radically different genre—i.e. from suspense to a fairy tale or a comedy or allow the children to come up another genre.

Then depending on the children's developed writing abilities, they might be given time to rewrite the story on their own or re-tell it in class prior to writing and illustrating it.

In the balanced literacy approach, this transformation of the story into another genre is done as part of the Writing Workshop component which uses the same reading material as the source for writing. The strategy results in the children having had the experience of an in-depth analysis of a particular genre as well as hands-on writing (or telling, if they can not yet write or can not yet write in English) experience of restyling that basic plot and characters into another genre. This authenticates the children's participation as readers and writers.

Strategy Two: Analyzing Story Elements

Story elements include plot (including conflict and resolution, setting (including time and place), characters (flat and round/static and dynamic), and theme (the main idea of the story). Students can use graphic organizers such as story maps, compare/contrast displays, and sequence boxes to display their understanding of these critical features of fiction.

Strategy Three: Analyzing Character Development

Characters in children's literature may be flat or round. A flat character is one-dimensional and is often defined by one characteristic. Rosie in *Rosie's Walk* is an example. A round character seems like someone you know, such as Jess in *Bridge to Terabithia*. Static characters do not change from the beginning to the end of the story, while dynamic ones do. Characters reveal themselves through their actions, their interactions, and through what they say.

Strategy Four: Interpreting Figurative Language

Similes are direct comparisons between two things using "like" or "as." "Her eyes were like stars" is a simile. Metaphors are indirect comparisons, such as "The earth is a big blue marble." Personification is giving human characteristics to non-animal beings. Frances, Shrek, or the animals in *Mr. Gumpy's Outing* are all examples of personification.

Strategy Five: Identifying Literary Allusions

Children can understand allusions best when they read a lot. A literary allusion when it appears in a story is also called *intertextuality*. That is when a reference, character, or symbol from one story appears or is alluded to in another. Recently, many popular children's books use literary allusions, from the Ahlbergs' *Each Peach Pear Plum* to Jon Scieszka's *The True Story of the Three Little Pigs*. Note that any character or plot element can become allusions, not just references from fairy tales.

Strategy Six: Analyzing the Author's Point of View

In fiction, point of view is the vantage point from which the narrator tells the story. We determine point of view by asking, where is the narrator standing in relation to the characters? Is the narrator inside or outside of the story? If inside, is the narrator one of the characters? This is *first person point of view.* If outside, can the narrator "see" into anyone else's mind besides his/her own? If the narrator cannot see into the mind and heart of other characters, then the point of view is *third person limited.* Narrators who can see what other characters are thinking and feeling are using *third person omniscient point of view*.

Use of Comprehension Strategies Before, During, and After Reading

Cooper (2004), Taberski (2000), Cox (2005) and other researchers recommend a broad array of comprehension strategies before, during, and after reading.

Cooper (2004) suggests a broad range of classroom posters on the walls plus explicit instruction to give children prompts to monitor their own reading. An example follows: My Strategic Reading Guide

I. Do I infer/predict important information, use what I know, think about what may happen or what I want to learn?
2. Can I identify important information about the story elements?
3. Do I generate questions and search for the answers?
4. Does this make sense to me? Does this help me meet my purpose in reading?
5. If lost, do I remember fix-ups?
   Re-read, read further ahead, look at the illustrations, ask for help, and think about the words, and evaluate what I have read.
6. Do I remember to think about how the parts of the stories that I was rereading came together?

Storyboard panels, which are used by comic strip artists and by those artists who do advertising campaigns as well as television and film directors, are perfect for engaging children K-6 in a variety of comprehension strategies before, during, and after reading. They can storyboard the beginning of a story, read aloud, and then storyboard its predicted middle or end. Of course, after they experience or read the actual middle or ending of the story, they can compare and contrast what they produced with its actual structure. They can play familiar literature identification games with a buddy or as part of a center by storyboarding one key scene or characters from a book and challenging a partner or peer to identify the book and characters correctly.

Use of Oral Language Activities to Promote Comprehension

Retelling

Retelling needs to be very clearly defined so that the child reader does not think that the teacher wants him or her to spill the WHOLE story back in the retelling. A child should be able to talk comfortably and fluently about the story he or she has just read. He or she should be able to tell the main things that have happened in the story.

When a child retells a story to a teacher, the teacher needs ways to help him or her assess the child's understanding. Ironically, the teacher can use some of the same strategies he or she suggests to the child to assess the child's understanding of a book which is not familiar to the teacher. These strategies include: back cover reading, scanning the table of contents, looking at the pictures, and reading the book jacket.

If the child can explain how the story turned out and provide examples to support these explanations, try not to interrupt him or her with too many questions. Children can use the text of the book to reinforce what they are saying and they can even read from it if they wish. It is also important to note that some children need to re-read the text twice and their re-reading of it is out of enjoyment.

When the teacher plans to use the retelling as a way of assessing the child, then the following ground rules have to be set and made clear to the child. The teacher explains the purpose of the retelling to determine how well the child is reading at the outset of the conference.

The teacher maintains in the child's assessment notebook or in his/her assessment record what the child is saying in phrases, not sentences. Just enough is recorded to indicate whether the child actually understood the story. The teacher also tries to analyze from the retelling why the child can not comprehend a given text. If the child's accuracy rate with the text is below 95 per cent, then the problem is at the word level, but if the accuracy rate for the text is above 95 per cent, the difficulty lies at the text level.

Development of the Reading Comprehension Skills and Strategies of Individual Students

ELL Learners bring to their classrooms different prior knowledge concerns than do their native English language speaking peers. Some of the ELL students have extensive prior knowledge in their native language and can read well on or above their chronological age level in their native language. Other ELL learners come to the United States from cultures where reading was not emphasized or circumstances did not give families native language literacy opportunities.

Rigg and Allen (1999) offer the following four principles regarding the literacy development and prior knowledge of ELL-second language learners:

1. In learning a language you learn to do the things you want to do with people who are speaking that language.
2. A second language, like the first, does not develop linearly, but rather globally.
3. Language can develop in rich context.
4. Literacy develops parallel to language, so as speaking and listening for the second language develops, so does writing and reading.

As far as retelling, it needs to be noted that English language learners have the problem of not bringing rich oral English vocabulary to the stories they are decoding. Therefore, often they "sound the stories out" well, but can not explain what they are about, because they do not know what the words mean.

Use of Oral Reading Fluency in Facilitating Comprehension

At some point it is crucial that just as the nervous, novice bike rider finally relaxes and speeds happily off, so too must the early reader integrate graphophonic cues with semantic and structural ones. Before this is done, the oral quality of early reader's has a stilted beat to it, which of course does not promote reading engagement and enjoyment.

The teacher needs to be at his/her most dramatic to model for children the beauties of voice and nuance that are contained in the texts whose print they are tracking so anxiously. Children love nothing more than to mimic their teacher and can do so legitimately and without hesitation, if the teacher takes time each day to recite a poem with them. The poem might be posted on chart paper and be up on the wall for a week.

First the teacher can model the fluent and expressive reading of this poem. Then with a pointer, the class can recite it with the teacher. As the week progresses, the class can recite it on their own.

Use of Writing Activities to Promote Literary Response and Analysis

In addition to the activities already mentioned, the activities below will promote literary response and analysis:
   * Have children take a particular passage from a story and retell it from another character's perspective.

- Challenge children to suggest a sequel or a prequel to any given story they have read.

- Ask the children to recast a story in which the key characters are male into one where the key characters are female (or vice versa). Have them explain how these changes alter the narrative, plot, or outcome.

- Encourage the children to transform a story or book into a Reader's Theater format and record it complete with sound effects for the audio-cassette center of the classroom.

- Have the children produce a newspaper as the characters of a given story would have reported the news in their community.

- Transform the story into a ballad poem or a picture book version for younger peers.

- Give ELL children an opportunity to translate stories into their native language or to author in English with a buddy a favorite story that was originally published in their native language.

SKILL 9.2 **Identifying strategies for developing and assessing students' responses to literature (e.g., using guided reading, reading logs, and discussions about literature; encouraging students to connect elements in a text to other sources, including other texts, their own experiences, and their background knowledge)**

There are numerous strategies for developing and assessing students' responses to various types of literature.

Guided Reading. Fountas and Pinnell as a technique to provide small group instruction to students on their reading levels introduced guided reading. It involves forming groups based on reading ability. During these groups you choose specific texts and take the students through a process to build their reading skills. Running records are taken on a regular basis and uses as the major assessment method.

Reading Logs. Reading logs can be used to encourage students to complete reading outside of the classroom setting and can take many different forms. A simple log of amount of time-spent reading is on the basic end of the spectrum. On the other end might be reader response logs, where the child is asked to respond specifically to something in the text they read. While these both seem like extremes, both strategies encourage students to develop their reading skills and for responses to literature.

Literature Discussion. Literature discussion groups, sometimes known as literature circles provide the students the opportunity to not only reflect on the reading, but also allow them to drive the discussion. In this strategy, the teacher is an ancillary member of the discussion. The content and its depth and breadth come directly from the participation of the students and their views on the items in the reading.

Making Reading Connections. As with all learning, it is important for a good reader to connect the item being read to other events. Guiding students to make these relationships is the role of the teacher. It is important that first, students draw from their background knowledge to better understand the vocabulary and content of the story. Sharing information across students can be helpful to those who may be lacking in certain background information. Connections also need to be made across texts. This can be done by comparing and contrasting more than one story. Sometimes it is helpful to look at the use of language by a specific author. In this case it would be beneficial to draw these comparisons across to books written by the same author. The most memorable connections are those that a child makes between the text and his/her own life. It is when they can relate to something on a personal level that the student can then truly understand the situations and ideas presented.

SKILL 9.3 Demonstrating knowledge of the elements of literary analysis and criticism (e.g., describing and analyzing story elements, recognizing features of different literary genres, determining mood and theme, analyzing the use of figurative language, analyzing the ways in which a literary work reflects the traditions, perspectives, and culture of a particular people or time period)

See skill 9.1 and 9.2

SKILL 9.4 Identifying appropriate literature and related activities to meet the reading needs of all students, including students who are learning English as a second language

As previously discussed, meeting the need of all learners provides a challenge to the reading specialist. Assessment data is the key place to begin to determine what appropriate activities should be implemented to help children to become better readers.

Beyond skills and progress, it is imperative that reading be fun and motivating for the students. Under this realm, it is important to select the appropriate literature to catch the interest of the students. For students lagging behind, publishers now make numerous serious of low reading level yet high interest texts to address these issues.

Different genders tend to read different types of books as well. Generally, boys may be drawn to more exciting books, even comic books or newspapers. It may not be the typical reading instruction that you see in schools, but the skills and activities can easily convey the knowledge you need to convey in a more inspiring manner.

It is also necessary to make sure that you address different genres. Exposing and reading poetry is just as important as reading the fiction and nonfiction stories. Reading plays and songs and other less traditional genres not only provide exposure for the children, but can also help address specific skill deficits.

Multicultural reading can help bridge any gaps that might exist with students for whom English is a second language. These types of books can help them to see themselves and thereby relate more to make the personal connections that are essential for good reading comprehension. Also, it provides the other students with insight into the cultural ways of different parts of society.

Selecting a wide range of literature allows the reading to become more meaningful and personal to the students completing it. Incorporating various activities to reinforce that any kind of reading is better than no reading. Having the students engaged and excited by reading is often ninety percent of the battle.

Once the excitement and desire is present, the teacher can spend her time and focus on designing activities through these texts to meet the skill needs of the students. It is important that the two are linked and that students see the connections between the two. Helping students make this generalization that these skills being taught go across all reading, is the step toward helping them to become life long readers in society.

COMPETENCY 10.0 THE TEACHER UNDERSTANDS STRATEGIES FOR PROMOTING CONTENT-AREA LITERACY.

SKILL 10.1 Identifying strategies for improving students' comprehension of content-area texts (e.g., text format, summarizing, semantic mapping, graphic organizers)

Reading does not end when one leaves the reading classroom; it in fact, is an inherent component of every subject area taught in schools today. Content area reading (science, social studies, etc.) can sometimes be much more difficult for students. Typically, the information is nonfiction and there is a great deal of knowledge contained in smaller amounts of text. Deciphering content area reading requires a unique set of strategies in order to best acquire the necessary information.

Text Format. Teaching children that nonfiction texts are laid out significantly different than fictional texts is an important skill. Often times the format of the text helps provide an automatic organizational tool to help chunk information. Key words or section headings can help provide students with catch phrases with which they can remember the information. They can also help students to scan a large amount of information to find smaller pieces they require to answer comprehension questions. Indexes and table of content skills can provide additional support with this.

Summarizing. As stated before content subjects generally attempt to convey a great deal of information in a smaller amount of text. This is where the idea of summarizing can be so valuable and productive. Teaching the students to be able to take larger amounts of information and break it down into four or five sentences allows them to manage more details and learning. It also helps them to make connections and compartmentalize the information.

Graphic Organizers. There a numerous different forms of graphic organizers. They can be defined as a pictorial method of organizing information to help the student remember it more efficiently. Graphic organizers can be complex or simple, provided to the student or drawn from memory. The key is that the method or organizing tool used will help the students classify the information to be learned into smaller pieces with common characteristics. They also help the students to begin to see relationships between the concepts. Graphic organizers work well as study aids to help students acquire more information. Some graphic organizers can use pictures or other visual cues to help the students remember the items to be learned.

Semantic Mapping. In this strategy of organizing information the students will use a visual representation to show how words or concepts are interrelated. This is a form of graphic organizer. In semantic mapping, the new knowledge is directly linked to the prior information. Sometimes called concept mapping, semantic maps allow the learner to see relationships between words or concepts and tie them to their own background knowledge in a meaningful manner.

SKILL 10.2 Recognizing different types and functions of texts and different purposes for reading

There are six different types of texts that are usually used in a school setting. Each type of text has a specific use within the classroom depending on the purpose for reading set forth by the teacher. The types of texts vary from the genres of reading and should not be confused.

Wordless Books. Wordless picture books are generally used to increase discussion and develop vocabulary. These books are good for generating ideas for writing or discussions among students. They provide pictures filled with details to serve as a springboard to oral language development or increasing the quality of description in writing.

Predictable Texts. Predictable texts allow the beginning reader to feel successful with the process of reading in a rapid manner. They provide the same words or phrases repeated over and over so that students can participate in the act of reading. They are also generally very much enjoyed by students due to the natural rhythm that develops by the repetitions. However, this type of text should be moved through rapidly so that children begin to attend to the words in reading and not rely on their auditory memory alone for what comes next.

Controlled Vocabulary Texts. Texts of this nature are usually used to increase the high frequency vocabulary of students. This sight word reading vocabulary is critical to later success with more advanced reading tasks. This type of book generally has a very slim plot or story line and is most beneficial for word recall than building comprehension.

Decodable Texts. Decodable texts are comprised of specific phonics skills. There is usually a range of the books that spans a great many different phonics skills. The stories are usually progressive as the skills learned in earlier books are reinforced in later books. As with controlled vocabulary texts, these books rarely have well developed story lines and are not well suited to comprehension development. They do however have a significant place in helping students unlock the code to reading.

Authentic Literature. This is the type of reading that most people are familiar with and the goal of all reading. All children should experience the reading of authentic literature or real stories. These can be fiction or nonfiction but provide numerous details and allow for the development of comprehensions skills. They range in difficulty and length, but are at the core of reading.

Created, Easy to Read Texts. This last text type would encompass teacher created reading passages or books to fill a specific purpose within the curriculum or for a group of students.

SKILL 10.3 Demonstrating knowledge of strategies for helping students identify and analyze common text structures (e.g., chronological, comparison/contrast, cause/effect)

There are five key strategies for child reading of informational/expository texts.

1.   Inferencing is a process that involves the reader making a reasonable judgment based on the information given and engages children to literally construct meaning. In order to develop and enhance this key skill in children, they might have a mini lesson where the teacher demonstrates this by reading an expository book aloud (i.e. one on skyscrapers for young children) and then demonstrates for them the following reading habits: looking for clues, reflecting on what the reader already knows about the topic, and using the clues to figure out what the author means/intends.

2.   Identifying main ideas in an expository text can be improved when the children have an explicit strategy for identifying important information. They can make this strategy part of their everyday reading style, "walking" through the following exercises during guided reading sessions. The child should read the passage so that the topic is readily identifiable to him or her. It will be what most of the information is about.

Next the child should be asked to be on the lookout for a sentence within the expository passage that summarizes the key information in the paragraph. Then the child should read the rest of the passage or excerpt in light of this information and also note which information in the paragraph is less important. The important information the child has identified in the paragraph can be used to formulate the author's main idea. The child reader may even want to use some of the author's own language in stating that idea.

3.   Monitoring means self-clarifying: As one reads, the reader often realizes that what he or she is reading is not making sense. The reader then has to have a plan for making sensible meaning out of the excerpt. Cooper and other balanced literacy advocates have a stop and think strategy which they use with children. The child reflects, "Does this make sense to me?" When the child concludes that it does not, the child then either re-reads, reads ahead in the text, looks up unknown words or asks for help from the teacher.

What is important about monitoring is that some readers ask these questions and try these approaches without ever being explicitly taught them in school by a teacher. However, these strategies need to be explicitly modeled and practiced under the guidance of the teacher by most, if not all child readers.

4. Summarizing engages the reader in pulling together into a cohesive whole the essential bits of information within a longer passage or excerpt of text. Children can be taught to summarize informational or expository text by following these guidelines. First they should look at the topic sentence of the paragraph or the text and ignore the trivia. Then they should search for information which has been mentioned more than once and make sure it is included only once in their summary. Find related ideas or items and group them under a unifying heading. Search for and identify a main idea sentence. Finally, put the summary together using all these guidelines.

Generating questions can motivate and enhance children's comprehension of reading in that they are actively involved. The following guidelines will help children generate meaningful questions that will trigger constructive reading of expository texts. First children should preview the text by reading the titles and subheadings. Then they should also look at the illustrations and the pictures. Finally they should read the first paragraph. These first previews should yield an impressive batch of specific questions.

Next, children should get into a Dr. Seuss mode and ask themselves a "THINK" question. Make certain that the children write down the question. Then have them read to find important information to answer their "think" question. Ask that they write down the answer they found and copy the sentence or sentences where they found the answer. Also have them consider whether, in light of their further reading through the text, their original question was a good one or not.

Ask them to be prepared to explain why their original question was a good one or not. Once the children have answered their original "think" question, have them generate additional ones and then find their answers and judge whether these questions were "good" ones in light of the text.

Strategies for Identifying Point of View, Distinguishing Facts from Opinions and Detecting Faulty Reasoning in Informational/expository Texts

Expository texts are full of information which may or may not be factual and which may reflect the bias of the editor or author. Children need to learn that expository texts are organized around main ideas. Expository content is commonly found in newspapers, magazines, content textbooks, and informational reference books (i.e. atlas, almanac, yearbook of an encyclopedia).

The five types of expository texts (also called "text structures") to which the children should be introduced through modeled reading and a teacher facilitated walk through are:

Description text: This usually gives the characteristics or qualities of a particular topic. It can be depended upon to be factual. Within this type of text, the child reader has to use all of his or her basic reading strategies, because these types of expository texts do not have explicit clue words.

Causation or Cause- Effect text: This text is one where faulty reasoning may come into play and the child reader has to use inferential and self-questioning skills to assess whether the stated cause-effect relationship is a valid one. Clue words to look for are: "therefore", "the reasons for", "as a result of", "because", "in consequence of", and "since." The reader must then decide whether the relationship is valid. For example, does the ventricle pump blood into the heart?

Comparison text: This is an expository text which gives contrasts and similarities between two or more objects and ideas. Many social studies, art, and science text books in class and non-fiction books include this contrast. Key words to look out for are: like, unlike, resemble, different, different from, similar to, in contrast with, in comparison to, and in a different vein. It is important that as children examine texts which are talking about illustrated or photographed entities can review the graphic representations for clues to support or contradict the text.

Collection text: This text presents ideas in a group. The writer presents a set of related points or ideas. This text structure is also called a listing or a sequence. The author frequently uses clue words such as first, second, third, finally, and next to alert the reader to the sequence. Based on how well the writer structures the sequence of points or ideas, the reader should be able to make connections. It is important the writer make clear in the expository text how the items are related and why they follow in that given sequence. Simple collection texts that can be literally modeled for young children include recipe making. A class of first graders, beginning readers and writers, were literally spellbound by a teacher's presentation of a widely known copyrighted collection text. The children were thrilled as the author followed the sequences of this collection text, and the children finally took turns stirring it until it was creamy and smooth. The children enjoyed eating their Cream Farina from a commercial cereal box which had cooking directions on it.

The children had constructed meaning from this five minute class demonstration and would now pay close attention to collection texts on other food and product instruction boxes because this text had become an authentic part of their lives.

Response structure expository texts present a question or response followed by an answer or a solution. Of course, entire mathematics text books and some science and social studies text books are filled with these types of structures. Again it is important to walk the child reader through the excerpt and to sensitize the child to the clue words which signal this type of structure. These words include, but are not limited to the problem is, the question is, you need to solve for, one probable solution would be, an intervention could be, the concern is, and another way to solve this would be.

Newspapers provide wonderful features which can be used by the teacher as read-alouds to introduce children grades 3-6 to point of view distinctions, specifically, editorials, editorial cartoons and key sports editorial cartoons. Children can also come to understand the distinction between fact and fiction, when they examine a newspaper advertisement or a supermarket circular for a product they commonly use, eat, drink or wear which includes exaggerated claims about what the product can actually do for the individual in question.

Finally the fact versus opinion distinction can be nicely explored if a teacher takes the children online to look at some star web sites and walks them through some exaggerated claims made about their particular movie star favorites. It is very important at some point, if the children have access to the internet, that the teacher show them how to examine web sites, look at who developed a particular web site and consider how credible the developers of the site are.

SKILL 10.4 Recognizing how to apply reading strategies for different reading purposes (e.g., skimming, scanning, in-depth reading)

Use of Reading Strategies for Different Texts and Strategies

As children progress to the older grades (3-6), it is important for the teacher to model for them that in research on a social studies or science exploration, it may not be necessary to read every single word of a given expository information text. For instance, if the child is trying to find out about hieroglyphics, he or she might only read through those sections of a book on Egyptian or Sumerian civilization which dealt with picture writing. The teacher, assisted by a child, should model how to go through the table of contents and the index of the book to identify only those pages which deal with picture writing. In addition other children should come to the front of the room or to the center of the area where the reading group is meeting. They should then, with the support of the teacher, skim through the book for illustrations or diagrams of picture writing which is the focus of their need.

Children can practice the skills of skimming texts and scanning for particular topics that connect with their grade Social Studies, Science and Mathematics content area interests.

Use of Comprehension Skills Before, After, and During Reading

Cooper (2004) advocates that the child ask himself or herself what a text is about before he or she reads it and even during reading of the text, what the text is going to be about. The child should be continually questioning himself or herself as to whether the text confirmed the child's predictions. Of course after completing the text, the child can then review the predictions and verify whether they were correct.

Using another strategy, the child reader looks over the expository text subheadings, illustrations, captions and indices to get an idea about the book. Then the child, still before reading the text, decides whether he or she can find the answer to his or her question.

Use of Oral Language Activities to Promote Comprehension

Taberski advocates using the "Stopping to Think About" strategy with expository texts as well as fictional ones.

This strategy is centered on the reader's using three "steps" as he or she goes through the expository text. These steps may be expressed as questions.

I. What do I, the reader, think is going to happen?
2. What clues in the text or illustrations or graphics lead me to think that this is going to happen?
3. How can I prove that I am right by going back to the text to demonstrate that this does happen or is suggested by actual clues in the text?

Taberski (2000) deliberately uses expository texts that relate to her grade's social studies and science lessons to model for children how to "stop and think" about the way an expository text is organized. She sometimes deliberately reads a section of a text or a non-fiction book aloud until the end of its chapter, so that the children can consider what they have learned about the topic and how it is organized. Then together as a whole class or as a whole guided reading group, they make predictions about what is coming next.

Development of Reading Comprehension Skills and Strategies of Individual Students

While all child readers can benefit from explicit expository reading strategies, the English Language Learner can truly get a gateway for understanding second language materials by working with a native English language speaking buddy on the question generating strategy. Both the buddy (a peer) and the teacher should alert and walk through with the English Language Learner student how much of a resource illustrations and pictures can be for constructing meaning. If the teacher has time to work individually with the English Language Learner, the day's daily newspaper which is replete with graphics, photos and text is a wonderful tool for honing expository reading skills using these strategies.

The five strategies for enhancing expository reading skills are not beyond use with learners with special needs. However, rather than be offered in an array, these strategies would have to be presented one at a time probably one on one with explicit teacher modeling and then done as shared reading and shared writing with the specific child.

Highly proficient readers might enjoy sharing their skills with other peers and could serve as the newspaper reading buddies for special needs students. They might not only support special needs grade level or younger peers in reading through a designated newspaper section every day, but might also collaborate or oversee their peers or younger peers in designing a word search or crossword puzzle based on that particular section of the newspaper.

Use of editorial sports page cartoons is a good way to introduce special needs learners to opportunities for identifying point of view. They can also create their own takes on the topics of the editorial cartoons using an accessible, non-threatening storyboard format for their commentary.

The Role of Oral Language Fluency in Facilitating the Comprehension of Informational/expository Texts

Children on the middle and secondary levels of education, who are studying social studies content, have been exposed to what social studies educators call re-enactments. This is a Reader's Theater- version of history and cultural study based completely on fact and established historical texts and documents.

Even young children will enjoy and gain tremendous additional expository comprehension facility when they are asked to dramatize a well known historical document or song. They may act out the preamble to the Constitution or read aloud as a chorus the Declaration of Independence or dramatize the Battle Hymn of the Republic. This gives children an opportunity to examine in deep form the vocabulary, syntactic, and semantic clues of these texts. They then have to use their oral instruments (voices) to express the appropriate expression for the texts.

If the children are in grades 4 and above, they can also be asked to "explain" in writing how they used the word, syntactic and semantic clues to interpret their oral language recitation. Recitation and writing can be a powerful experience for children grades 4 and up as they build their expository reading and writing skills.

Use of Writing Activities to Promote Comprehension

K-W-L Strategy

This is a graphic organizer strategy which activates children's prior knowledge and also helps them to target their reading of expository texts. This focus is achieved through having the children reflect on three key questions.

Before the child read the expository passage:
"What do I *K*now?" and
"What do I or we *W*ant to find out?"

After the child has read the expository passage:
"What have I or we *L*earned from the passage?"

What is excellent about this strategy, which is broadly used and easily implemented in almost any classroom, is that it is almost totally student-centered and powerfully focuses the child's attention on the actual reading of expository passages. The K-W-L strategy also helps the child prepare for a potential writing task.

When the teacher first introduces the K-W-L strategy, the children should be allowed sufficient time to brainstorm what all of them in the class or small group actually know about the topic. The children should have a three-columned K-W-L worksheet template for their journals and there should be a chart up front to record the responses from class or group discussion. The children can write under each column in their own journal, and should also help the teacher with notations on the chart. This strategy involves the children actually gaining experience in note taking and having a concrete record of new data and information they have gleaned from the passage about the topic.

Depending on the grade level of the participating children, the teacher may also want to channel them into considering categories of information they hope to find out from the expository passage. For instance, they may be reading a book on animals to find out more about the animal's habitats during the winter or about the animal's mating habits.

When children are working on the middle-section (*W*ant) strategy sheet, the teacher may give them a chance to share what they would like to learn further about the topic and help them to express it in question format.

K-W-L is useful and can even be introduced as early as grade 2 with extensive teacher support. It not only serves to support the child's comprehension of a particular expository text, but also models for children a format for note taking. Beyond note taking, when the teacher wants to introduce report writing, the K-W-L format provides excellent outlines and question introductions for at least three paragraphs of a report.

Cooper (2004) recommends this strategy for use with thematic units and with reading chapters in required science, social studies, or health text books.
In addition to its usefulness with thematic unit study, K-W-L is wonderful for providing the teacher with a concrete format to assess how well children have absorbed pertinent new knowledge within the passage (by looking at the third *Learn* section). Ultimately it is hoped that students will learn to use this strategy, not only under explicit teacher direction with templates of K-W-L sheets, but also on their own by informally writing questions they want to find out about in their journals and then going back to their own questions and answering them after reading.

Use of Text Features (e.g. Index, Glossary) - Graphic Features (e.g. Charts, Maps) and Reference Materials

Traditionally, the aspects of expository text reading comprehension have been taught in a dry format using reference books from the school or public library, particularly, the Atlas, Almanac, and dusty large geography volumes, to teach these necessary and meaningful skills.
Although these worthy library and perhaps classroom library books can still be used, it is much easier to take a simple newspaper to introduce and provide children with daily ongoing, authentic experiences in learning these necessary skills as they also keep up with real world events that affect their daily lives.

They can go on a chronological hunt through the daily newspaper and discover the many formats of schedules contained therein. For instance, some newspapers include a calendar of the week with literary, sports, social, movie and other public events. Children can also go on scavenger hunts through various sections of the newspaper and on certain days find full blown timelines detailing famous individual's careers, business histories, and milestones in the political history of a nation or even key movies made by a famous movie director up for an Oscar.

The nature of the newspaper reportage and the public's need to know the why and wherefore behind the story of natural disasters, company takeovers, political downfalls and uprisings leads newspapers to represent events graphically and to use cause /effect diagramming and comparison/contrast wording. If the teacher specifically wants to make certain that the students come away with this material, he or she can pre-clip "teaching" stories from the news for the child and introduce them in a special NEWS center.

After children have been walked through these comparison/contrast news writings and cause/effect diagramming as it has appeared in the newspaper, they can be challenged to find additional examples of these text structures in the news or challenged to reframe or rewrite familiar stories using these text structures. They can even use desktop publishing to re-author the stories using the same text structures.

If a class participates in a local Newspaper in Education program, where the children receive a free newspaper two to three times a week within the classroom, the teacher can teach index skills using the index of the newspaper and having children compete or cooperate in small groups to find various features.

Map and chart skills take on much more relevance and excitement when the children work on these skills using sport charts detailing the batting averages and pass completions of their favorite players or perhaps the box scores of their older siblings' football and baseball games. Maps dealing with holiday weather become meaningful to children as they anticipate a holiday vacation.

Ability to Apply Reading Skills for Various Purposes

What is really intriguing about the use of newspapers as a model and an authentic platform for introducing children into recognizing and using expository text structures, features and references, is that the children can demonstrate their mastery of these structures by putting out their own newspapers detailing their school universe using some of these text structures.
They can also create their own timelines for projects or research papers they have done in class using newspaper models.

Application of Comprehension Strategies for Electronic Texts

If the class gets newspapers in the classroom as part of an ongoing Newspapers in Education program, it is natural and easy for the teacher to take the time to show children how their same news is covered online. All of the newspapers have e-news. Children can first do a K-W-L on what they know or think they know about e-news and then actually review their specific daily newspaper's site. With the support of the teacher or an older peer, they can examine the resource and perhaps note the following differences in electronic text:

- Use of moving pictures and video to document events
- Use of sound clips in addition to written text
- Use of music/sound effects not in printed text
- Links to other web resources and to other archived articles

Of course, this can lead to much rich discussion and to further detailed web versus print news resource analysis. For children in grades 5 and 6, this might even include a research investigation of a particular news story or event including broadcast media coverage.

Development of Reading Comprehension Skills and Strategies of Individual Students

Both English Language Learners and struggling readers can benefit from the structure and format of the K-W-L approach. It allows them to share their prior experiences and knowledge of the topics covered in the expository text through natural conversation. It provides them with a natural device for the teacher or tutor to customize and to scaffold instruction to meet their linguistic and experiential backgrounds. Through the discussion and sharing of other children's comments, struggling readers and children from ELL backgrounds have an opportunity to learn how to use questions to "walk through" and take notes on expository writing.

Highly proficient readers can do a comparative expository news event study between print accounts, e-news reportage, and broadcast media coverage. They can prepare charts and their own news mock-up to show the similarities and contrasts between what aspects of the event get covered in what media format. They may also want to write to actual reporters and editors from the different media to share their insights and see if these professionals are willing to respond.

"If we want children to become strategic readers, then we create classrooms that reinforce the strategies we've demonstrated and allow children to practice on books that match their needs."
Sharon Taberski

SKILL 10.5 Demonstrating knowledge of study skills to help readers locate, analyze, and recall information from reference materials, content-area texts, graphs, charts, and maps

With the advent of the Internet the art of research and study skills in texts is becoming lost. It is however a skill that needs to be emphasized and explained to students. Understanding reference materials will provide the students with the necessary foundational skills to better prepare them for future learning.

Students need to be able to locate the information that they need for projects or to further their learning. In order to be able to find the information they need, students will need knowledge of using indexes, table of contents and other time saving helpers.

Furthermore, students need to be taught how to read and interpret graphs, charts and maps that will be found within reference materials and content specific materials. Being able to correctly interpret these types of information will better allow the student to draw the appropriate conclusions. It will enhance the knowledge the student gains from reading and provide further clarification.

Once the children understand how to access and interpret the information contained in content specific materials or reference materials they can then begin to analyze it to clarify their thinking process and make the connections to their own life or information from other texts. Sometimes, the students will find conflicting pieces of information that they will be able to then look at in a more in depth manner.

Processing information in this way, takes the level of reading to an even higher more involved level. It also requires students to find their own method for integrating it into their personal schema for later recall.

Teaching students specific study skills like: note taking, summarizing, using graphic organizers, semantic mapping, and time management will allow for effective use of the reference materials available to them.

COMPETENCY 11.0 THE TEACHER UNDERSTANDS STRATEGIES FOR PROMOTING STUDENTS' INDEPENDENT READING.

SKILL 11.1 Recognizing ways to motivate all students to read independently at school and at home

There are many ways teachers can encourage reading for pleasure in their classrooms. One of the best ways is to read aloud from a novel each day, even with grades as young as Grade 2. For Kindergarten and Grade 1, choosing picture books by one author at a time will help students realize that different authors write on different topics and in different ways. Author studies in all grades will encourage students to seek out books by that author and read them on their own.

Even within the content areas, there is a wealth of fiction that relates to the theme at hand and provides the students with background information that will help them with their studies. For example, when studying Colonial America in Social Studies, there are many picture books that teachers can use as introductions for the lessons. Using part of the class to read aloud from a novel about that period in history will help students to develop an interest in reading about the themes and help them understand how much enjoyment that reading can bring.

Monthly book clubs are also an excellent way of getting age-appropriate reading material into the students' hands. Since these book clubs offer the books at fairly inexpensive prices, parents realize that they can get more value for their money when they order each month. Book fairs at school provide students with the chance to win books for themselves and their classrooms.

Read-a-thons encourages reading because the students realize that by reading they are helping a cause. Some of these offers include prizes for the students or the teacher or school could initiate this kind of motivation.

Responding to literature is one of the most important parts of reading. By the responses that students give to what they have read, teachers can determine the level of comprehension. It takes practice for students to be able to respond critically to a text because they have the idea that all published authors are perfect and they should not criticize what they write.

Some of the strategies that teachers can use to provide opportunities for students to give creative and personal responses to their reading include:

1. Reading conferences – ask a student to read a section of the text and then tell why he/she chose that section. Teachers can also ask students why they are reading a certain book or ask about their favourite author.
2. Reading Surveys – Teachers can devise a list of questions to find out what students are reading, how they decide what books to read, and how students feel about the topics or language used in the book.
3. Daily reading time – This could be a set time when everyone in the class is reading, including the teacher or it could be a center activity for a small group of children.
4. Literature Circles – using the role sheets developed by Harvey Daniels in Voice and Choice in a Student-Centered Classroom, students take on different roles each day. They discuss the chapter or book, find new vocabulary words, illustrate a scene or pose questions for the group.
5. Reader's Theatre – students adapt part of the book or story and make it into a choral reading with expression that shows how they felt about what they have read.

SKILL 11.2 Identifying appropriate methods for determining students' reading interests and helping students develop selection criteria for independent reading

One of the simplest most efficient ways for the teacher to get to know his/her students is to conduct an entry survey. This is a record that provides useful background information about the students as they enter a class or school. Collecting information through an entry survey will give valuable insights into a student's background knowledge and experience. Teachers can customize entry surveys according to the type of information considered valuable.

In the case of reading, it would be beneficial to conduct some sort of an interest survey to determine what subject areas students want to read. As previously discussed, finding texts that are of interest to students will provide the motivation and encouragement students need to continue to read. This is especially true for those students struggling.

In helping children determine appropriate leveled books for independent reading, many teachers garner a color coding system and suggest different colors to the students. Teachers may suggest that for a quick easy read a child pick from one colored books, but if the child would like to challenge himself he should pick from a different colored book.

The teacher varies the levels throughout the year increasing the level of the difficulty for the students as their skills improve. The color-coding systems seems the most time friendly and least threatening method for helping children select appropriate texts. Students do not have to feel negative connotations that they might feel if they were functioning several grade levels behind and books were labeled by grade.

It could be quite disheartening for a student to be told to choose from the first grade basket. However, when told to pick from any basket but pick an orange stickered book, the student's privacy and independence stay in tact.

SKILL 11.3 Demonstrating knowledge of strategies for encouraging students who are learning English as a second language to read independently

See skill 11.1

SKILL 11.4 Identifying strategies for selecting and organizing a range of reading materials (e.g., fiction, nonfiction, poetry, drama, reference) at various levels of difficulty

Another method is to sort your classroom library by different subjects. This allows the students to go to a basket or crate on a specific subject of their interest and find several books. In this way, the students can explore different topics throughout the school year. Additional baskets could be created beyond subject by genre.

A basket filled with poetry might inspire some students to try their hand at writing poetry. The drama basket might provide students the opportunity to put on a small play or reader's theatre for fellow classmates. Other genres can be explored in similar manners.

Some teachers also include author baskets or series baskets. In this way, if students enjoy the way a specific author writes, they can explore other titles by that author. The same is true for books in a series.

When utilizing this basket strategy, it does not matter the reading level of text, but simply the genre, subject, author, etc. As previously discussed, it is through a color-coding system that teachers can distinguish different levels of text difficulty.

Another method is to have different baskets labeled with tags that indicate easy readers, just right readers, and challenge readers. Though less reliable it does continue to allow students to choose from texts at various levels.

SUBAREA IV.	SUPPORTING READING THROUGH ORAL AND WRITTEN LANGUAGE DEVELOPMENT

COMPETENCY 12.0 THE TEACHER UNDERSTANDS THE RELATIONSHIPS AMONG READING, WRITING, AND ORAL LANGUAGE, AND USES INTERRELATED INSTRUCTION IN THESE AREAS TO PROMOTE READING PROFICIENCY.

SKILL 12.1 Applying knowledge of the relationships among reading, writing, listening, and speaking to reinforce learning across the curriculum for all students, including students who are learning English as a second language

Reading skills are developed along with listening, speaking and writing skills. The materials consist, for the most part, of the student's skills. The philosophy of language experience includes:
1. What students think about, they can talk about.
2. What students say, they can write, or have someone write.
3. What students write or have someone write for them, they can read.

SKILL 12.2 Identifying oral language activities to enhance students' reading development (e.g., read alouds, language play, group discussions, questioning, sharing information)

Language Experience Approach
The language experience approach is similar to the whole language in that reading is considered as a personal ac, literature is emphasized, and students are encouraged to write about their own life experiences. The major difference is that written language is considered a secondary system to oral language, while whole language treats the two as parts of the same structure. The language experience approach is used primarily with beginner readers, but can also be used with older elementary and with other older students for corrective instruction.

Students dictate a story to a teacher as a group activity. Ideas for stories can originate from student artwork, news items, personal experiences, or they may be creative. Topic lists, word cards, or idea lists can also be used to generate topics or ideas for a class story. The teacher writes down the story in a first draft and the students read them back. The language patterns come from the students and they read their own written thoughts. The teacher provides guidance on word choice, sentence structure and the sounds of the letters and words. The students edit and revise the story on an experience chart. The teacher provides specific instruction in grammar, sentence structure, and spelling, if the need arises, rather than using a specified schedule. As the students progress, they create their individual storybooks, adding illustrations if they wish. The storybooks are placed in folders to share with others. Progress is evaluated in terms of the changes in the oral and written expression as well as in mechanics.

There is no set method of evaluating student progress. That is one disadvantage of the language experience approach. However, the emphasis on student experience and creativity stimulates interest and motivates the students.

Individualized Reading Approach
Students select their own reading materials from a variety, according to interest and ability, and they are more able to progress at their own individual rates. Word recognition and comprehension are taught, as the student needs them. The teacher's role is to diagnose errors and prescribe materials, although the final choice is made by the students. Individual work may be supplemented by group activities with basal readers and workbooks for specific reading skills. The lack of systematic check and developmental skills and emphasis on self-learning may be a disadvantage for students with learning problems.

See also competencies 9.0 and 10.0

SKILL 12.3 Recognizing how to provide authentic, relevant writing opportunities that enhance students' development as readers

Developing the writing of students is a complex process. As with any other aspect of teaching, it's important to provide as many realistic opportunities as possible. When students read for an authentic purpose, the reading becomes more important and there is an increased interest in completing the task.

In writing, teachers often spend time having the students complete journals, write stories or complete other assignments. While all of these types of writing provide skill development and can be important to complete with students, it is when you can find ways to incorporate authentic and relevant writing that students can find that same increased interest and the importance of writing.

Sometimes in schools these realistic reasons to write automatically present themselves. There will be times when the students are dissatisfied with a rule or decision that has been made within the school. During such a situation, the students could expand upon their persuasive writing skills to attempt to change the rule with which they disagree.

In other cases, students may keep pen pal letters with kids in another state or country. This type of correspondence even if accomplished via email, develops letter-writing skills in a more realistic setting than asking the students to write a fictitious letter for the teacher.

Similarly, the students could write jokes to be used on the announcements. They could add their own books to the library or even write books to share with younger students. Writing contests would provide another chance for teachers to provide a more realistic reason for writing to students.

In the end, it is not the type of writing to be completed or the reason for which it is completed that is important. It is the understanding that children take away from the process that writing has a purpose in society. That writing is a relevant skill that needs to be developed.

Using these authentic methods, children will begin to see the relevance in their own lives. They will then be able to come up with their own ideas and reasons to write. This takes the skill to the next level, that of application. Bringing students to the application level is the goal of education.

SKILL 12.4 Recognizing ways in which oral language skills can be transferred to written language (e.g., language-experience activities, note taking, dialogue writing, journaling, dictation)

Some of the activities that teachers can use to integrate language arts into the content areas of the curriculum include:

- Use thematic units that incorporate reading, writing, Math, social studies and science with activities that are interrelated
- Have a quick write at the end of content area instruction in which students record what they learned in this class. This is often referred to as using a Learning Log.
- Use shared reading with students paired for reading the text
- Introduce content area topics by reading from a picture book about the topic
- Use process writing for all writing activities across the curriculum
- Use interactive writing
- Oral reports
- Use of cartoons in writing assignments
- Written retellings of the text material
- Math journals (Science journals, Social Studies journals)
- Write informational texts
- Jot notes for research

Media's impact on today's society is immense and ever increasing. As children, we watch programs on television that are amazingly fast-paced and visually rich. Parent's roles as verbal and moral teachers are diminishing in response to the much more stimulating guidance of the television set. Adolescence, which used to be the time for going out and exploring the world first hand, is now consumed by the allure of MTV, popular music, and video games. Young adults are exposed to uncensored sex and violence.

But media's affect on society is beneficial and progressive at the same time. Its affect on education in particular provides special challenges and opportunities for teachers and students.

Thanks to satellite technology, urban classrooms and rural villages can receive instructional radio and television programs. CD-ROMs can allow students to learn information through a virtual reality experience. The Internet allows instant access to unlimited data and connects people across all cultures through shared interests. Educational media, when used in a productive way, enriches instruction and makes it more individualized, accessible, and economical.

COMPETENCY 13.0 THE TEACHER UNDERSTANDS STRATEGIES FOR PROMOTING VOCABULARY DEVELOPMENT.

SKILL 13.1 Recognizing how to help students expand their vocabulary knowledge and skills by listening to and reading a wide variety of texts

One way to explore the relationship between oral vocabulary and the comprehension of written words is through the use of Oral Records (which are discussed at length in the appendix).

In *On Solid Ground: Strategies for Teaching Reading K-3*, Sharon Taberski (2000) discusses how oral reading records can be used by the K-3 teacher to assess how well children are using cueing systems. She notes that the running record format can also show visual depictions for the teacher of how the child "thinks" as the child reads. The notation of miscues in particular shows how a child "walks through" the reading process. They indicate if and in what ways the child may require "guided" support in understanding the words he or she reads aloud. Taberski notes that when children read they need to think about several things at once. First, they must consider whether what they are reading makes sense (semantic or meaning cues). Next, they must know whether their reading "sounds right" in terms of Standard English (syntactic and structural cues). Third, they have to weigh whether their oral language actually and accurately matches the letters the words represent (visual or graphophonic cues).

In taking the running record and having the opportunity first-hand to listen to the children talk about the text, the teacher can analyze the relationship between the child's oral language and word comprehension. Information from the running record provide the teacher with a road map for differentiated cueing system instruction.

For example, when a running record is taken, a child often makes a mistake but then self-corrects. The child may select from various cueing systems when he or she self-corrects. These include: "M" for meaning, "S" for syntax, and "V" for visual. The use of a visual cue means that the child is drawing on his or her knowledge of spelling patterns. Of course, Tabereski cautions that any relationship between oral language and comprehension that the teacher draws from an examination of the oral-reading records, must be drawn using a series of three or more of the child's oral reading records, taken over time, not just one.

A teacher can review children's running records over time to note their pattern of miscues and which cues they have the greatest tendency to use in their self-corrections. Whichever cueing system the children use to the greatest extent, it is necessary for the teacher to offer support in also using the other cueing systems to construct correct meaning. Taberski suggests that while assessing running records to determine the relationship between oral language and meaning, the children read from "just right" books.

Strategies for Promoting Oral Language Development and Language Comprehension

Read-Alouds (This is the corner piece of the balanced literacy approach for teaching reading. Therefore it is advised that the teacher candidate and new teacher read this material carefully. This may well appear as an essay topic in the Constructed Response section).

Comments:

Within the context of the Balanced Literacy Approach and the Literacy Block, the Read Aloud is part of the Whole Class Activities. The book selected should be one taken from the classroom library, which is appropriate for a read aloud. Before reading the book to the class, the teacher needs to be familiar with it. The teachers should also "plan" or at least "know" what nuances of content, style, rhythm, and vocabulary that will be emphasized in the reading.

In addition, specifically for the younger grades, the teacher should select a text which also enhances the development of phonemic awareness. This might include a text that can be used to teach rhyming, alliteration, or poetry.

Sometimes, read-aloud texts are selected for their tie-ins with the science, social studies and mathematics curriculum.

Generally teachers aim to teach one strategy during the read-aloud, which the children will practice in small groups or independently. Among these strategies for the first grader could be print strategies and talking about books.
As the teacher reads aloud, the teachers' voice quality should highlight his or her enjoyment of the read-aloud and involvement with its text. Often in a balanced literacy classroom, the teacher reads from a specially decorated Reader's Chair, as do the guest readers. This chair's decorativeness, complete with comfortable throwback pillows or rocking chair style frame, is meant to set an atmosphere that will promote the children's engagement in and love for lifelong reading.
The balanced literacy approach also advocates that teachers select books which children will enjoy reading aloud. Particularly accessible texts for the elementary school classroom read-alouds are collections of poetry.

Teachers must allow time for discussion during and after each Read Aloud period. After the children have made comments, the teacher should also talk about the reading.

Knowledge of Common Sayings, Proverbs and Idioms

Strategy: The Fortune Cookie Strategy (Reissman, 1994). Grades 3 and up

Distribute just before snack (fortune cookies) to the children. Have them eat the cookies and then draw their attention to the fortunes which are enclosed.

First, the teacher will model by reading aloud and sharing his/her own fortune. After reading the fortune aloud, the teacher will explain what the fortune means using its vocabulary as a guide. Finally the teacher can share whether or not the teacher agrees with the statement made in the fortune.

Children can either volunteer to share their fortunes or each can read the fortune aloud, explain the saying and tell whether he or she agrees with the proverb.

Next, children can be asked to go home and interview their parents or community members to get family proverbs and common sayings.

Once the children return with the sayings and proverbs, they can each share them and explain their meaning. The class as a whole can discuss to what extent these sayings are true for everyone. Proverbs and Sayings can become part of a word wall or be included in a special literacy center. The teacher can create fill in, put together, and writing activities to go with the proverbs. They tie in nicely with cultural study on the grade 3-6 level including Asian, Latin American, and African nations.

What makes proverbs particularly effective for vocabulary development are the limited number of words in their texts and the fact these short texts allow for guided and facilitated reading instruction.

This strategy also highlights in a positive way the uniqueness and commonality of the family proverbs which are contributed by children from ELL backgrounds. If possible their proverbs can also be posted in their native languages as well as in English.

See for further proverbs: **http://www.serve.com/shea/germusa/prov1.htm**

Write like a Babylonian:
http://www.upennmuseum.com/cuneiform.cgi

Write like an Egyptian:
http://www.upennmuseum.com/hieroglyphsreal.cgi

Knowledge of Foreign Words and Abbreviations Commonly Used in English (e.g. RSVP)

Strategy: RSVP your foreign language in English literacy

Of course, the English language is replete with abbreviations that are shortened forms of words from other languages. Not only can this be used for expanding children's vocabulary and writing variety; but also it can help to positively highlight the bilingual and sometimes trilingual abilities of ELL students.

The teacher should develop a word strip mix and match game with commonly found foreign words and abbreviations. These items should, if possible, be cut out of newspapers and flyers to highlight their authenticity as part of every day life objects. Among those common words and abbreviations might be: perfume, liqueur (chocolate, of course), latte, cappuccino, panni, brioche, latkes, etc. Food, local Starbucks, coffee houses, and bakeries are excellent sources of these abbreviations. To get sufficient material to cut out to start the game, just get an extra Sunday newspaper or pick up a few circulars from a large supermarket.

Model for the children how to play the game and find out the common words or abbreviations meaning and foreign derivation using the dictionary.

Next have the children as a whole class or in small groups, work to identify the derivations of the foreign words and even map them on a world map.

As part of additional, foreign word center activities, children can opt among a number of choices. These can include: maintaining a BIG BOOK OF FOREIGN WORDS or ABBREVIATIONS, to which many contribute, using the weekly food circulars and collecting labels with foreign words which can then be collaged with an accompanying product list, authoring stories and true accounts featuring as many foreign words as possible.

What is productive about this strategy is that it enhances vocabulary development while it also highlights the extent to which the English language as spoken, used and written in the United States currently, is embedded with foreign language words and terms. This of course, makes the native language talents of the ELL child positive and important ones.

Extending a Reader's Understanding of Familiar Words

Dictionary Use:

Dictionaries are useful for spelling, writing, and reading.
It is very important to initially expose and habituate students to enjoy using the dictionary.

Cooper (2004) suggests that the following be kept in mind as the teacher of grades K-6 introduces and then habituates children to a lifelong fascination with the dictionary and vocabulary acquisition.

Requesting or suggesting that children look up a word in the dictionary should be an invitation to a wonderful exploration, not a punishment or busy work that has no reference to their current reading assignment.

Model the correct way to use the dictionary for children even as late as the third – sixth grade. Many have never been taught proper dictionary skills. The teacher needs to demonstrate to the children that as an adult reader and writer, he or she routinely and happily uses the dictionary and learns new information that makes him or her better at reading and writing.

Cooper believes in beginning dictionary study as early as kindergarten and this is now very possible because of the proliferation of lush picture dictionaries which can be introduced at that grade level. He also suggests that children not only look at these picture dictionaries, but also begin to make dictionaries of their own at this grade level filled with pictures and beginning words. As children join the circle of lexicographers, they will begin to see themselves as compilers and users of dictionaries. Of course, this will support their ongoing vocabulary development.

In early grade levels, use of the dictionary can nicely complement the children's mastery of the alphabet. They should be given whole class and small group practice in locating words.

As the children progress with their phonetic skills, the dictionary can be used to show them phonetic re-spelling using the pronunciation key.

Older children in grades 3 and beyond need explicit teacher demonstrations and practice in the use of guide words. They also need to begin to learn about the hierarchies of various word meanings. In the upper grades, children should also explore using special content dictionaries and glossaries in the backs of their books.

SKILL 13.2 Demonstrating knowledge of criteria for selecting appropriate vocabulary words (e.g., words that are related to one another, words needed to comprehend a reading selection)'

The Role of Systematic, Noncontextual Vocabulary Strategies

Strategy One: Hierarchical and Linear Arrays

The very complexity of the vocabulary used in this strategy description, may be unnerving for the teacher. Yet this strategy included in the Cooper (2004) literacy instruction is really very simple once it is outlined directly for children.

By using the term "hierarchical and linear" arrays, Cooper really is talking about how some words are grouped based on associative meanings. The words may have a "hierarchical" relationship to one another. For instance, an undergraduate or a first grader is lower in the school hierarchy than the graduate student and second grader. Within an elementary school, the fifth grader is at the top of the hierarchy and the pre K or kindergartener is at the bottom of the hierarchy. By the way, the term for this strategy obviously need not be explained in this detail to K-3 children, but might be shared with some grade and age appropriate modifications with children in grades 3 and beyond. It will enrich their vocabulary development and ownership of arrays they create.

Words can have a linear relationship to one another in that they run a spectrum from bad to good-for example from K-3 experiences, pleased-happy-overjoyed. These relationships can be displayed in horizontal boxes connected with dashes. Below is another way to display hierarchical relationships.

Once you get past the seemingly daunting vocabulary words, the arrays turn out to be another neat, graphic organizer tool which can help children "see" how words relate to one another.

To use this graphic organizer, the teacher should pre-select a group of words from a read aloud or from the children's writing. Show the children how the array will look using arrows for the linear array and just straight lines for the hierarchy. In fact invite some children up to draw the straight hierarchy lines as it is presented, so they have a role in developing even the first hierarchical model. Do one hierarchy array and one linear array with the pre selected word with the children. Talk them through filling out (or helping the teacher to fill out) the array. After the children have had their own successful experience with arrays, they can select the words from their independent texts or familiar, previously read favorites to study. They will also need to decide which type of array, hierarchical or linear, is appropriate. For 5th and 6th graders, this choice can and should be voiced using the now "owned" vocabulary words "hierarchical array" and "linear array."

This strategy is best used after reading, since it will help the children to expand their word banks.

Contextual Vocabulary Strategies

Vocabulary Self-Collection. This strategy is one in which children, even on the emergent level from grade 2 and up, take responsibility for their learning. It is also by definition, a student centered strategy, which demonstrates student ownership of their chosen vocabulary.

This strategy is one that can be introduced by the teacher early in the year, perhaps even the first day or week. The format for self-collection can then be started by the children. It may take the form of a journal with photocopied template pages. It can be continued throughout the year.

To start, ask the children to read a required text or story. Invite them to select one word for the class to study from this text or story. The children can work individually, in teams or in small groups. The teacher can also do the self-collecting so that this becomes the joint effort of the class community of literate readers. Tell the children that they should select words which particularly interest them or which are unique in some way.

After the children have had time to make their selections and to reflect on them, make certain that they have time to share them with their peers as a whole class. When each child shares the word which he or she has selected, have them provide a definition for the word. Each word that is given should be listed on a large experiential chart or even in a BIG BOOK format, if that is age and grade appropriate. The teacher should also share the word he or she selected and provide a definition. The teacher's definition and sharing should be somewhere in the middle of the children's recitations.

The dictionary should be used to verify the definitions. When all the definitions have been checked, a final list of child-selected (and single teacher-selected) words should be made.

Once this final list has been compiled, the children can record it in their word journals or they may opt to record only those words they find interesting in their individual journals. It is up to the teacher at the onset of the vocabulary self-collection activity to decide whether the children have to record all the words on the final list or can eliminate some. The decision made at the beginning by the teacher must be adhered to throughout the year.

To further enhance this strategy children, particularly those in grades 3 and beyond, can be encouraged to use their collected words as part of their writings or to record and clip the appearance of these words in newspaper stories or online. This type of additional recording demonstrates that the child has truly incorporated the word into his/her reading and writing. It also habituates children to be lifelong readers, writers, and researchers.

One of the nice things about this simple but versatile strategy is that it works equally well with either expository or narrative texts. It also provides children with an opportunity to use the dictionary.

Assessment is built into the strategy. As the children select the word for the list, they share how they used contextual clues and through the children's response to the definitions offered by their peers, their prior knowledge can be assessed.

What is most useful about this strategy is that it documents that children can learn to read and write by reading and writing. The children take ownership of the words in the self-collection journals and that can also be the beginning of writer observation journals as they include their own writings. They also use the word lists as a start for writers' commonplace books. These books are filled with newspaper, magazine, and functional document clippings using the journal words.

This activity is a good one for demonstrating the balanced literacy belief that vocabulary study works best when the words studied are chosen by the child.

SKILL 13.3 Demonstrating knowledge of instructional activities and materials to promote vocabulary development (e.g., word sorts, word banks, classification, semantic mapping)

Vocabulary is an integral part of all reading instruction. Comprehension is heavily reliant on understanding the vocabulary of the story. Vocabulary building can be done through word games, crossword puzzles, and board games like Scrabble, Scattergories or others and many other ways.

Vocabulary in reading has two levels. First, there is reading vocabulary, which is simply recognizing and knowing the words in the text. In the lower grades this is mostly made up of high frequency and sight words.

Word Sorts. Sorting words helps children to begin to recognize patterns in words or similar sounds. Students are given one to three rules and a list of words, which they must sort into groups according to the provided rules. For example, if the rules given would be words with the long e sound and words with the short e sound, the students would then read each word to determine which sound would be found in the word.

Classification. Classifying words can be very similar to word sorts at a primary level. Words could be classified by tense or in other similar ways. Students could use graphic organizers to classify words. In older grades, students may classify words by roots, suffixes, prefixes or even by meaning.

Second, there is definitional vocabulary. These are words that are found in books where the students need to understand the meaning of the words in order to better understand the story itself.

Word Banks. Word banks can be very helpful when completing vocabulary activities. They provide a limited choice of words for the students to draw from to complete various activities including cloze activities. Cloze activities consist of reading passages where certain words have been replaced with a blank line. Word banks also provide a narrower list of terms for the students to master.

Semantic Mapping. As previously discussed, semantic mapping allows students to generate a visual representation of how words and concepts interrelate. In this case, it can be an indispensable tool for the students to make comparisons and see the connections betweens words in their reading.

Overall, vocabulary development can be completed using a variety of instructional activities across many grade levels. It is important to vary the activities and materials used to reach more of the students in the classroom. One approach is generally not successful for all students and teachers have to use a varied approach to reach more students.

SKILL 13.4 Applying knowledge of strategies for gaining and extending meaning from unfamiliar words in connected text (e.g., word analysis, use of context)

When reading, often times students will come across words with which they are unfamiliar. In some cases, the students will be able to accurately decode the word provided, but will be unable to determine the meaning after a first read. At this point, students could turn to the dictionary and look up the meaning of the word before proceeding, but though a valid method, it is not the most efficient means for gaining meaning. The students need to use the remainder of the sentence, paragraph or even page to attempt to construct a rough meaning for the unknown.

Word Analysis. Analyzing the word itself is one strategy students can use to successfully derive meaning from words. Looking at the word itself, students can begin to recognize prefixes and suffixes in words. As the teacher, taking time to teach the meanings of the most common prefix and suffixes used in the English language will allow students to make generalizations to unknown words. In the same vein, teaching word derivations can be quite beneficial. Many English words are derived from the Latin and Greek language. Again, by teaching the meanings of Latin and Greek root words, teachers can help students simplify words that are unknown into smaller known parts. Finally, combining the known definitions of root words and combining them with known prefix and/or suffix meanings will provide the students with a solid foundation with which to attack unknown words for comprehension.

Use of Context. Teachers often talk about using context, or the other words in a sentence or passage to figure out unknown words, but sometimes they do not take the time to specifically teach this skill. For many students, it becomes a naturally developing skill. Many proficient readers are even unaware of how they reached the conclusion as to the meaning of the word when they use context clues. However, for the struggling readers, they lack this innate sense of arriving at the same conclusions. Students need to be taught very specifically methods for using contextual clues to determine meaning. The most effective strategy is to use a think aloud approach. In this approach, the teacher models out loud her entire thinking process for the students. She walks them through each thought she would have about determining the meaning. The teacher needs to provide key questions for the students that they can use later to reflect. Some examples of questions might include: Do any of the other words in the sentence help me to understand what this word may mean? If I finish reading the paragraph, does that help me understand better? Can I tell if this word is a noun, verb, and adjective by its placement in the sentence? Does the word have any endings that can tell me what tense it may be or if it means more than one?

By answering questions like these for students, the teacher can lay the foundation for contextual understanding. Eventually, the teacher then moves into the background and the students step in to complete the activities. When reading often times, students will come across words with which they are unfamiliar. In some cases, the students will be able to accurately decode the word provided, but will be unable to determine the meaning after a first read. At this point, students could turn to the dictionary and look up the meaning of the word before proceeding, but though a valid method, it is not the most efficient means for gaining meaning. The students need to use the remainder of the sentence, paragraph or even page to attempt to construct a rough meaning for the unknown.

The strategies necessary to develop vocabulary in students for whom English is not the primary language mirror the strategies that work for other students. There is no one set of approaches that work best for second language students, it is only through a combination of strategies and approaches that students' success can be assured.

Keeping in mind and as previously discussed, students who are learning English as a second language require some additional time in order to make the transition. For those students who have received education in their primary language the time is shortened, typically five years. While students who receive no formal instruction in their primary language, it may take as long as seven years.

Vocabulary development in any case, needs to be meaning based instruction. With or without schooling in their primary language, these students do have a mental framework of what words mean and of concepts. It is by tying the new information to these existing structures that allows the students to progress and gain more skills in English.

This transfer between languages is not an easy process and requires time and both meaning based and explicit teaching strategies. The general list of vocabulary words to memorize along with their meanings will not be a useful strategy for these students. A more significant approach is to tie the vocabulary into the context of the reading or situation. It is through contextual situations that students will better be able to progress.

Since the English language has many roots derived from the Latin and Greek languages as do many other languages, these parallels can be explicitly shown to students. Through this manner, they will be able to find the necessary hooks in their own language with which to connect the English variation. Students whose primary language also has many Latin and Greek derivatives will make the transition to English easier than those whose primary language is not of these roots.

As with any group of students, diversity is going to be present and a key factor in the educational process. Using teaching methodologies of a variant nature will be the most successful approach to helping second language students become fluent in English. Vocabulary instruction needs to be flexible, sometimes explicit, and still other times be based in context.

COMPETENCY 14.0 THE TEACHER UNDERSTANDS HOW KNOWLEDGE OF ENGLISH LANGUAGE STRUCTURES AND CONVENTIONS RELATES TO THE DEVELOPMENT OF READING PROFICIENCY.

SKILL 14.1 Identifying strategies for helping students understand the similarities and differences between language structures used in spoken and written English (e.g., formal vs. informal tone and style)

It is an important part of the process of teaching integrated language arts skills to students to spend some time introducing the children to the differences between language structures in both oral and written English. Too often, students believe that all communication is equal, when in fact there are differences dependent upon the purpose of the communication.

Informal. Informal language refers to the way students communicate to each other. The use of slang terms is common in informal language. When writing to each other, students may write in a short hand, with phrasing that is somewhat unclear. Using first person terms, such as I, is also common in informal communication. In today's more mobile society, emails, mobile text messaging and/or instant messaging systems have their own abbreviations, which are also a form of informal communication. Students need to be taught and understand when informal language is appropriate and when it is not.

Formal. Formal communication, whether spoken or written, is most often the format students will use in schools. Students are expected to speak and write refraining from using slang or other less informal words. They are asked to convey clearly their ideas and generally write in third person. There is typically an audience to which the student is writing or communicating and the conventions of language are expected to be used with integrity. There are however, exceptions, when creating fictional works, there may be more license to use informal language to set tone or as part of the style of writing.

Tone. Sometimes referred to as voice, the tone of oral or written language sets the mood. It is the attitude conveyed to the people listening or reading. In oral language, the same words can be said with different inflections and convey significantly different meanings. Tim Rasinski, professor at Kent State University in Ohio, has been heard to use the example, of the word dude. Think to yourself how you would say dude to convey excitement, now say the same word but use different inflection to mean disappointment. In written language, the voice of the writing also helps to give the reader the mood.

Style. Style is without a doubt the most subjective of the described strategies. You could provide the same piece of writing to several professors to review and get many different comments about style. It involves looking at the word choice, verbage used, and vocabulary present. It is important to teach students to be clear when writing and avoid unnecessary wordiness. Also, teaching correct verb usage maintaining correct tense helps the style of writing to be more accepted. Finally, correct use of vocabulary is needed. Some students believe using multi-syllabic words is the key and will then use terms they are not familiar with inappropriately, causing the reader to cringe. So, while subjective, there are some key components to style, students need to be instructed in their proper use.

SKILL 14.2 Applying knowledge of strategies for promoting students' understanding of basic syntax and semantics

Language requires the use of the concepts of syntax and semantics in order for the intended meaning to be conveyed to the recipient. In this manner, it is part of the essential curriculum for all students that time is spent defining and providing examples of these ideas. Introduction should begin with oral language then slowly be transferred into the written form of communication.

Syntax. Syntax by definition involves the way words are put together to form the language. It includes the idea of nouns, verbs, adjectives, adverbs and all of the other labels given to specific categories of words. There are bodies of research on polar opposite ends of the spectrum when it comes to the direct teaching of syntax. One camp believes that it is important for students to be given specific instruction in this area. They believe that explicit and specific instruction provides the foundation students need to later develop appropriate skills. Some strategies used include: diagramming sentences, word sorts, and categorizing groups of words. The other side of the fence judges the identification of words by these labels as pointless. They believe that through practice and modeling of appropriate language with correct syntax, students will develop these skills naturally. Generally, they think that students will be able to use nouns and adjectives correctly whether or not they can identify and name the specific words as either nouns or adjectives.

Semantics. Semantics refers to the meaning of words and the manner in which they are put together to convey meaning. Semantics can vary by changing one or more words in a sentence. Even if the main nouns and verbs are not changed and simply conjunctions or modifiers are changed, the meaning of the sentence can be significantly altered.

In reality, instruction and modeling in both semantics and syntax are equally important. They are interdependent for both oral and written language. Students who have difficulty grasping the understanding of these skills may require more explicit teaching in this area.

For students for whom English is not their primary language, this may also be a concern. The semantics and syntax of each language varies and applying the rules for one language to another can send misleading and confusing messages. Sometimes, it can be helpful to simply point out the differences and devise comparison and contrast charts, which the students can use and refer to when completing a writing assignment.

SKILL 14.3 Identifying strategies for helping students apply knowledge of English grammar, spelling, and other language conventions in reading, writing, listening, and speaking contexts

Generalization of tasks from specific skill instruction to broader areas is a complex skill that some students have difficulty obtaining. Understanding how English grammar, spelling and the other language conventions previously discussed cross all of the language arts disciplines is a skill students need to be successful.

Reading. In reading students will be exposed to all of the grammar, spelling and other conventions on a regular basis. As the teacher, it is important to take time to point out these areas to the students who may otherwise pass them by without a second thought. One important strategy for helping in this area is called Directed Reading Thinking Activities (DRTA). This strategy developed by Russell Stauffer (1969) allows the teacher to guide the thinking of the student usually in making predictions and improving comprehension. An adaptation to this strategy would allow the teacher to guide the thinking of the students to recognize and identify the conventions.

Writing. Since writing is a more formal skill than oral language, the conventions will be slightly different. Many times students will write the same way they speak which is usually unacceptable for written language. The editing process is probably the most effective method for helping students achieve improved use of grammar, spelling, syntax and semantics. Peer editing and teacher editing provide excellent tools for students.

Listening. Listening is an art. Many times it is obvious that students are hearing what the speaker is saying, but are not truly listening. Setting the purpose for an oral presentation and providing graphic organizers are strategies that help structure listening activities. Having a purpose for listening with a graphic organizer allows the students to better filter out relevant and irrelevant information. Demonstration of correct language conventions and incorrect ones would provide the students with the opportunity to complete a comparison and contrast situation.

Speaking. When orally presenting information, it is important the student realize the necessity of using correct language. Having the students practice the presentation out loud into a tape recorder is a technique that will allow the students the opportunity to critique themselves or others and provide valuable feedback.

SKILL 14.4 Identifying methods for assessing students' understanding of English language structures and conventions

When considering the assessment of students' understanding of English language structures and conventions, the most commonly used method is rubrics.

Rubrics can be commercially, teacher, or even student created to be used as an assessment tool. A rubric is a tool that defines in writing the teacher's expectations for assignments. The language on rubrics should be clearly thought out and leave little room for misinterpretations. Rubrics provide different levels of criteria to obtain different levels of proficiency. In this way, students clearly understand why their work was assessed in the manner it was without needing further clarification.

Rubrics also provide consistency when assessing assignments that could otherwise be viewed subjectively, as is the case with English language and conventions, particularly style.

Well-developed rubrics tell the criteria for evaluation while giving performance expectations, ratings and descriptors. They cover a range from the unacceptable to the acceptable providing students with a clear picture of all possible scores.

Another assessment method to use with considering English language structures and conventions is a list of essential questions to refer to as the evaluator. When using this strategy, the teacher prepares a list of essential questions that he feels when answered affirmatively will demonstrate the appropriate skills to show master of these skills.

When developing these questions, most teachers derive them as yes or no questions directly from the curriculum and/or state standards that specifically pertain to their grade level. In this way, the teacher can use one piece of writing or one oral presentation and be able to show others how he determined the proficiency level of a student.

The use of yes and no questions limits the variability of ratings and tying it directly to the curriculum ensures that what is to be taught has been taught.

Both methods of assessment discussed provide the opportunity for the teacher to go back and determine what if any skills or information may need to be retaught in order for students to achieve competence.

COMPETENCY 15.0 THE TEACHER UNDERSTANDS STRATEGIES FOR SUPPORTING AND PROMOTING THE READING DEVELOPMENT OF STUDENTS WHO ARE LEARNING ENGLISH AS A SECOND LANGUAGE.

SKILL 15.1 Recognizing how to interrelate elements of language arts instruction to support the reading development of students who are learning English as a second language (e.g., using preview-review, visual aids, charts, real objects, word organizers, graphic organizers, outlining)

There are many different ways to support students who are learning English as a second language in their development of reading.

Preview-Review. Background knowledge is essential when reading for adequate comprehension to occur. Before reading a text, it can be helpful to preview vocabulary, phonics concepts, or other language arts elements with the students. This preview provides them a heads up so to speak and the ability to have some minor background knowledge. After reading the selection, it is just as important to go back and review the information to ensure understanding.

Visual Aids, Charts and Real Objects. For all students, but particularly those learning English as a second language, whenever it is possible to provide a nonverbal visual representation it will enhance the instruction. Often times, the students have a framework of understanding about certain topics, but do not have the language skills or vocabulary to define that concept. With pictorial representations, the language component is eliminated and therefore the students can draw more conclusions and better understand the concepts. The visual may be a picture, a chart or if possible the real object.

Word Organizers. Semantic mapping can help to provide students with a deeper understanding of the interrelationship between words and concepts. Seeing these relationships on paper can help the students make additional generalizations and draw conclusions.

Graphic Organizers. The flexibility of graphic organizers to span multiple subjects makes them an invaluable tool to students and teachers. The fact that a graphic organizer helps put a visual representation to a concept or arrange multiple concepts into a more manageable manner provides the student learning English with the opportunity to connect new learning with old learning or to connect English with their native language.

Outlining. Outlining is an organizational tool that is very sequential and concrete. The use of this tool with students for whom English is a second langue provides a clear path for them to follow. Whether it is a prepared outline showing the concepts to be covered with room for the students to take notes, or their own prepared outline for upcoming writing assignments, students will find the sequential nature of the outline to leave little room for misinterpretation.

No matter the organization tool, students acquiring English will begin to see the interrelationship across language arts skills.

SKILL 15.2 Demonstrating familiarity with and cultural sensitivity to the ways in which languages differ

The multicultural facets of society provide wonderful opportunities for learning and depth and breadth of knowledge about the world. As more and more languages are represented within this country, teachers must have a solid understanding of the various cultural differences of these languages.

In order to provide support to students for who English is not the primary language, teachers must help students make connections within their first language. For many teachers, it would be impossible to speak and understand at a fluent level all of the languages that are present within their classrooms.

However, it is beneficial to have a basic level of understanding of the fundamentals of these languages. Without at least a basic understanding of the structure of these languages it will be difficult to help students draw parallels.

For example, if the language places its adjectives after the nouns, students might exhibit this same order of words when they begin to write or speak in English. The teacher, who is unfamiliar with the language conventions of the first language, might think this very odd and refer the child for additional evaluations, when in fact there is no problem. The child simply needs to be instructed in the differences in word order between their primary language and English.

This type of cultural awareness and sensitivity allows the students to begin to feel comfortable within the English learning environment. It can be very intimidating for a student to be thrown into a classroom where they cannot speak the language nor understand it. These students sometimes act out physically due to the frustration of being unable to communicate with anyone.

Students will sometimes resort to a gesturing system to attempt communication. Having other students available who speak the same language as the student, if possible, can also help to build comfort for the students. Bridging these types of gaps show the students that teachers care about them.

Cultural sensitivity is important for all students regardless of their language proficiency.

SKILL 15.3 Demonstrating an understanding of the factors and processes involved in transferring literacy competencies from one language to another

Several times it has been discussed that students for whom English is not the primary language require additional time to transfer the literacy skills. There are several factors that can be involved in the progress students make. The one that seems to stand out, as the most relevant seems to be the level of schooling received in the primary language.

Research indicates that it takes between five and seven years for students to make the successful acquisition of the new language. The difference seems to be related to the amount of education received in their primary language before learning the second language.

Scaffolding learning can be a key factor to helping increase the likelihood of transferring the skills across domains. In this approach, the teacher provides more supports at the beginning of the learning process, and then slowly weans the students from those supports until they are completing them independently.

Additional factors can include: time exposed to the second language, teaching methodologies utilized and home language support. Social and motivation factors can also affect the transference of literacy skills for students.

Assessment is also a key factor. Literacy skills can be making great strides but if measured through invalid tests and measures that have a cultural bias it may be difficult to demonstrate the actual growth patterns.

Overall, as discussed in previous sections and briefly here, students learning a second language require additional time and support to become readers of English.

SKILL 15.4 Demonstrating familiarity with strategies for promoting the transfer of language skills from one language to another

See skills 15.1, 15.2, and 15.3

GLOSSARY

These definitions are critical for success on all multiple choice questions on the examinations. Proper use of these terms, is crucial for success in tackling a constructed response involving balanced literacy.

ABILITY GROUPING- grouping of children with similar needs for instructional purposes. Ability groups do not remain constant throughout the year, but change as the children's needs within them change.

ALLITERATION- occurs when words begin with the same consonant sound, as in *Peter Piper picked a pair of pickled peppers*.

ALPHABETIC PRINCIPLE- the idea that written spellings represent spoken words.

ANCHOR BOOK- a balanced literacy term for a book that is purposely read repeatedly and used as part of both the reading and writing workshop.

It is a good idea to use certain books that become the children's familiar and cherished favorites for both reading and then to inspire children's writing.

ASSONANCE- Occurs when words begin with the same vowel sound.

AUTHENTIC ASSESSMENT- assessment activities which reflect the actual workplace, family community and school curriculum.

BALANCED LITERACY LESSON FORMAT- The Balanced Literacy Approach has its own specific format for the delivery of the literacy lesson, whether it is a reading or writing workshop lesson. The format begins with a 10-15 minute mini-lesson which the teacher delivers to the whole class. This mini-lesson is then followed by a thirty-minute small group (when the children break into small groups to work) lesson. It concludes with a 10-minute share during which the whole class reconvenes to share what they have done in the small groups.

One can refer to this format as the whole-small-whole group approach.

BENCHMARKS- school state, or nationally mandated statements of the expectations for student learning and achievement in various content areas.

BICS-BASIC INTERPERSONAL COMMUNICATION SKILLS (ELL term-Bilingual Education)- learning second language skills and becoming proficient in a second language through face to face interaction-translation through speaking, listening, and viewing.

BLENDING- the process of hearing separate phonemes and being able to merge them together to read the word.

BOOK FEATURES- children need to be familiar with the following book features: front and back cover, title and half- title page, dedication page, table of contents, prologue and epilogue, and foreword and after notes. For factual books, children need to be familiar with: labels, captions, glossary, index, headings and subheadings of chapters, charts and diagrams, and sidebars.

CHECKLIST- an assessment form which lists targeted learning and social behaviors as indicators of achievement, knowledge or skill. They can be professionally- or teacher-prepared.

CINQUAIN- a five line poem that can be read and then used as a model for writing. Generally line 1 of this format is a single word, line 2 has 2 words, which describe the title of line 1, line 3 is comprised of 3 words which are movement words, line 4 has 4 words which express feeling and line 5 has a single word which is a synonym for line 1's single word.

COMPREHENSION- this occurs when the reader correctly interprets the print on the page and constructs meaning from it. Comprehension depends on activating prior knowledge, cultural and social background of the reader, and the reader's ability to use comprehension monitoring strategies.

CONCEPTS ABOUT PRINT- include: how to handle a books, how to look at print, directionality, sequencing, locating skills, punctuation, and concepts of letters and words.

CONSONANT DIAGRAPHS- two consecutive consonants that represent one new speech sound. In the word "digraph" the *ph* which sounds like /f/ is a digraph.

CONTEXTS- sentences deliberately prepared by the teacher which include sufficient contextual clues for the children to decipher meaning.

CONTEXTUAL REDEFINITION- using context to determine word meaning.

COOPERATIVE READING- Children read with a partner or buddy. It can be silent or oral reading.

CRISSCROSSERS- an ELL term for second language learners who have a positive attitude toward both first language and second language learning. These second language learners, children from ELL backgrounds, are comfortable navigating back and forth between the two languages as they learn.

CUES- as they self monitor their reading comprehensions, readers have to integrate various sources of information or cues to help them construct meaning from text and graphic illustrations.

DECODING- "sounding out" a printed sequence of letters based on knowledge of letter sound correspondences.

READING

DIPHTHONGS- two vowels in one syllable where the two sounds are heard. For instance in the word *house* both the "o" and the "u" are heard.

DIRECTIONALITY-children use their fingers to indicate left to right direction and return sweep to the next line.

DIFFERENTIATED INSTRUCTION- The need for the teacher, based on observation of individual student's work, progress, test results, fluency, and other reading/literacy behaviors, to provide modified instruction and alternative strategies or activities. These activities are specifically developed by the teacher to address the individual student's different needs.

EARLY READERS- recognize most high frequency words and many simple words. They use pictures to confirm meaning. Using meaning, syntax, and phonics, they can figure out most simple words. They use spelling patterns to figure out new words. They are gaining control of reading strategies. They use their own experiences and background knowledge to predict meanings. They occasionally use story language in their writing. This stage follows emergent reading.

EMERGENT READERS- the stage of reading in which the reader understands that print contains a consistent message. The reader can recognize some high frequency words, names, and simple words in context. Pictures can be used to predict meaning. The emergent reader begins to attend to left to right directionality and features of print and may identify some initial sounds and ending sounds in words.

ENCODE- to change a message into symbols. For example, readers encode oral language into writing.

ENGLISH as a SECOND LANGUAGE- a way of teaching English to speakers of other languages using English as the language of instruction.

EXPOSITORY TEXT-. is non-fiction that provides information and facts. This text type is what newspapers, science, mathematics and history texts use. Currently there is much focus, even in elementary schools, on teaching children how to comprehend and author expository texts. They must produce brochures, guides, recipes, and procedural accounts on most elementary grade levels. The teaching of reading of expository texts requires working with a particular vocabulary and concept structure that is very different from that of the narrative text. Therefore time must be taken to teach the reading of expository texts and contrast it with the reading of narrative texts.

FIRST LANGUAGE- an ELL term for the language any child acquires in the first few years of life. It is through this acquired language that the child acquires phonological and phonemic awareness.

FLUENT READERS- identify most words automatically. They can read chapter books with good comprehension. They consistently monitor, cross-check, and self-correct reading. They can offer their own interpretations of text based on personal experiences and prior reading experiences. Fluent readers are capable of reading a variety of genres independently. Furthermore, they can respond to texts or stories by sharing pertinent examples from their lives. They can also readily make connections to other books which they have read. Finally, they are capable of beginning to create spoken and written writings which are in the style of a particular author.

FORMAL ASSESSMENT- a test or an observation of a performance task which is done under controlled and regulated conditions.

FUNCTIONAL READING- the reading of instructions, recipes, coupons, classified ads, notices, signs, and other documents which we have to read and correctly interpret in school and in society.

GRADE EQUIVALENT/GRADE SCORE- a score transformed from a raw score on a standardized test into the equivalent score earned by an average student in the norming group.

GRAPHIC ORGANIZERS- graphic organizers express relationships among various ideas in visual form including: sequence, timelines, character traits, fact and opinion, main idea and details, differences and likenesses. Graphic organizers are particularly helpful for visual learners.

GUIDED READING- one of the key modes of instruction in the balanced literacy theory approach. During guided reading, the teacher "guides" the child through silent reading of a text by giving them prompts, target questions, and even helping the child start an answer to a specific prompt or question. At the end of each guided reading section or excerpt of the text, the child stops to talk with the teacher about the text. By definition, guided reading is an interactive discussion between the child and the teacher. This mode of reading instruction is generally used when children need extra support in constructing meaning because the text is complex or because their current independent reading capacities are still limited.

HIGH FREQUENCY- frequently used words. These words appear many more times than do other words in ordinary reading material. Examples of such words include: *as, in, of,* and *the*. These words are also sometimes called service words. These words are also part of sight vocabulary words. A classic best-known high frequency word list was generated by Dolch (1936).

INDEPENDENT READING- a set period of time within the daily literacy block when children read books with 95%-100% accuracy on their own. This reading of books by themselves which they can understand without teacher support promotes lifelong literacy and love of learning, which enhances reading mileage, builds fluency, and helps children orchestrate integrated cue strategies.

INFORMAL ASSESSMENT- observations of children made under informal conditions; these can include kid watching, checklists, and individual child/teacher conversations.

INFORMAL READING INVENTORY (IRI) - a series of reading excerpts that can be used to determine a child's reading strengths and needs in comprehension and decoding. Many published reading series have an IRI to go with their series.

JUSTIFIED PRINT- the positioning of print on the page so that each line ends either a sentence or a phrase.

KID WATCHING- term used within the balanced literacy approach for the teacher's deliberate, detailed, and recorded observations of individual student and class literacy behaviors., often done during small group work. The teacher then reconfigures lessons on experiences to meet the students' individual and group needs.

KINESTHETIC- learning is tactile; as contrasted with an activity where the learner sits still or attempts to sit still in one place. Cutting and moving syllable or word strips or using sandpaper letters are kinesthetic activities.

LANGUAGE EXPERIENCE- Children giving dictation to the teacher who writes their words on a chart or their drawings. This shows children that words can be written down.

LEARNING LOGS- daily records of what students have learned.

LISTENING POST- sets of headphones attached to a single tape player. Children can go to centers where they listen to audiotapes of books while reading the print book. These posts are in many libraries as well.

LITERATURE CIRCLES- a group discussion involving four to six children who have read the same work of literature (narrative or expository text). They talk about key parts of the work, relate it to their own experience, listen to the responses of others, and discuss how parts of the text relate to the whole.

MANIPULATION- moving around or switching sounds within a word or words within a phrase or sentence.

MEANING VOCABULARY- words whose meanings children understand and can use.

MISCUE- an oral reading error made by a child which differs from the actual printed text.
MISCUE ANALYSIS- the teacher keeps a detailed recording of the errors or inaccurate attempts of a child reader during a reading assessment. These are recorded within a running record. This helps the teacher see whether the cues-syntactic, semantic, or graphophonemic-the child is using are accurate.

MONITORING READING- various strategies that children use to monitor their readings. A sample are maintaining fluency by bringing prior knowledge to the story to make predictions, using these predictions to do further checking, searching, and self-correcting as the story progresses, and using problem-solving word study skills to make links from known words to unknown words.

MORPHEMES- the smallest units of meaning in words. There are two types of morphemes; free morphemes, which can stand alone such as *love,* and bound morphemes, which must be attached to another morpheme to carry meaning such as *ed* in *loved.*

NARRATIVE TEXT- one of the two basic text structures. The narrative text tells or communicates a story. Narrative texts are novels, short stories and plays. Some poems are narratives as well. The narrative text needs to be taught differently than the expository text because of its structure.

ONE TO ONE MATCHING- matching one spoken word with one written word.

ONSET-RIME BLENDING –ONSET-Everything before the vowel and RIME (the vowel and everything after it). For example, the word "sleep" can be broken into /sl/ and /eep/. Word families are build using rimes. The /eep/ word family would include *jeep, keep* and *weep*.

ORTHOGRAPHY- a method of representing spoken language through letters and diacritics.

PERCENTILE- if a child scores at the 56th percentile for his/grade level, his/her score is equal to or above that of 56 percent of the children taking that standardized test and below that of 46 percent of the children on whose scores the test was normed.

PERFORMANCE ASSESSMENT- having children do a task that demonstrates their knowledge, skills and competency. Having children author their own alphabet book on a particular topic would be a performance assessment for knowledge of the alphabet.

PHONEME- The speech sound units that make a difference in meaning. The word "rope" has three phonemes /r/, /o/, and /p/. Change one phoneme, say /r/ to /n/, and you have a different word *nope.*

PHONEMIC AWARENESS- the understanding that words are composed of sounds. Phonemic awareness is a specific type of phonological awareness dealing only with phonemes in a spoken word.

PHONICS- the study of relationships between phonemes (speech sounds) and graphemes (letters) that represent the phonemes. It is also decoding or the sounding out of unknown words. that are written.

TEACHER CERTIFICATION STUDY GUIDE

PHONOLOGICAL AWARENESS- the ability to recognize the sounds of spoken language and how they can be blended together, segmented, and switched/manipulated to form new combinations and words.

PHONOLOGICAL CUES- readers use their knowledge of letter/sound and sound/letter relationships to predict and confirm reading.

PHONOLOGY- the study of speech structure in language that includes both the patterns of basic speech units (phonemes) and the tacit rules of pronunciation.

PORTFOLIOS- collections of a child's work over time. They include a cover letter, reflections from the child and teacher, and other supportive documents including standards, performance task examples, prompts and sometimes peer comments.

PRIMARY LANGUAGE- (ELL term)- the language an individual is the most fluent in and at ease with. This is usually, but not always the individual's first language.

PROMPTS- when the teacher intervenes in the child's independent reading to help the child pronounce or comprehend a specific word or prompt. On a reading record, the teacher notes the prompt. When the teacher wants to match a child with a particular book or determine the child's stage of reading/level, the teacher does not use prompts.

QUESTION GENERATING STRATEGY FOR AN EXPOSITORY TEXT- first the child previews the text by reading titles, subheads, looking at pictures or illustrations, and reading the first paragraph. Next the child asks a "think" question which he or she records. Then the child reads to find information that might answer the "think" question. The child may write down the information found or think about another question that is answered by what the child is reading. The child continues to read using this strategy.

READING FOR INFORMATION- Reading with the purpose of extracting facts and expert opinion from the text. Children should be introduced to the following information reading resources: web resources that are age and grade appropriate for children, the concept of the table of contents, chapter headings, glossaries, pictures, maps, charts, diagrams and text structures in an information text. They should be taught to use notes, graphs, organizers, and mind maps to share information extracted from a text.

RECODE- To change information from one code into another, as recoding writing into oral speech.

RECOGNITION VOCABULARY- the group of words which children are able to correctly pronounce, read orally and understand on sight.

READING

RECORD OF READING BEHAVIOR – (running record) an objective observation during which the teacher records, using a standard set of symbols, everything the child reader says as the child reads a book selected by the teacher.

REFLECTION- to analyze, discuss, and react to one's learning on any grade or age level.

RETELLING- retelling can be written or oral. Children are expected and encouraged to tell as much of a story as they can remember. Re-telling is far more extensive than just summarizing. Children should include the beginning, middle and end plot lines and should be able to tell about the book's characters.

RUBRIC- a set of guidelines or acceptable responses for the completion of any task. Usually a rubric ranges from 0 to 4 with 4 being the most detailed response and 0 indicating a response to the task which lacked detail or was in other ways insufficient.

SCAFFOLDING- refers to the teacher support necessary for the child to accomplish a task or to achieve a goal which the child could not accomplish on his/her own. Vygotsky termed this window of opportunity the "zone of proximal development." Ultimately as the child becomes more proficient or capable, the scaffold is withdrawn. The goal of scaffolding is to help the child to perform the reading task independently and internalize the behavior. During SHARED READING, the task is scaffolded by the teacher's reading to the children aloud. As the teacher reads, the teacher scaffolds the initial decoding and helps with the meaning making/construction.

SEARCHING- children pause to search in the picture, print, or their memory for known information. This can happen as the child tackles an unknown word or after an error.

SECOND LANGUAGE-(ELL term)-A language acquired or learned simultaneously with or after a child's acquisition of a first language.

SEGMENTING- the process of hearing a spoken word and identifying its separate phonemes or syllables.

SELF-CORRECTION- children begin to correct some of their own reading errors. Generally this behavior is accompanied by the re-reading of the previous phrase or sentence.

SEMANTIC CUES- children use their prior knowledge, sense of the story, and pictures to support their predicting and confirming the meaning of the text.

SEMANTIC WEB- a visual graphic organizer that the teacher can use to introduce a reading on a specific topic. It visually represents many other words associated with a target word. The web can help activate the children's prior knowledge and extend or clarify it. It can also serve to check new learning after guided or independent reading.

SPATIAL LEARNING- Using images, color, or layout to help readers whose learning style is spatial.

STANDARD SCORE- how far a child's grade on a standardized test is from the average score (mean) on the test in terms of the standard deviation. If a child scores 70 on a standardized test and the standard deviation is 5 and the average (mean) score is 65, the child is one standard deviation above the average.

STANDARDIZED TEST- a test given under specified conditions allowing comparisons to be made. A set of norms or average scores on this test will be used for comparisons.

STOP AND THINK STRATEGY- a balanced literacy strategy for constructing meaning. As the text is being read, the child asks himself or herself, does this make sense to me? If it does not make sense to me, I should then try to re-read it or read ahead. I can also look up words that I don't know or ask for help. Generally the teacher models this strategy with the whole class as a mini lesson and then it is posted prominently in the classroom for continued reference by the children.

STRATEGIC READERS- as defined by researchers Marie Clay and Sharon Taberski, strategic readers are self improving and do the following as they read:

(A lengthy glossary explanation of this term has been provided because it can appear in a variety of multiple choice questions on the examination as well as part of a constructed response question).

- Monitor their reading to see if it makes sense semantically, syntactically, and visually.
- Look for and use semantic, syntactic, and visual clues.
- Uncover and identify new things about the text.
  Cross check and use one cueing system against another.
- Self-correct their reading when what they first read does not match the semantic, syntactic and visual clues
- Solve for and identify new words using multiple cueing systems

Beyond these behaviors, a strategic or self-improving reader uses many strategies to construct meaning. When their reading experience is going well-they know the words and understand the text or story-they are working continuously (even if they are not conscious of it) at maintaining meaning. If and when the strategic or self-improving reader runs into an unfamiliar word, then the reader has many strategies to identify that word. Becoming a successful strategic reader is a goal that can and should be shared with children as early as the middle of the first grade, although the term "self-improving reader" might be used at that point.

TEXT FEATURES- children need to be alerted to the following text features which may initially appear strange to them. The features of text include: a period which marks the end of a "telling sentence;" a question mark that is at the end of a sentence that asks a question, an exclamation mark used to express surprise or excitement at the end of a sentence, capital letters which begin a sentence and the names of persons, places, and things; bold italicized or underlined text to highlight key ideas; quotation marks which show dialogue, a hyphen used to break a long word up into its syllables, a dash used to show a break in an idea, or to indicate a parenthetical element or an omission; an ellipse, which shows an omission or break in the text; and a paragraph in nonfiction which shows a new point being made.

TRANSITIONAL READERS- recognize an increasing number of "hard" words that are content related. They can provide summaries of the stories that they read. They are more at ease with handling longer, more complex, connected text with short chapters. Transitional readers can read independent level texts with correct phrasing, expression, and fluency. When they encounter unfamiliar words, they have a variety of strategies to figure out the unfamiliar words. Their reading demonstrates that they are able to integrate meaning, syntax and phonics in a consistent manner so that they can understand the texts they are reading.

VENN DIAGRAM- a diagram consisting of two or three intersecting circles to visually represent similarities and differences for texts, characters and topics. No author study is complete without VENN DIAGRAMS comparing different author's works. This is the most commonly used graphic organizer in elementary schools today. It can be used effectively as part of an answer to a constructed response question.

VISUAL CUES- readers use their knowledge of graphemes to predict and confirm text. The graphemes may be words, syllables or letters.

WORD ANALYSIS- the analysis of words employing letters, phonic structures, contextual clues, or dictionary skills.

WORD IDENTIFICATION- how the reader determines the pronunciation, and the meaning of an unknown word.

WORD RECOGNITION- The process of determining the pronunciation and some degree of the meaning of an unknown word.

WORD WORK- the term that the balanced literacy approach uses for the study of vocabulary.

Directory of Theorists and Researchers

Introduction
Many questions on the teacher certification examinations can only be correctly answered if you know the theorist or the research that is referenced. The teaching of reading owes much to the work, principles and guidelines of teacher educators and university field researchers who have changed the style, methods and practice of teaching reading. While those listed in this directory are by no means all the major researchers (page constraints would make a complete listing impossible), the individuals listed below are those whose contributions are frequently referenced on the certification tests and whose work is evident in today's elementary classroom teaching and learning of reading.

PHONICS CENTERED APPROACH

In 1955 Rudolph Flesch gained national prominence when he publishedx *Why Johnny Can't Read*. This book went on to become a best seller and has now become a classic which is readable and speaks to current concerns. Flesch became the spokesperson for a war that periodically resurfaces in the reading world.

Flesch, Chall (1967) Stahl (1992), Adams (1990), and Johnson and Bauman (1984) believe that a phonics-based approach is crucial for reading success. Flesch and others feel that the balanced literacy advocates are seriously undermining the crucial role that phonics plays in the children's development as successful decoding readers. However, it must be noted that while balanced literacy does emphasize the use of literature based reading programs, it in no way dismisses phonics from its reading program; indeed phonics is included in the crucial "word work" component of the reading and writing workshop.

The phonics advocates point to the fact that most research shows that early and systematic instruction in phonics skills results in superior reading achievement in elementary school and beyond.

Adams (1990) detailed what type of phonics instruction is needed.

To learn to read skillfully, children need practice in seeing and understanding decodable words in real reading situations and with connected text.... phonics instruction {needs to be} part of a reading program that provides ample practice in reading and writing. Encouraging children with connected text can also show them the importance of what they are learning and make the lessons in phonics relevant and sensible. Phonics centered advocates believe that children should begin to learn letter associations in kindergarten with most useful phonics skills being taught by first grade. These basic skills should then be reviewed in second grade and beyond.

Consonant sounds should be taught first, since they are more reliable in their letter-sound associations.

READING

Short vowel sounds appear more frequently in beginning reading materials, so they should be introduced before long vowels. Phonics advocates believe that most beginning readers need to be taught letter sound associations explicitly. Phonics advocates also believe that beginning readers need to read stories that have words to which phonics skills apply. This allows them to practice their phonics skills as they write and spell words. They should also play lots of letter-sound association games.

Phonics advocates claim that when phonics is abandoned reading scores drop and balanced literacy advocates counter with the fact that they have never advocated abandoning the teaching of phonics.

As Jeanne Chall, a professor at Harvard's Graduate School of Education notes: "a beginning reading program that does not give children knowledge and skill in recognizing and decoding words will have poor results."

Theorists and Researchers:

Adams, Marilyn Jager
Noted for her research on early reading, Adams lists five basic types of phonemic awareness tasks which should be covered by the end of first grade. These include: ability to hear rhymes and alliterations, ability to do oddity tasks, ability to orally blend words, ability to orally segment words, ability to do phonemic manipulation tasks.

Clay, Marie M. Marie
A New Zealand born researcher, in the field of special needs emergent literacy and in the development of assessment tools for these children. Her research in this field is felt throughout the Reading Recovery movement and involves the use of her, *Reading Recovery: A Guidebook for Teachers in Training,* in the majority of graduate emergent literacy courses and in many classrooms in the US including those that do not have a Reading Recovery teacher.

Her doctoral thesis focused on what was to become her life's work, emergent reading behavior. At the crux of her research for the dissertation, Clay reviewed and detailed the progress week by week of one hundred children during their first year of school (1966). An important outcome of the dissertation was her development of reliable observation tools for the assessment and analysis of changes over time in children's literacy learning. These assessments are the crux of *An Observation Survey of Early Literacy Achievement* (1993) which is an essential work for the primary school educator. The assessments have been validated and reconstructed for learners from the Spanish, Maori and French languages. A special appendix in this guide includes the *Record of Reading Behavior* tool she created with Kenneth Goodman.

Reading Recovery is a key Clay contribution to the field of foundations of reading teaching. The movement, which is discussed in detail in this section, was born out of the concerns of classroom educators who were upset that even with excellent programs and expert teaching, they were not able to positively influence the literacy progress of some of their young children. Clay posed the question of investigating what would happen if the design and delivery of traditional reading education were changed for these struggling young learners.

The whole thrust of the Reading Recovery movement has been to improve the early identification and instructional delivery for these struggling young readers. Her goal was to develop a system which would bring those children scoring the lowest in assessment measures to the level of the average readers within their classes.

With the support of Barbara Watson and others, the program was developed in three years. The first field tests of the program took place in the late 1970's in Auckland schools. To date, circa 2005, the program is operating in most English speaking countries and has been reconstructed for use in Spanish and French.

Janet S. Gaffey and Billie Askew have said of Marie Clay (1991) that her contribution "has been to change what is possible for individual learners when teaching permits different routes to be taken for desired outcomes."

Reading Recovery has been identified by the International Reading Association as a program that not only teaches children how to read, but also reduces the number of children who are labeled as "learning disabled." It further lowers the number of children who are placed in remedial reading programs and classes.

Clay Reading Recovery lessons are designed to promote accelerated learning so that children can catch up to their peers and continue to learn independently.

The hallmark of the Reading Recovery program is that the Reading Recovery teacher works with one student at a time over a 12 to 20 week period. Each daily 30 minute lesson is tailored to address the needs of the individual student. Therefore Reading Recovery teachers generally teach no more than four or five students per day in individual lessons.

The Clay Observation of Early Childhood Achievement (1993) is used to assess children's strengths and weaknesses. Reading Recovery teachers devote the first ten minutes of their sessions with individual children to assessment as the children engage in reading and writing. A running record of the child's progress is taken every day and is used to plan future lessons.

The lessons themselves include the use of familiar stories. Children engage in assembling and in sequencing cut up stories. They work with letters or write a story. Teaching style involves the teacher demonstrating strategies and the child then developing effective strategies to continue reading independently. Key components of each lesson include: phonemic awareness, phonics, spelling, and comprehension study. Much time is devoted to problem solving so that the children's decoding is purposeful. Children are given time to practice and demonstrate fluency skills.

Ultimately what sets Reading Recovery aside is the fact that it is one-to-one tutoring. This is also what makes it effective for children, and of course, what raises issues about it are costs for the school systems which may want to adopt it. Obviously the districts and education systems have to decide whether they want to pay the costs of this and other individualized tutoring systems now in the primary school years or pay later as these children become adults whose literacy skills are not sufficient for proactive citizenship.

Fountas, Irene C and Gay Su Pinnell

These two researchers have developed a leveling system for reading texts, which arranges them by level of difficulty. Beyond a specific analysis of set titles, the theorists have explained in several published works how to use their leveling system to meet and assess the progress of various readers. They also provide detailed explanations and support for reading teachers of young children K-3 in using reading records and benchmark texts.

They are the key articulators of the balanced literacy model that includes reading and writing workshop. Among their other contributions to the field are: guidelines for creating sets of leveled books, assessment rubrics, strategies for fostering "word solver" skills in child readers, and methods for teaching phonics and spelling in the literacy classroom.

Routman, Regie

Routman's contributions to Reading Foundations are the result of over three decades of experience as an elementary school teacher, a reading specialist, a learning disabilities tutor, a Reading Recovery teacher, a language arts and mentor teacher and a staff developer. Due to these various experiences, her insights into reading resonate with a broad spectrum of school community members.

Routman's works are conversational, teacher to teacher sharings of her daily experiences in classrooms. In her published books on the teaching of reading (i.e. *Reading Essentials*-Heinemann, 2002), Regie shows teachers how to teach consistent with the findings in reading research, yet also with highly practical "scripted lessons" and teaching tips which make the classroom come alive. She advocates literature based teaching and meaning centered approaches for learning.

In addition, she is a strong advocate of using poetry from grades one and beyond as an integral thread for a reading program. She is the author of *Kids' Poems: Teaching Children to Love Writing Poetry* (Scholastic, 2000) which includes separate volumes of poetry for grades K-4.

Routman believes in teaching reading to meet specific children's needs regardless of the particular reading program in place. She is a strong advocate for the use of small guided reading groups and reading for understanding. Phonics and other word analysis strategies are part of her reading framework, but not at its core. Her focus for the reading classroom is on the development and the use of the classroom library as the center for an independent reading program, shared reading and reading aloud.

Routman has designed informal reading evaluations on books/texts her students are reading (her published works are known for their appendices replete with templates for evaluations, projects, reports, book lists, suggested texts by topics etc.). Her classroom model includes matching children with specific library books as well as linking assessment with instruction. Finally she is a researcher who sees reading as intimately linked to writing.

Routman is also involved with the politics of literacy. This vision of literacy involves the image of the teacher, as an informed professional, who regularly reads the latest professional books, collaborates with colleagues in school and beyond, and deals with the most recent research developments. Interestingly, Routman is one researcher who also feels that an informed professional can and should know when to question research. Other aspects of the politics of literacy as Routman conceptualizes them are: communicating effectively with parents and dealing with testing and standards mandates.

Two of her published works, *Conversations: Strategies for Teaching, Learning, and Evaluating* (Heinemann, 2000) and *Invitations: Changing as Teachers and Learners k-12* (Heinemann, 1991 and 1994) are essential for the elementary reading teacher's bookshelf and can take the teacher through several years of work.

Taberski, Sharon

Taberski is an experienced elementary teacher educator who is also a member of the Primary Literacy Standards Committee run by the National Center on Education and the Economy and the University of Pittsburgh. Her works in the field are served up as wonderfully accessible and necessary advice from "the veteran teacher across the hall" who loves her students and is delighted to help a new colleague.

Unlike many theorists in the field of reading, Taberski's work is not focused around a prescribed set of skills, but rather around a series of interconnected interactions with the learner.

Among these interactions which are detailed and clearly communicated in her book *On Solid Ground* (2000-Heinemann) are:

- Assessment- Procedures for assessing children's reading, and to inform teaching, scheduling and managing reading conferences, taking oral reading records, and using retellings as discussion tools.
- Demonstration- Taberski developed and field tested strategies for using shared reading and read aloud as platforms for figuring out words and comprehending texts. She is a strong advocate of small group work- guided reading, word-study groups and teaching children one on one.
- Practice- In the Taberski framework, independent reading is used as a time for practice. Students play key roles in this practice and Sharon has a set of detailed and easily adaptable guidelines for matching children with books for independent reading. Her work includes booklists and ready to use information that is available for reproduction.
- Response- It's important for students to know that they are doing well and where they must focus their efforts to improve skills. Taberski explains how her students use writing and dialogue as tools for independent reading.

Vail, Priscilla
Noted for her research in the study of dyslexia and its myths, Vail has articulated ways in which children can develop their reading skills as they cope with this disorder and techniques parents and educators can use to support reading development. She has also worked on specific test taking skills for children coping with dyslexia and other special needs. Her strategies can be infused in the regular education program to enhance all students' reading achievement schools. She is a proponent of phonics instruction and skills within the context of an integrated whole language approach (once called integrated language arts).

Another focus of Vail's research is the link between language and thinking. She is concerned with how a child's receptive language, expressive language and metacognition can be fostered. She has developed assessment methods for each of these capacities and activities to help strengthen them in children grades k-4.

BIBLIOGRAPHY OF PRINT RESOURCES

PROFESSIONAL BOOKS:

Adams, M. (1990). *Beginning to read: Thinking and Learning about Print.* Cambridge, MA: MIT Press.

Anders, P., & Bos, C. (l986). Semantic Feature Analysis: An Interactive Strategy for Vocabulary Development and Reading Comprehension, *Journal of Reading*, 29, 610-616.

Blevins, W. (l997). *Phonemic Awareness Activities for Early Reading Success.* New York: Scholastic.

Boyd-Bastone, P. (2004). Focused Anecdotal Record Assessment (ARA): A Tool for Standards Based Authentic Assessment. *Reading Teacher, 58* (3), pp. 230-239.

Calkins, Lucy McCormick. (2001). *The Art of Teaching Reading.* New York: Longman.
    This is the woman who beautifully explains the reading workshop and its relationship to the writing workshop as she shares wonderful snapshots of mini lessons, conferring, conferencing, independent reading, guided reading, book talks, prompts, coaching, and classroom library use. Exceedingly readable and direct.

Campbell, Robin. (2004). *Reading and Writing for Real Purposes.* Portsmouth, NH: Heinemann.
    This work focuses on how children who deftly absorb and interconnect symbols and sounds of their universes can be supported in K-1 classes to extend this ability into phonics learning. Campbell demonstrates how immersion in a highly literate classroom filled with print and language stimuli allows kids to build accurate letter-sound relationships. The book provides a framework for teaching phonics using proven field-tested Campbell strategies.

    Among these strategies are: early mark making, read-alouds, playing with language in rhyme and song, writing and reading in a variety of genres, exploring environmental and classroom print, and using students' own names. Samples of student work are included.

Chancey, C. (l994). Language development, metalinguistic awareness, and emergent literacy skills of 3 year old children in relation to social class. *Applied Psycholinguistics*, 15, 371-394.

Clay, Marie M. (1993). *An Observation Survey of Early Literacy Achievement.* Portsmouth, NH: Heinemann.

Clay, Marie M. (l993). *Reading Recovery: A Guidebook for Teachers in Training.* Portsmouth, NH: Heinemann.

Cooper, J. David. (2004). *Literacy-Helping Children Construct Meaning.* Boston, MA: Houghton Mifflin. (5th Edition).

This book explains with numerous charts, tables, templates, and excerpts form actual texts, what the balanced literacy approach to the teaching of reading and writing is. It offers the new teacher: exact schedules, strategies, guidelines, assessment tools, bibliographies, research, and even scripts for conferring with children.

Cooper is a clear and crisp writer who does not overwhelm the reader, but rather engages the reader. Even veteran teachers would return again and again to this text for support and refreshing insights.

Cox, Carole. (2005). *Teaching Language Arts.* Boston, MA: Pearson.

A compendium of state of the art lesson plans, web resources, online case studies, teaching ideas and extensive templates. All of these materials are aligned to the balanced literacy reading and writing workshop model.

The book also includes teaching ideas for the ELL reader, children with learning disabilities, and speakers of non- standard dialects. The book also features snapshots of second language learners as well as bi-literacy web resources.

Cullinan, Bernice E. (1998). *Three Voices-An Invitation to Poetry Across the Curriculum.* New York: Stenhouse. K-6 and beyond.

Two classroom educators and a noted researcher in children's literature demonstrate how poetry can be used in the classroom to teach various aspects of reading and to nurture lifelong literacy. Thirty-three grade and age appropriate strategies are included which have been field tested in classrooms across the country.

Ezell, H. K., & Justice, L. M. (2000). Increasing the Print Focus of Adult -Child Shared Book Reading through Observational Learning. *American journal of Speech Pathology*, 9, 36-37.

Flesch, Rudolf. (1985). *Why Johnny Can't Read* New York: Harper and Row.

Fountas, Irene C., & Gay Su Pinnell. (2001). *Guiding Readers and Writers 3-6.* Portsmouth, NH: Heinemann.

This work includes 1000 leveled books with guidelines for using them as part of a reading and writing workshop. The book explains how to use various genres in the classroom and how to use visual graphic organizers for the teaching of reading and writing.

Fountas, Irene. C., & Gay Su Pinnell. (1999). *Matching Books to Readers Using Leveled Books in Guided Reading K-3.* Portsmouth, NH: Heinemann.

This major contribution to the field has a list of 7, 500 grade and age appropriate books. In addition the authors include word counts to be used for keeping running records, text characteristics, guidelines for leveling of additional books and suggestions for developing classroom library collections.

Other works by these researchers also published by Heinemann include: *Voices on Word matters: Learning about Phonics and Spelling in the Literacy Classroom* (1999) and *Word Matters-Teaching Phonics and Spelling in the Reading/Writing Classroom* (1998).

Fry, Edward Bernard, Kress, Jacqueline, Fountakidis, Dona Lee. (2000). *The Reading Teacher's Book of Lists*. San Francisco, CA: Wiley Press.

    This book is an invaluable one for the working classroom educator. It includes ready to use lists that cover a multiplicity of teacher needs. Among them are: spelling demons, readability graphs, phonics, useful words, reading math, vowel lists, anagrams, portmanteaus (do you know what they are and how well they can work in word study?), web sites, classic children's literature, etc. Even a veteran teacher educator will find useful and new resources. Also wonderful for developing independent word study investigations and literature explorations.

Ganske, Kathy. (2000). *Word Journeys-Assessment-Guided Phonics, Spelling, and Vocabulary Instruction*. New York, NY: Guilford Press.

    This book offers a practical approach for assessing children's spelling. The author has created a DSA (Development Spelling Analysis) tool which teachers can use to evaluate individual children's spelling progress and to differentiate instruction. The book includes snapshots of children at different levels of spelling development.

Hall, Susan. (1994). *Using Picture Books to Teach Literary Devices*. Westport, CT: Oryx Press.

How to Help Every Child Become a Reader. Just Publishing. K-6 and beyond.

    This accessible text draws on materials developed by the US Department of Education to share research, resources, referrals and suggestions for supporting all children to become lifelong and engaged readers. It offers specific suggestions and resources for assisting struggling readers including those with special needs and those from ELL backgrounds.

Labov, L. (2003). When Ordinary Children Fail to Read. *Reading Research Quarterly*, 38, 128-31.

Macmillan, B. M. (2002). Rhyme and Reading. A Critical Review of the Research Methodology. *Journal of Research in Reading*, 25(1), 4-42.

Makor, Barbara. *Primary Phonics Readers*.
Short storybooks that K-2 can own and read independently.

    They feature phonetically controlled texts, sounds and spellings that are grade and age appropriate and high interest child-centered themes. As children progress through the series of twenty titles, they review and enhance their mastery of phonetic elements, sight words, and sequences at a more rapid pace. This material is compatible with the majority of phonics programs.

Munro, J. (1998). Phonological and Phonemic Awareness: Their Impact on Learning to Read Prose and Spell. *Australian Journal of Learning Disabilities*, 3, 2, 15-21.

    Paperback Nursery Rhyme Sampler-Whispering Coyote Press-Essential for a Prek-1 classroom and useful even in grades 1 and 2; these classic nursery rhymes promote phonemic and phonological awareness and children's ownership of their reading through song and movement.

Routman, Regie. (2000). *Conversations: Strategies for Teaching, Learning, and Evaluating*. Portsmouth, NH: Heinemann.

Routman, Regie. (1994). *Invitations: Changing as Teachers and Learners K-12.* Portsmouth, NH. Heinemann.

Routman, Regie. (1996). *Literacy at the Crossroads: Crucial Talk About Reading, Writing, and Other Teaching Dilemmas.* Portsmouth, NH: Heinemann.

Routman, Regie. (2002). *Reading Essentials.* Portsmouth, NH: Heinemann.

Statman, Ann. *Handprints-Leveled Storybooks for Early Readers Educators Publishing Service-*Grades K-2.
> These fifty titles which come with five teacher's guides were leveled using the Fountas and Pinnell Guided Reading Leveling System. The stories reflect real world situations and people young readers know. They include: sentence structure, pictures and cues that focus strategic reading. Print size, sentence positioning, and word spacing is appropriate for the level of the particular storybook. The titles build a strong sight vocabulary through the use of high frequency words. Language used within the series progresses from natural to formal book language.

Schumm, Heanne Shay. *The Reading Tutor's Handbook.* Free Spirit. K-6 and beyond.
> This guide offers step by step instructions, templates and handouts for providing children with differentiated reading support. It is not only helpful for teachers, but also can be shared with paraprofessionals, teachers, interns, and parents as a support framework for the classroom reading program.

Taberski, Sharon. (2000). *On Solid Ground: Creating a Literacy Environment in Your K-3 Classroom.* Portsmouth, NH: Heinemann.
Terban, Marvin. *Time to Rhyme-A Rhyming Dictionary.* Boyd Mills Press. Grades 1-3.
> This book is easily enough formatted so that it can be used to introduce children in the early elementary grades to the use of a rhyming dictionary as a reference tool. Its simple word groupings encourage writing which can also reinforce and reciprocally enhance reading skills through the reading and writing workshop.

Vail, Patricia. *Reading Comprehension-Students Needs and Teacher's Tools.* Educators Publishers Service K-6 and beyond.
> This is a compendium of explanations of specific instructional practices, terms, student projects, learning games and resources which are critical for successfully teaching reading.

ALPHABET BOOKS

A major genre of fiction and non-fiction for the teacher of reading is the alphabet book. These books' appeal, concepts, and efficiency as models for reading and writing merit them a special section in this bibliography. Even those whose text is simple enough for Prek-2, can serve as anchor books and models for writing workshop in grades 3-6.

Aigner-Clark, Julie. (2002). *Baby Einstein- The ABCs of Art*. Illustrations by Nadeen Zaidi. New York: Hyperion Books.

Beaton, Clare. *Zoe and Her Zebra*. Barefoot Books. Prek-1.
   This board book features a character young children can identify with named Zoe. Her adventures are told in a simple, repetitive text with a soft literally "touchy" felt art.

Bunting, Eve. *Girls A to Z*. Boyd Mills Press. PreK-1.
   This book uses the alphabetic format to promote the opportunity for girls to select various professions and careers ranging from astronaut to zookeeper. Bunting's text is breezy and rhymes.

Cheney, Lynne. (2002). *America- A Patriotic Primer*. New York: Simon and Schuster Books. Illustrated by Robin Priess Glasser.

Cheney, Lynne. *A Is For Abigail: An Almanac of Amazing American Women*. New York: Simon and Schuster Books. Ages 4-8.

Glaser, Milton. (2003). *The Alphazeds*. Miramax. Ages 4-8.

Grimes, Nikki. *C is for City*. Illustrated by: Pat Cummings. Boyd Mill Press. K-3.
   This alphabet rhyme book doubles as a guide to city activities. With its built in invitations to readers to search for alphabetical items, it is perfect for use as an informal assessment tool or an interactive/paired reading anchor text.

Inkpen, Mick. (2000). *Kipper's A to Z*. San Diego: Harcourt. Ages 3-7.

Isadora, Rachel. (1999). *ABC Pops! (Picture Books)*. Disney Press. Ages 4-8.

Johnson, Stephen. (1995). *Alphabet City*. Penguin Books. All ages.

Kelley, Marty. *Summer Stinks*. Zino Press. Prek-1.
   This work describes the summer season in terms of things which "stink" about it, including ants, bugs, and sweat. Fun to read and add to as the alphabet letters are learned and vocabulary is built up.

Martin, Mary Jane. *From Anne to Zach*. Boyd Mills Press.
   In this captivating book which can serve as a touchstone text for model collaborative authoring, children learn the letters of the alphabet through other children's names.

Melmed, Laura Krauss and Frane Lesser. (2003) *Capital! Washington DC from A to Z*. New York: Harper Collins.

Musgrove, Margaret. (1976). Illustrated by Leo and Diane Dillon. *Ashanti to Zulu. African Traditions.* New York: Dial Books for Young Readers.
   This is a Caldecott-winning book which uses the alphabetic format for a richly detailed and researched study of 26 African Peoples. It includes a map and pronunciation guide and illustrations that were researched in the Schomberg Center and the American Museum of Natural History. Even the frame design for each illustration reflects the African Kano knot which signifies endless searching.

Paratore, Colleen. *26 Big Things Hands Do*. Minneapolis, MN: Free Spirit.
   What is delightful about this alphabet book is that it presents the alphabet letters as positive actions children can perform with their own small hands to help others. These actions include: applauding, giving gifts, planting, and volunteering. Of course, alphabet study can continue with adding other "helping actions" to the word wall or substituting them in the text.

Pelham, David, (1991). *A is for Animals*. New York: Simon and Schuster

Seeley, Lorna. *The Book of Shadow Boxes*. Peachtree.
   Within the shadow of each letter's shadow box lies a hidden treasure for the young reader to find. The book is intricately and exquisitely designed and conceptualized by Ms. Seeley. Its visual fascination extends well beyond the elementary grades as it of course fosters not only the alphabetic principle, but also reading comprehension and literacy response.
Sneed, Brad. (2002). *Picture a Letter*. New York: Penguin Books.

Seuss. *ABC*. Random House. Ages 2-up.

Thornhill, Jim. *The Wildlife ABC and 123: A Nature Alphabet and Counting Book*. Maple Tree Press. K-1 with additional nature notes on the species for the teacher/parent.
   In addition to fostering the alphabetic principle, the book nicely mixes geographic, multicultural, and scientific knowledge into a beautifully designed text. It uses children's fascination with nature to foster reading and math literacy.

Zschock, Martha and Heather. (2002). *Journey Around New York from A to Z. Beverly.* Mass: Commonwealth Editions

Zschock, Martha. (2001). *Journey Around Boston from A to Z.* Beverly Mass: Commonwealth Editions.

TRADE BOOKS

These books foster particular aspects of reading skills, fluencies and competencies.

Blackstone, Stella. *Where's the Cat?* Barefoot Books. Prek-k.
   This book which focuses its primary school readers on searching for a lost cat provides excellent use of repetitive language and encourages interactive reading.

Campbell, Bebe Moore. (2003). Sometimes *My Mommy Gets Angry. New York, New York: G. P. Putnam's Sons.*

This is a moving story about a young girl whose mother suffers from mental illness. It is told in a way that is easy to read, along with beautiful illustrations. The main character is Annie. Sometimes her mother is very happy and other times very angry and sad. Annie has learned what to do when her mom is having a bad episode. She has books to read, a special stuffed animal and some secret snacks. Annie also has a strong support system in place with friends, neighbors, her teacher and grandmother.

This book is a good introduction to the issue of mental illness. It is especially important in that students see how this young girl is able to cope with this difficult part of her life. "Sometimes by mommy has a dark cloud inside of her. I can't stop the rain from falling, but I can find sunshine in my mind."
Teachers can introduce students to this issue with this poignant book. Students can brainstorm different scenarios and discuss how they can be resolved. They can discuss who their support network includes and what it takes for a person to be strong enough to weather such a storm.

The book is a much needed resource for children in times where Annie's situation is far more common than is generally known. Annie's capacity to make effective, affirming social decisions makes the work an inspirational touchstone for other peers who need to confront their parents' emotional crises. Children might be inspired to author poetry or create deliberately fictionalized narrative accounts about how they have confronted various crises.

In offering an upper elementary grade and age appropriate narrative of a peer dealing with an emotionally ill parent, this book provides readers confronting similar family and caregiver issues with an opening for discussion and for hopeful outreach. Just reading this account may well be the first step necessary to assist a youngster in acknowledging a "hidden problem" and getting crucial adult assistance in dealing with the crisis.

Garza, Carmen Lomas. (1990). *Family Pictures Cuadros de familia*. Children's Book Press.

This book tells the story of the author's childhood growing up in a Hispanic community in Texas. The book is written in both Spanish and English, accompanied by the author's most incredible paintings. The paintings are unique, somewhat folksy, colorful, and totally entrancing. They bring you into Carmen's world. Once inside it, you don't want to leave.

There is so much to explore in this book; it works well with the study of "myself and family", community, communities around the world, Mexico, family traditions and customs. It emphasizes social and emotional learning and how a young girl can find her way in the world. The traditions followed by her community and family were not necessarily accepted or understood by white America. Yet these values gave her the strength to be her own person and to rely on both her relationships and rich inner life to express herself.

There are so many activities that this book inspires. Children can study the origins of the piñata, and make one. They can make a cookbook of recipes from Mexico or from their own homes. Children can also be encouraged to design their own book of family pictures. They can emphasize special occasions that they celebrate or focus on family traditions which reflect their cultural backgrounds. The richness and lushness of the paintings invites the readers to construct meaning and to create their own narratives, procedural accounts, poetry, and dialogues inspired by one or more of the paintings.

Picture walk through the illustrations. Given the Spanish/English text, this strategy can be an engaging spatial entry point for descriptive and narrative spoken and written presentations. The lushly detailed illustrations of family rites and celebrations can be springboards for children's literary and artistic renditions of equivalent family pictures and events which are prompted by Carmen's selections.

Use of dual language text for the book validates children's and family member's responses in languages other than English. Obviously, this book and its format are inspirational for ELL/Bilingual learners and for special needs learners who can be captivated by the paintings.

The power of this book lies in its accessing and modeling the magic of family rites and rituals for a broad spectrum of linguistics, intrapersonal, spatial, and kinesthetic learners from monolingual, bilingual and special needs backgrounds. Common to all of its audience members are the social and emotionally celebratory components of Family Pictures.

Glaser, Shirley, & Glaser, Milton. (2003). *The Alphazeds Words*. Hyperion Books. This book is incredible in so many ways! It is an alphabet book that can be read by or to little ones and not so little ones. It starts with an empty room. One by one, each letter of the alphabet enters the room, each with its own distinct look, fantastic illustrations and typography by the designer Milton Glaser. Each of these letters also has its own distinct personality. A is angry, B is bashful, J is jealous, and so on. The room gets quite crowded. How do all of these different personalities manage to get along and coexist? Not too well apparently, as there is shouting, pushing, hitting and kicking. In the midst of all the chaos, the light in the room goes out and there is silence.

> "When the light came back on, something extraordinary had happened. Four letters had gotten together to comfort one another. Together they had managed to create something larger and more important than themselves.
> *"They had made the first word."*

This is a great lesson on how each of us can be an individual, yet when we work together, something wonderful can happen. This book illustrates an incredible lesson in social and emotional maturity, and helps the child realize that it isn't just about "me."

There are many different activities that a teacher can use with this book. The children can work in groups to make their own alphabet book of emotions. They can then present the book as a group, discussing the roles each of them played, and how they each used their unique talents to make the book.

Older children grades 3 and up, can research and present as a group some important discoveries that were made more special because they involved people working together. They can also work on a project about cooperative learning, perhaps surveying class and schoolmates on how they feel they learn the best.

Hest, Amy. (1985). *The Purple Coat*. New York: Macmillan Publishing Co.
In the autumn of every year, Gabrielle travels with her mother to New York City to visit her Grandpa who owns a tailor shop. Once there, he always makes her a new coat, but this year Gabrielle decides the usual navy blue coat won't do. The Purple Coat follows Gabrielle in her attempt to establish her own identity.

Lionni, Leo. (1980). *Inch by Inch*. Astor-Honor Publishing Co. Inc.
In *Inch by Inch*, an inchworm (which is a caterpillar, or larval stage, of the fall cankerworm, which becomes a moth) keeps itself from being eaten by various birds by proving its worth as a measuring device.

Lupton, Hugh. *The Story Tree- Tales to Read Aloud.* Barefoot Books. K-3

These seven multicultural stories are accessible enough to children to encourage their eventually taking over the read aloud sharing on their own. This book is also a good one for family literacy sessions and for parent volunteers to read aloud in the classroom.

Martin Jr., Bill, & John Archambault. (1966). *Knots on a Counting Rope.* New York, New York: Henry Holt and Company.

This beautifully illustrated book reaches out in so many different directions, and we can all learn so much from it. Knots on a Counting Rope is the story of a Native-American boy who is blind and is learning from his grandfather how to survive in this world. Boy-Strength-of-Blue-Horses insists on hearing the story of his birth over and over again.

Every time his grandfather retells the story of the boy's birth, he adds a knot to his counting rope. Each time he hears the story, Boy- Strength-of-Blue-Horses gains more confidence in himself. The story emphasizes the Native-American tradition of storytelling, and there are numerous art, math and social studies lessons that offshoot from this book.

Of course, the telling and retelling of the story celebrate the young blind hero's strengths and weaknesses and ability to set goals with optimism. Stories of one's birth related by others are powerful demonstrations of social skills of the highest order.

This book also deals extensively with social and emotional learning. Children learn that those with disabilities need to be treated with sensitivity while learning to find their place in the world. One way in which children's social and emotional learning is strengthened is by understanding themselves and those around them. In order to facilitate this, each child will interview at least one family member about when he/she was born. The accounts collected with appropriate photos or memorabilia can then be shared in class and perhaps even authored into a *Knots on a Counting Rope* style book format.

Children can also retell the story of the boy using the counting system of cultures other than Native American. This literary response will incorporate cultural study, respect and empathy into ongoing reading and writing workshop efforts.

McCully, Emily Arnold. (1992). *Mirette on the High Wire.* G.P. Putnam's & Sons.

Mirette helps her mother run a boardinghouse for acrobats, jugglers, actors and mimes. Her life changes when she discovers a boarder crossing the courtyard on air. She begs him to teach her how he does it. He refuses to teach her, but she begins practicing on her own. As she improves, he begins to help her. In the end she helps him overcome his fear of the high wire.

Rabe, Bernice. (1981). *The Balancing Girl*. E.P. Dutton.
>Margaret, a girl in a wheel chair is excellent at balancing all kinds of objects. Margaret shows her friend Tommy how good she is at balancing at the school carnival.

Ringgold, Faith. (1991). *Tar Beach.* New York, New York: Crown Publishers.
>This book is one of my favorites, and it is moving in its words, art, and the beautiful story it tells. This is an effective book to use for younger grades to connect with myself, my family and my community. It can also be used in connection with a mapmaking unit. The children can be encouraged to make a map of their neighborhood from an aerial view.
>
>A starting point for a discussion would be why the author portrayed New York from such a vantage point. In this beautiful book, the narrator, Cassie Louise Lightfoot, lets her dreams and ambitions take her to places in New York City that she ordinarily would not be able to be part of because of her circumstances. As a result of her self-motivation and self-awareness, Cassie is able to go as far as her dreams will let her. In this book Cassie also shows strengths in the areas of emotional sensitivity, as well as inter and intra-personal relationships.
>
>Children can author their own Tar Beach equivalent night fantasies and then share them with one another through an exhibit or big books. Although Cassie's family is obviously poor since they have to picnic on their roof, Cassie's dreamlike lushly illustrated flight over Harlem validates the beauty of their family life and of the city landscape which is accessible to all. This is an invaluable lesson in the importance of the wealth inherent in the appreciation of family connections and the beauty of nature and public architectural designs! A song of family and of the city!

Schories, Pat. *Breakfast for Jack/Jack and the Missing Piece*. Front Street.
>These wordless stories help pre-literate children, ELL learners new to this country and special needs children explore the basic elements of story-character, setting and plot. The lack of words allows the children to "construct their own meaning," and create their own different stories which "fit" the illustrations.

Steinberg, Laya. *Thesaurus Rex*. Barefoot Books.
>This book introduces a dinosaur with an interest in words whose story is told through a wonderful rhyming text which can be used for fostering phonemic awareness and for choral readings.

Uhlberg, Myron. *The Printer*. Peachtree.
>This story celebrates the conventions of print in that the boy narrator's father is a deaf man who speaks with his hands and as a job chooses to turn lead type letters into words and sentences. An excellent book to support family literacy and an appreciation for the conventions of print.

Van Allsburg, Chris. (1988). *Two Bad Ants*. Houghton Mifflin Co.
   In *Two Baxd Ants*, news comes to the ant world of a great discovery in a far away place. A delicious crystal has been found. A group of ants set out to bring back this crystal to their queen. Two ants are overwhelmed by the treasure and stay behind in this dangerous alien world. It is a tale of choices, consequences and the discovery of life's real treasures.

Walter, Mildred Pitts. (2004). Illustrated by Larry Johnson. *Alec's primer*. Lebanon, NH: University Press of New England.
   This is the true account of a Virginian slave who was taught to read by his owner's daughter. He later fought in the Civil War on the Union side and became a landowner himself in Vermont. The beautifully written narrative is complemented by the vibrant paintings of Larry Johnson which include authentic period details.

Webliography

Reading Online
http://www.readingonline.org
This online web resource which is sponsored by the International Reading Association is full of specific reading teaching ideas, lessons and new research. It includes summaries of conference presentations and even tips on how to use technology to teach reading.

Balanced Literacy
http://www.thekcrew.net/balancedliteracy.html
Established in 1996, this site is organized according to the components of the balanced literacy approach. It also has an excellent listing of professional books that can assist with various aspects of teaching reading.

Carol Hurst
http://www.carolhurst.com/index.html
This is a terrific resource for exploring the children's literature works which are at the crux of author and genre study. It can be used for material to supplement period studies and discussions of authors' lives. Older children will be able to explore it on their own.

Read, Write, Think
http://www.readwritethink.org/lessons/
This resource maintained by the NCTE, National Council of Teachers of English, has a growing database of age and grade specific literacy lesson plans. It also includes all the graphic organizers cited in this book and many more, ready to download.

Inspiration Software
http://www.inspiration.com
http://www.inspiration.com/freetrial/index.cfm
This is the home site for the Inspiration and Kidspiration mind mapping software. These online templates and capacities assist the reading teacher with customizing the various graphic organizers discussed throughout the book, and with gaining the ability to design customized graphic organizers for a particular theme, study or student group. A free trial version of this resource which is child friendly can be downloaded.

Visual Thesaurus
http://www.visualthesaurus.com/online/
This is really both an online dictionary and a thesaurus.

Resources for Read Aloud, Shared Reading, and Independent Reading available on the Internet include the following:

http:// www.mightybook.com/library_4to6.htm.
This is a library of books read aloud by the computer. Children can listen to these books or practice reading with a buddy as the computer broadcasts the text. Of course, this type of read aloud would only be used IN ADDITION to the vibrant read-aloud of the teacher.

http://www.enchantedlearning.com/Rhymes.html
These are online nursery rhymes ready for reading to the children and posting throughout for room or for literacy center display.

SEDL-RCI Framework of Reading
http://www.sedl.org/reading/framework/assessment.html
This is an excellent resource for readings in the theories and methods of foundations. There are topic aligned links to specific theorists which can be included at the close of your lesson planning and may be reviewed before certification tests.

TEACHER CERTIFICATION STUDY GUIDE

TOOLS TO HELP YOU TEACH THE FOUNDATIONS OF READING AND SUCCEEDING IN CONSTRUCTED RESPONSE CERTIFICATION EXAMINATIONS

Appendix 1- The Record of Reading Behavior- A close up look at a key assessment tool.

Often in the constructed response question on a foundations of education certification test or on a general elementary certification test; the educator is asked to analyze a record of reading behavior or to construct an appropriate one from data given in an anecdote. Furthermore with the current climate of accountability, it is a good idea for new teachers and for career changers to examine closely the basic elements of recording reading behavior.

While there are various acceptable formats for emergent literacy assessment used throughout the country, the one selected for use here is based on the work of Marie Clay and Kenneth Goodman. These two are key researchers in the close observation and documentations of children's early reading miscues (reading mistakes).

It is important to emphasize that the teacher should not just "take the Record of Reading Behavior " and begin filling it out as the child reads from a random book prior to beginning of the observation. There are specific steps for taking the record and analyzing its results.

1. Select a text
If you want to see if the child is reading on instructional level, choose a book that the child has already read. If the purpose of the test is to see whether the child is ready to advance to the next level, choose a book from that level which the child has not yet seen.

2. Introduce the text
If the book is one that has been read, you do not need to introduce the text, other than by saying the title. But if the book is new to the child, you should briefly share the title and tell the child a bit about the plot and style of the book.

3. Take the record
Generally with emergent readers' grades 1-2, there are only 100-150 words in a passage used to take a record. Make certain that the child is seated beside you, so that you can see the text as the child reads it.

If desired, you may want to photocopy the text in advance for yourself, so you can make direct notations on your text while the child reads from the book. After you introduce the text make certain that the child has the chance to read the text independently. Be certain that you do not "teach" or help the child with the text, other than to supply an unknown word that the child requests you supply. The purpose of the record is to see what the child does on his or her own.

READING

As the child reads the text, you must be certain to record the reading behaviors the child exhibits using the following notations.

In taking the record, keep in mind the following: Allow enough time for the child to work independently on a problem before telling or supplying the word. If you wait too long, you could run the risk of having the child lose the meaning and his/her interest in the story as he or she tries to identify the unknown word.

It is recommended that when a child is way off track, you tell him or her to "Try that again" (TTA). If a whole phrase is troubling, put it into square brackets and score it as only one error.

The notation for filling out the Record of Reading behavior involves noting the child's response on the top with the actual text below it.

Comprehension Check

This can and should be done by inviting the child to retell the story. This retelling can then be used to ask further questions about characters, plot, setting and purpose which allow you to observe and to record the child's level of comprehension.

Calculating the Reading Level and the Self-correction Rate

Calculating the reading level lets you know if the book is at the level on which the child can read it independently or comfortably with guidance or if the book is at a level where reading it frustrates the child.

Generally, an accuracy score of 95-100% suggests that the child can read the text and other books or texts on the same level.

An accuracy score of 90-94% indicates that the text and texts likely will present challenges to the child, but with guidance from you, a tutor or parent, the child will be able to master these texts and enjoy them. This is instructional level.

However, an accuracy score of less than 89% tells you that the material you have selected for the child is too hard for the child to control alone. Such material needs to be shared with the child in a shared reading situation or read to the child.

KEEPING SCORE ON THE RECORD

Insertions, omissions, substitutions, and teacher told responses, all count as errors. Repetitions are not scored as errors. Corrected responses are scored as self corrections.

No penalty is given for a child's attempts at self correction that results in a finally incorrect response but the attempts should be noted. Multiple unsuccessful attempts at a word score as one error only.

The lowest score for any page is zero.
If a child omits a line or lines, each word omitted is counted as an error. If the child omits a page, deduct the number of words omitted from the total number of words which you have used for the record.

Calculating the Reading Level

Note the number of errors made on each line on the Record of Reading Behavior in the column marked E (for Error).

Total the number of errors in the text and divide this number into the number of words that the child has read. This will give you the error rate.

If a child read a passage of 100 words and made 10 errors, the error rate would be 1 in 10. Convert this to an accuracy percentage, or 90%.

Calculating the Self Correction Rate

Total all the self-corrections.
Next, add the number of errors to the number of self-corrections and divide by the number of self-corrections.

A self correction rate of 1 in 3 to 1 in 5 is considered good. This rate indicates that the child is able to help himself or herself as problems are encountered in reading.

Analyzing the record

This record should assist the educator in developing a detailed date specific picture of the child's progress in reading behavior. It should be used to help the educator individualize instruction for the specific child.

As the errors are reviewed, consider whether the child made the error because of semantics (cues from meaning), syntactic (language structure), or visual information difficulties.

As self-corrections are analyzed, consider what led the child to make that self-correction. Check out and consider what cues the child does use effectively and which the child does not use well.

Consider the ways in which the child tackles a word which is unknown. Characterize that behavior and consider how the teacher can assist the child with this issue.

If a child can retell at least three quarters of a story, this is considered adequate for retelling.

Analysis of reading behavior records can and should support the educator in designing appropriate mini lessons and strategies to help the child with his or her recorded errors and miscues.

Sample Test

1) The major difference between phonemic and phonological awareness is:

   A) One deals with a series of discrete sounds and the other with sound-spelling relationships.

   B) One is involved with teaching and learning alliteration and rhymes.

   C) Phonemic awareness is a specific type of phonological awareness that deals with separate phonemes within a given word.

   D) Phonological awareness is associated with printed words.

2) The theorist in early reading (emergent reading) who has identified five tasks for phonemic awareness is:

   A) John Munro

   B) Brian Cambourne

   C) Marilyn Jager Adams

   D) Lucy Calkins

3) An oddity task is one in which children:

   A) Identify the odd number in a mathematical series and talk about how they did it.

   B) Perform a creative exercise designed for differentiated learning styles.

   C) Recognize which sound is odd in a series of like sounds.

   D) Design a different activity for themselves.

4) All of the following are true about phonological awareness EXCEPT:

   A) It may involve print.

   B) It is a prerequisite for spelling and phonics.

   C) Activities can be done by the children with their eyes closed.

   D) It starts before letter recognition is taught.

5) Ms. James is seated with a child by her side. The child is reading aloud from an open book. Ms. James is teaching in a school that has embraced the Balanced Literacy Approach. Therefore it is most likely that Ms. James is writing and recording:

A) The child's use of expression in reading aloud.

B) The child's errors and miscues.

C) Her observations of the child's attitude toward reading.

D) The child's feelings about the particular passage being read.

6) Most of the children in first-year teacher Ms. James's class are really doing well in their phonemic awareness assessments. However, Ms. James is very concerned about three children who do not seem to be able to distinguish between spoken words that "sound alike," but are different. Since she is a first year teacher, she feels her inexperience may be to blame. In truth, the reason these three children have not yet demonstrated phonemic awareness is most likely that:

A) They are not capable of becoming good readers.

B) They are bored in class.

C) They may be from an ELL background.

D) Ms. James does not pronounce the different phonemes clearly enough.

7) Ms. Ramsey has forgotten her credit cards and has limited cash in her wallet. She is buying supplies for her reading classroom that she wants to have annotated with the children's names by the first day of school. She should buy all of the following with her cash except:

A) Folders.

B) Markers.

C) Rulers.

D) Index cards.

8) Ms. Rivers is preparing for a parent teacher conference. She does all of the following EXCEPT:

A) Collects individual child running records.

B) Puts away all the book bags and leveled pots so the classroom will be more spacious.

C) Puts out by each child's seat the child's weekly log and spelling folder.

D) Sets up work samples by each child's place.

9) In terms of a balanced literacy classroom, a "leveled bin" indicates:

A) A plant set at child's eye level for descriptive writing purposes.

B) A bin with books the child has selected.

C) A bin with books leveled by the teacher.

D) A bin with all kinds of reading materials including magazines and packaging on a child's level.

10) Mark Garner has been told that he will have to support some special needs readers in his classroom in addition to the rest of the students. He can expect to have:

A) Gifted children who are accelerated in reading skills for their grade and age.

B) Children who have disabilities and will need special support in accessing the content and methods he uses with the rest of the class.

C) Children who come from native language backgrounds other than English.

D) Children who display the capacities and needs detailed in a and b.

11) Julia has been hired to work in a school that serves a local public housing project. She is working with kindergarten children and has been asked to focus on shared reading. She selects:

A) Chapter books.

B) Riddle books.

C) Alphabet books.

D) Wordless picture books.

12) It is 4 PM, yet Francine is still in her classroom. The seats in her classroom are filled with adults of various ages who are holding books. They are seated two by two with both holding copies of the same book. Francine probably is:

A) Explaining to parents how she will teach a particular story.

B) Demonstrating shared reading with a buddy for volunteer parents.

C) Hosting a parents organization meeting for her grade level.

D) Distributing old books from the class library to parents.

13) The work of Chard and Osborn (1999) in establishing guidelines for children with reading disabilities has shown that it is essential for them to:

A) Read wordless picture books.

B) Learn at least 10 sight words.

C) Work intensely on the alphabetic principle.

D) Focus on using syntactic clues.

14) A key theorist whose work has helped teacher's document children's oral reading progress throughout the school year is:

A) Jerome Bruner.

B) Daniel J. Chard.

C) J. David Cooper.

D) Marie Clay.

15) The first grade class is on a neighborhood walk. As the children approach the neighborhood Kentucky Fried Chicken chain, Danny reads from the store window "Kentucky Fried Chicken Hot and Crunchy." Danny has never read or been taught to read this before. The most likely explanation for Danny's being able to read this is that he is:

A) An advanced reader who is self improving.

B) His parents have taught him to read the signs and materials at the Kentucky Fried Chicken store.

C) He is in the logographic phrase of phonics learning.

D) This was just a lucky guess on his part.

16) An observer enters Julia's first grade classroom. Children are working with oaktag strips and placing the word letters on these strips on a sentence strip holder. Then they seem to be involved in some kind of counting. The observer is confused. This activity is taking place during the reading block. Julia explains:

A) The children are counting letters.

B) This is word sorting and the children are grouping words by length, common letters and sound.

C) The children are combining mathematics counting and word study.

D) The children are doing a strategy sheet based on a particular word family.

17) As he walks up and down the hallway, Mr. Adams, the new Assistant Principal, continually hears Ms. Brown telling her children to go to the wall. Mr. Adams looks briefly at the literacy block schedule and continues on his walk through the building. He realizes that Ms. Brown's children are at work on:

A) A new hall display.

B) Taking down an old display and then redoing it for a new theme.

C) Adding words to their spelling word wall.

D) Measuring the height of plants for a mathematics lesson.

18) Randy is proud of how many new vocabulary words he has learned. He enjoys playing with a device his teacher has, since it helps him to show all the words he can create from various letters. The device is a:

A) Word strip.

B) Letter holder for making words.

C) Word mask.

D) None of the above.

19) Ability grouping means:

A) Grouping of children according to the results of an IQ test.

B) Grouping of children with similar test results for instructional purposes.

C) Grouping of children according to their oral reading accuracy rate.

D) Grouping of children wit similar needs for instructional purposes.

20) Tim is not in the same ability group as his best friend Alex. He starts to cry even though he is a second grader. The teacher comforts him by telling him the truth that:

A) He is just as smart as Alex.

B) He can play with Alex during recess.

C) Ability groups change as the children's needs in them change during the year.

D) Tim is smarter than his best friend Alex.

21) "Beautiful Beth is the Best Girl in the Bradley Bay area." This sentence could be used to help children learn about:

   A) Assonance.

   B) Alliteration.

   C) Rhyming pairs.

   D) None of the above.

22) Greg Ball went to an author signing where Faith Ringgold gave a talk about one of her many books. He was so inspired by her presence and by his reading of her book *TAR BEACH*, that he used the book for his reading and writing workshop activities. His supervisor wrote in his plan book, that he was pleased that Greg had used the book as an/a _____ book.

   A) Basic book.

   B) Feature book.

   C) Anchor book.

   D) Focus book.

23) A delegation from the United Kingdom has come to the United States and since they are considering adapting the balanced literacy approach, they are very interested in seeing the small group demonstrated. Mr. Adams knows that he should bring them into Greg's room when Greg is doing which activity?

   A) A mini lesson.

   B) A conference with individual students.

   C) A time when children are divided into small and independent study groups.

   D) A read-aloud.

24) As the visitors from the United Kingdom tour the school, they are pleased to hear a sing-song chant "Don't fall asleep at the page, don't forget the _____" Mr. Adams explains to them that the first graders are learning about pointing at words and moving from the left to the right, this is called:

   A) Directionality

   B) Return sweep

   C) Top to bottom

   D) Line for line reading

25) Andrew is just starting school, but it looks like he will be successful in reading because:

   A) He comes from a family which cares about his progress.

   B) He is phonemically aware and knows his alphabet.

   C) He has been in pre-school.

   D) He is well behaved.

26) Gracie seems to be struggling with her reading, even in first grade, although her mother works at a publishing firm and her dad is an editor. Her speech is also full of mispronunciations, although her parents were born in the school neighborhood. Gracie should be checked by:

   A) A reading specialist.

   B) A speech therapist or an audiologist

   C) A pediatrician.

   D) A psychologist.

27) Ronald's parents are hearing impaired. He probably will need:

   A) Extensive work with the use of picture cues

   B) Work with songs, rhymes and read alouds to promote phonemic awareness.

   C) No extra work or support.

   D) None of the above.

28) Maria was an outstanding student in her elementary school in Brazil. Now she is nervous about starting fourth grade in the US, although she learned English as a second language in Brazil. She and her parents should be relieved to know that:

   A) She will get extra help in the United States with her English.

   B) There is a positive and strong correlation between a child's native language and his/her learning of English.

   C) Her classmates will help her.

   D) She will have a few months to study for the reading test.

29) Paul is a new teacher. He has just started his logs and assessments for his children's phonemic awareness. He asks a reading teacher to look over his log, but the log is returned to him:

A) Paul gave the log to the wrong colleague.

B) The colleague would not help him out by reviewing it.

C) The log did not have the dates the child's behavior was observed and had no stated performance standards.

D) The log didn't have a cover letter from Paul.

30) **The term graphophenemic awareness refers to:**

A) Handwriting skills.

B) Letter to sound recognition.

C) Alphabetic principle.

D) Phonemic awareness.

31) A stationery store owner in the neighborhood of the school is amused by the fact that the children on a school walk, are rushing up to various store signs and street signs. The children are probably exploring:

A) The alphabetic principle.

B) The principle that print carries meaning.

C) Letter sound recognition.

D) Phonemic awareness.

32) As Ms. Maxwell enters a first grade class, the teacher is busily writing down what the children are saying. The teacher is probably doing this to:

A) Demonstrate how to copy down speech.

B) Make a connection and promote awareness of the relationship between spoken and written language.

C) Authenticate the children's comments.

D) Raise the children's self esteem.

33) A district observer notes that fifth graders are showing younger peers in the third grade how to hold a book and walk around with it, they assume:

A) That the fifth graders are particularly theatrical.

B) That the fifth graders are proud of how they read stories aloud.

C) That the fifth graders are training the younger children in book holding.

D) That this has nothing to do with instruction.

34) Environmental print is available at all of the following except:

A) Within a newspaper.

B) On the page of a library book.

C) On a supermarket circular.

D) In a commercial flyer.

35) Book handling skills include ALL of the following except:

A) Putting a cellophane or plastic cover on a book.

B) Identifying the back cover of the book.

C) Reading the book jacket.

D) Reading dedication page and the title page of the book.

36) The best way for a primary grade teacher to model directionality and one to one word matching would be:

A) Using a regular library or classroom text book.

B) Using her own person reading book.

C) Using a big book.

D) Using a book dummy.

37) As far as the balanced literacy movement is concerned the "WHOLE" is:

A) All the reading themes to be covered that day.

B) The whole class meeting for the mini lesson.

C) The complete unit to be covered over the month.

D) All of the reading and writing work to be done in connection with one book.

38) The "TO, WITH, BY" continuum means:

   A) The teacher works with the children.

   B) The children work Independently.

   C) Everything is led by the teacher and taught to the children.

   D) The teacher first teachers to the children, then works with them and ultimately the children learn by themselves.

39) Factual book features children should learn include:

   A) Captions.

   B) Glossaries.

   C) Diagrams.

   D) All of the above.

40) When they are in 6th grade, children should be able to independently go through an unfamiliar collection and:

   A) Use only the table of contents.

   B) Use the first line indices, and find a poem by author and subject.

   C) Use only the glossary.

   D) None of the above.

41) At a faculty meeting Ms. Riley found out that she might have crisscrossers in her class and that Mr. Brown had them and he was happy about it:

   A) Crisscrossers are students who have skipped a grade.

   B) Crisscrossers are students with excellent skills in reading and in Math.

   C) Crisscrossers are second language learners who have a positive attitude toward first and second language learning.

   D) Crisscrossers are second language learners who are only positive about English Language Learning.

42) Cues in reading are:

   A) Vowel sounds.

   B) Digraphs.

   C) Sources of information used by readers to help them construct meaning.

   D) None of the above.

43) As part of a study for a unit on the history of Massachusetts, Mr. Gentry is using the early childhood book *26 Letters and 99 Cents* by Tina Hoban. He wants his readers to study it and create a more detailed guide to their state using its concept. This is a technique frequently used in:

   A) Reading and writing workshop.

   B) Writing process instruction.

   C) Readers workshop.

   D) Technical writing.

44) A key theorist who supports a phonics centered approach is:

   A) Marie Clay.

   B) Sharon Taberski.

   C) Shelley Harwayne.

   D) Rudolf Flesch.

45) To decode is to:

   A) Construct meaning.

   B) Sound out a printed sequence of letters.

   C) Use a special code to decipher a message.

   D) None of the above.

46) To encode means that you:

   A) Decode a second time.

   B) Construct meaning from a code.

   C) Tell someone a message.

   D) None of the above.

47) There are two basic types of text structure:

   A) Fiction and non-fiction.

   B) Primary and pre-k.

   C) Expository and narrative.

   D) Wordless and text rich.

48) While the supervisor is pleased overall with Barbara's first year of teaching, he feels that given the fact that two of her students are transfers from Mexico and one student has a hearing impairment, she has to plan for:

   A) Extra homework for all of them.

   B) Extra time for the hearing impaired child.

   C) A buddy to work with the two students from Mexico.

   D) Differentiated instruction to meet these students varied special needs.

49) The district is emphasizing that all students in grades 3-6 must focus this month on the reading of functional documents. Ms. Ramirez just smiles and scoops up a handful of free newspapers which she gets on subscription. This is Wednesday and there is a food section. She plans to use:

   A) The main news stories.

   B) The sports pages.

   C) The recipe pages.

   D) The comics.

50) Ms. Ramirez also wants the children to share their functional reading skills with their families, so she asks that they take the newspapers home to focus on the:

   A) Advice columns.

   B) Fill in coupons.

   C) Metropolitan news briefs.

   D) Weather section.

51) Mr. Adams was pleased with Ms. Ramirez's reading lesson, but he realized that she would have visually represented the comparisons she was trying to get the children to make better, if she had used:

   A) a big book.

   B) More expressive language.

   C) A better literary example.

   D) A graphic organizer.

52) Margaret is the winning Ps 123 orator. She loves reciting poetry by Shel Silverstein. Who would guess that she is also a poet in her first language? Margaret's first language is definitely:

   A) English.

   B) French.

   C) Spanish.

   D) NOT English.

53) A teacher is asking children to look at the beginning letters of words. She then asks the child to connect the beginning letter to the text and story and to think about what word would make sense there. This is an example of:

   A) A balanced literacy approach.

   B) A phonemic approach.

   C) A phonic approach.

   D) AN ELL differentiated approach.

54) The teacher is watching the children go from oral speech into writing. The teacher says, "Great job:"

   A) A good decoding.

   B) A good recoding.

   C) A good encoding.

   D) All of the above.

55) By November the first graders have a vocabulary of words which they can correctly pronounce and read aloud. These words are their:

   A) Sight vocabulary.

   B) Recognition vocabulary.

   C) Personal vocabulary.

   D) Working vocabulary.

56) As the child is reading and has made an incorrect attempt, the teacher prompts:

   A) That is a mistake, do it again.

   B) No, you are stupid... why can't you get it?

   C) Does that make sense to you?

   D) Forget it, this is too hard for you.

57) Asking a child if what he or she has read makes sense to him or her, is prompting the child to use:

   A) Phonics cues.

   B) Syntactic cues.

   C) Semantic cues.

   D) Prior knowledge.

58) When you ask a child, if what he or she has just read "sounds right" to him or her, you are trying to get that child to use:

   A) Phonics cues.

   B) Syntactic cues.

   C) Semantic cues.

   D) Prior knowledge.

59) By definition, which children in a classroom will have trouble with syntactic cues?

   A) Those from families who do not have household libraries.

   B) Those not in a top reading group.

   C) Those from ELL backgrounds.

   D) All of the above.

60) "Self correct" in reading means:

   A) The teacher corrects on the record the errors the child makes.

   B) The child goes back and corrects errors made in a running record.

   C) The reading specialist teaches this to the child.

   D) a and b.

61) A natural role for a highly proficient reader would be:

   A) To assist the teacher with cleaning the classroom and organizing the student folders.

   B) To develop charts for the teacher by copying needed poems for full class study.

   C) Tutor and support struggling readers.

   D) Work on his/her own interests while the teacher works with the rest of the class.

62) A theorist who believes that there is a finite body of approved literature children should be taught on various grade levels and has produced books about what everyone needs to know to be literate on various grade levels is:

   A) Rudolf Flesch

   B) J. David Cooper

   C) John Dewey

   D) E. D. Hirsch

63) Children "own" words when all of the following happen except:

   A) They find these words on their own.

   B) The teacher provides a mandated word list.

   C) They use the words in their own writings.

   D) The words appear in literature that interests them.

64) A discussion circle can convene:

   A) After the children have finished reading a text as a group.

   B) Before the children read a text as a group.

   C) While the reading of the text is going on.

   D) All of the above.

65) To promote word study, children can:

   A) Be required to go to the dictionary at least once or twice a day.

   B) Collect and share words of interest they find in their readings.

   C) Do vocabulary work sheets from a basal reader or commercial vocabulary book.

   D) Do all of the above.

66) In order to get children to compile specialized vocabulary, they can use:

   A) Newspapers.

   B) Internet resources and approved web-sites that focus on the special interest.

   C) Experts they can interview.

   D) All of the above.

67) If children are engaged in creating a museum within classroom project to exhibit their work, they are:

   A) Not doing any reading or writing.

   B) Doing many authentic reading, writing, and researching tasks.

   C) Not likely to visit a real museum.

   D) All of the above.

68) Teachers should select at least ___ words for pre-reading vocabulary discussion:

   A) 12.

   B) 15.

   C) 2-3.

   D) 8-10.

69) The teacher should choose words for pre-story discussion and exploration based on:

   A) The teacher's interest.

   B) Whether the teacher feels the children have prior knowledge of or experience with the words.

   C) A pre-existing grade level required vocabulary list.

   D) Words that will impress his or her supervisor.

70) Two steps a teacher might take before selecting words for study are:

   A) Reading the story and story mapping.

   B) Asking advice from a veteran teacher and the grade leader.

   C) Looking in a teacher's guide and copying out the words listed there.

   D) All of the above are correct

71) A teacher discovers after considering his class's prior knowledge of the story material that he would need to teach 12 words at least before he starts teaching the story to the whole group. This indicates:

   A) The children will need a read-aloud.

   B) The children will need independent reading.

   C) The children will need guided reading.

   D) The children will need shared reading.

72) The teacher is very concerned about identifying a book that is "just right" for Jay to read independently. This means that Jay should be able to read this book with:

   A) Below 92% accuracy

   B) 100% accuracy

   C) 95-100% accuracy

   D) 92-97% accuracy

73) Jay really wants to read a book that he can only read with 94% accuracy. He could get to read this book as:

   A) An independent reading.

   B) A guided reading.

   C) A shared reading.

   D) All of the above.

74) When taking a child's running record, the kinds of self corrections the child makes:

   A) Are not important, but the percentage of accuracy is important.

   B) May show something about which cueing systems the child relies on.

   C) Can be meaningful if analyzed over several records.

   D) Both b and c

75) A "decodable text" is:

   A) A text that a child can read aloud with correct pronunciations.

   B) A text that a child can answer comprehension questions about with a high percentage of accuracy.

   C) Text written to match the sequence of letter-sound relationships that have been taught.

   D) None of the above.

76) Once a teacher has carefully recorded and documented a running record:

   A) There is nothing further to do as long as the teacher keeps the running record for conferences and documentation of grades.

   B) The teacher should review the running record and other subsequent ones taken for growth over time.

   C) The teacher should differentiate instruction for that particular student as indicated by growth over time and evidence of other needs.

   D) Both b and c

77) The reliability of a test is measured by:

   A) The number of children who can pass it.

   B) The number of children who fail it.

   C) The degree to which it measures what it is supposed to measure over time.

   D) None of the above

78) A quartile on a test is:

   A) A quarter of the grades grouped.

   B) The division of the percentiles into four segments each of which is called a quartile.

   C) 25 of the tests scored.

   D) b and c

79) Validity in assessment means:

   A) The test went off without any previewing of the questions or leaks on its contents.

   B) The majority of test takers passed.

   C) The correct time was allowed for the children to complete the test.

   D) The test assessed what it was supposed to assess and measure.

80) Vocabulary should be introduced after reading if:

   A) The children have identified words from their reading which were difficult and which they need explained.

   B) The text is appropriate for vocabulary building.

   C) The teacher would like to teach vocabulary after the reading.

   D) a and b

81) The teacher is working on a life science unit in grade five and using many print and electronic sources for information. Some of these words have a linear and some of them a hierarchical relationship to one another. The teacher has spent much time explaining how the words connect with one another. At this point, it would be a good idea to:

   A) Use a root family diagram or tree.

   B) Work with the base words.

   C) Use hierarchical and linear arrays.

   D) Start semantic mapping for a particular concept.

82) **Direct teaching of a concept or strategy means:**

   A) The teacher teaches the concept or strategy as part of a genre lesson.

   B) The teacher teaches the concept as part of the writing workshop.

   C) The teacher explicitly announces to the class that this strategy will be taught.

   D) The teacher teaches the strategy to a small group of children or to an individual child.

83) **The word "bat" is a ___ word for "batter-up":**

   A) Suffix.

   B) Prefix.

   C) Root word.

   D) Inflectional ending.

84) **"Ballgame" is a _____ word. Its meaning is derived from the combination of "Ball" and "Game":**

   A) Contraction.

   B) Compound.

   C) Portmanteau.

   D) Palindrome.

85) **In a balanced literacy classroom, new vocabulary would most likely appear on:**

   A) An experiential chart.

   B) A class newspaper.

   C) The word wall.

   D) Outside the room on a bulletin board.

86) **An effective way to build vocabulary and to make connections with mandated science and mathematics material is to teach Greek and Latin roots using:**

   A) Semantic maps.

   B) Hierarchical arrays.

   C) Linear arrays.

   D) Word webs.

87) **As a parent walked through the first grade floor of her school, she kept hearing repeated clapping. Most likely the children were:**

   A) Clapping to show respect for one another.

   B) Rehearsing for how they would clap at a play.

   C) Clapping out syllables of multi-syllabic words.

   D) All of the above.

88) As part of study about the agricultural products of their state, children have identified 22 different types of apples produced in the state. They can use a _____ to compare and contrast these different types of apples:

   A) Word web.

   B) Semantic map.

   C) Semantic features analysis grid.

   D) All of the above.

89) Based on individual conferences with many children, the teacher realizes that although they are all self-improving readers, they need help in better use of the context to define words. The teacher decided to try the use of:

   A) A dictionary to look up words.

   B) A thesaurus to use with the dictionary.

   C) Contextual redefinition training.

   D) Instruction in how to effectively use a dictionary.

90) The parents of Ramon, a child who has grown up in Puerto Rico and studied English there as a second language, ask that the teacher provide him with individual support in context redefinition. Ramon is scoring above grade level in reading. His mother, who is also a teacher of reading, argues that:

   A) He should get extra help because he has just transferred from another country.

   B) Being walked through the process of using contexts is helpful for an ELL student.

   C) He needs to work with a peer on this skill.

   D) None of the above.

91) A bound morpheme is:

   A) A prefix.

   B) A contraction.

   C) An inflectional ending that can be added to a base word to change its case, gender, number, tense or form.

   D) A root word.

92) A second grader is writing his first book review. He has conferred with his teacher several times while he was writing the book review. Now he is rehearsing it with the teacher before he reads it aloud to the class. The child's learning of how to compose and deliver a book review has been:

   A) Done independently.

   B) Assisted by family support.

   C) Done in a cooperative group setting.

   D) Scaffolded by the teacher.

93) One of the many ways in which a child can demonstrate comprehension of a story is by:

   A) Filling in a strategy sheet.

   B) Retelling the story orally.

   C) Retelling the story in writing.

   D) All of the above.

94) A strategy is:

   A) A practice or routine the teacher can continually refer to.

   B) A practice or routine a child can continually refer to or use.

   C) A sheet or template for a practice the child can continually fill out.

   D) All of the above.

95) The Stop and Think Strategy means that the child reader will:

   A) Read through until the end of the story or text.

   B) Ask himself or herself if what he or she has read makes sense to him or her.

   C) Stop after reading some text and write down his/her concerns.

   D) All of the above.

96) Taking responsibility for a child's own learning, will usually involve the child in:

A) Reading and writing on his/her own.

B) Developing a personal literacy project which will later be shared with the teacher and peers and family.

C) Putting away books and materials when directed.

D) a and b.

97) "Sounds right" can sound wrong to:

A) Any reader who is not a fluent or early reader.

B) AN ELL reader.

C) A struggling reader.

D) None of the above.

98) "Bias" in testing occurs when:

A) The assessment instrument is not an objective, fair and impartial one for a given cultural, ethnic, or special needs participant.

B) The testing administrator is biased.

C) The same test is given with no time considerations or provisions for those in need of more time or those who have handicapping conditions.

D) All of the above.

99) Norm-referenced tests:

A) Give information only about the local samples results.

B) Provide information about the local test takers did compared to a representative sampling of national test takers.

C) Make no comparisons to national test takers.

D) None of the above.

100) If you get your raw score on a test, you will get:

A) The actual number of points you scored on the test.

B) The percentage score of the number of questions you answered correctly.

C) A letter grade for your work on the test.

D) An aggregated score for your performance on the text.

101) The data coordinator of the district who is concerned with federal funding for reading will probably want to start aggregating scores immediately because:

A) It is interesting to crunch more data.

B) By aggregating, the individual scores can be combined to view performance trends across groups.

C) This will help the district determine which groups need more remedial instruction.

D) b and c

102) A standardized test will be:

A) Given out with the same predetermined questions and format to all.

B) Not be given to certain children.

C) If given out in exactly the same format with the same content, may be taken over a lengthier test period (i.e. 4 hours instead of three or two).

D) All of the above.

103) Mr. Mandrake is subbing for Ms. Matley. He sees by the schedule that he is supposed to start the day after the morning meeting with a Read-Aloud. He notes a large picture on the easel and grabs the book just two minutes before the Read-Aloud is to start. He shouldn't heave a sigh of relief because:

A) He needs to be familiar with the book so that he can plan the read-aloud.

B) He does not know if the class has already heard this book.

C) He has not planned vocabulary, themes, or activities to go with the book.

D) All of the above.

104) The science fair is coming up and Ms. Gardner is trying to find time in her busy schedule to work on her class's earth worm diary project. With all of the mandated tests and assemblies, she has not found time to start her students on their earth worm research. Within the context of reading instruction, she can:

A) Begin a thematic study unit.

B) Start with a read aloud of the *Diary of an Earth Worm* by Doreen Cronin.

C) Scaffold the research process by going online with her children using an approved search engine to find matches for earthworm sites.

D) All of the above.

105) Annie's mother has been invited to class to serve as a guest reader. She scoops up her favorite books from her family bookshelf and rushes off to school. When she gets to Annie's classroom, she is greeted and ushered into a rocking chair and given a special hat to wear. The explanation is:

A) The children are excited to have a volunteer and are bored with their teacher day in and day out.

B) This is a class designated author's chair and an author's hat has been worked on by the whole class for anyone who comes to read to them or who reads his/her own writings.

C) Both a and b

D) None of the above.

106) Four of Ms. Wolmark's students have lived in other countries. She is particularly pleased to be studying Sumerian proverbs with them as part of the sixth grade unit in analyzing the sayings of other cultures because:

A) This gives her a break from teaching and the children can share sayings from other cultures they and their families have experienced.

B) This validates the experiences and expertise of ELL learners in her classroom.

C) This provides her children from the US with a lens on other cultural values.

D) All of the above.

107) As Ms. Wolmark looks at the mandated vocabulary curriculum for the 6th grade, she notes that she can opt to teach foreign words and abbreviations which have become part of the English language. She decides:

A) To forego that since she is not a teacher of foreign language.

B) To teach only foreign words from the native language of her four ELL students.

C) To use the ELL students' native languages as a start for an extensive study of foreign language words.

D) To teach 2-3 foreign l language words that are now in English and let it go at that.

108) As Mr. Adams exits his school building, he notices that Mr. Mark, a new teacher, is leading a group of happy looking fifth graders back into the building. They are carrying all kinds of free pamphlets and circulars from a local coffee house. Mr. Adams immediately asks Mr. Mark why the class went to that coffee house during the lunch break. When he hears Mr. Mark's answer, he is delighted:

A) Mr. Mark says they went looking for environmental print and words with a café and latte root.

B) Mr. Mark says they didn't spend any money and got free hot chocolate.

C) The children will have to summarize a pamphlet as homework.

D) All of the above.

109) Mr. Adams has complained to Mr. Mark that there are too many newspapers piled up in his classroom. Mr. Mark has responded that he does not want to throw away these piled up newspapers because:

A) They can be used for letter –sound correspondence.

B) They represent environmental print.

C) They can be used to create print-meaning signs.

D) All of the above.

110) In Ms. Francine's class, dictionary use is a punishment. Mr. Adams is:

A) Pleased with the way that Ms. Francine approaches dictionary use

B) Unconcerned with this approach to the use of the dictionary

C) Convinced that the teacher should model her own fascination and pleasure in using the dictionary for the children.

D) Delighted by the fact that children are being forced to use the dictionary.

111) Dictionary study:

A) can begin in grades 1 or 2.

B) can begin in pre-K using the lush picture dictionaries.

C) should start on grade three level.

D) a and b.

112) An excellent research project that can combine dictionary study with science research would be:

A) A student authored dictionary terms and phrases about earthworms.

B) A teacher developed specialized dictionary of words and phrases about. earthworms.

C) A collection of articles on earthworms put together by the school librarian.

D) b and c.

113) A veteran teacher waited for her adult daughter outside of her daughter's first class in the Teaching of Reading. As she and her daughter talked about the first session of the course, the teacher never heard an explicit mention of the teaching of reading. All she heard about was:

A) Learning about narratives.

B) Dealing with text structures.

C) Constructing meaning.

D) All of the above.

114) Making inferences from the text means that the reader:

A) Is making informed judgments based on available evidence.

B) Is making a guess based on prior experiences.

C) Is making a guess based on what the reader would like to be true of the text.

D) All of the above.

115) Sometimes children can be asked to demonstrate their understanding of a text in a non-written format. This might include all of the following except:

A) A story map.

B) A Venn diagram.

C) Storyboarding a part of the story with dialogue bubbles.

D) Retelling or paraphrasing.

116) A very bright child in a grade one class came from a family which did not a have a strong oral story telling or story reading tradition in its native language. This child would need support in developing:

A) Letter-sound correspondence skills.

B) Schemata for generic concepts most children have in their memories and experiences based on family oral traditions and read a loud.

C) Oral expressiveness.

D) b and c.

117) The concerned parent whose child had a visual impairment wanted as much help for him as the teacher and the school district could give her. She begged: "Please, he didn't attend pre-school, he has no prior knowledge." Strictly speaking this is:

A) Correct, since he didn't get pre-school experiences.

B) Incorrect, since prior knowledge covers everyone's experiences.

C) Incorrect, since he did have prior knowledge experiences but these didn't match those of many of his peers, so he would need to enhance his prior knowledge.

D) b and c

118) Mr. Mark is a brand new teacher who is not from the neighborhood where his school is located. He is a bit nervous as this is his first teaching assignment. He does not yet know how to relax enough to get his students to activate prior experience. He should:

A) Try a free recall question: Tell us what you know about...

B) Try an unstructured Question: Let's talk About...

C) Use word association: What do you associate X with?

D) All of the above.

119) Among the literary strategies that teachers can use to activate prior knowledge are:

A) Predicting and previewing a story.

B) Story mapping.

C) Venn diagramming.

D) Linear arrays.

120) Ms. Angel has to be certain that her fourth graders know the characteristics of the historical fiction genre. She can best support them in becoming comfortable with this genre by:

A) Providing sequel and prequel writing opportunities using that genre.

B) Reading them many different works from that genre.

C) a and b.

D) Having them look up the definition of that genre in a literary encyclopedia.

121) Author's viewpoint questions stump Gary. His teacher can help him by asking him during their reading conferences:

A) If Gary feels the book he is reading, is it just right for him.

B) What the author would say about what the character is doing in the story.

C) How the story can be changed to another genre.

D) If Gary wants to read more books by this author.

122) Ms. Clark is seen by outside observers from her district, seated in front of her class of sixth graders with a notebook in her lap and an easel. She reads aloud from a book and then writes down a series of questions. As she reads along, she sometimes writes down the answers to her own questions. This is most likely:

A) A sign that Ms. Clark is uncertain of her own comprehension capacity.

B) She is modeling self questioning for the children.

C) She is aware that she is being watched and wants to make a good impression.

D) All of the above.

123) Bill has been called up to the teacher for an individual conference. She asks him to retell one of the books he has listed on his weekly log. He begins and is still talking 7 minutes later. Most probably, Bill:

A) Told the entire story with all its details and minor characters.

B) May or may not have really gotten the main points and perspectives of the story.

C) May have really liked the Story.

D) None of the above.

124) Ms. Ancess used to take time to have her children memorize major poems and even had an assembly for parents and school staff where the children dramatically recited various poems. Now that she is worried about the children's reading scores, she doesn't want to waste time with this memorization. Actually if she still includes this high interest, child-centered experience:

A) The children can use their oral fluency and her modeling as a bridge for enhanced comprehension.

B) The children can get a sense of "ownership" of the words.

C) Children and parents will have a "break" from worrying about the test.

D) None of the above.

125) To help children with "main idea" questions, the teacher should:

A) Give out a strategy sheet on the main idea for children to place in their reader's notebooks.

B) Model responding to such a question as part of guided reading.

C) Have children create "main idea questions" to go with their writings.

D) All of the above.

Answer Key

1. C	47. C	93. D
2. C	48. D	94. D
3. C	49. C	95. B
4. A	50. B	96. D
5. B	51. A	97. B
6. C	52. D	98. D
7. B	53. C	99. B
8. B	54. B	100. A
9. C	55. B	101. D
10. D	56. C	102. D
11. D	57. C	103. D
12. B	58. B	104. D
13. C	59. C	105. B
14. D	60. B	106. D
15. C	61. C	107. C
16. B	62. D	108. D
17. C	63. B	109. D
18. B	64. A	110. C
19. D	65. D	111. D
20. C	66. D	112. A
21. B	67. B	113. C
22. C	68. C	114. A
23. C	69. B	115. D
24. B	70. D	116. B
25. B	71. C	117. D
26. B	72. D	118. D
27. B	73. A	119. A
28. B	74. D	120. C
29. C	75. A	121. B
30. C	76. C	122. B
31. B	77. C	123. A
32. B	78. B	124. A
33. C	79. D	125. D
34. B	80. D	
35. A	81. C	
36. C	82. C	
37. B	83. C	
38. D	84. B	
39. D	85. C	
40. B	86. D	
41. C	87. C	
42. C	88. D	
43. A	89. C	
44. D	90. B	
45. B	91. C	
46. B	92. D	

Rationales for Sample Questions

1. This is a sheer memorization question. By definition, phonemic awareness falls under the phonological awareness umbrella. All of the other choices do not deal with the DIFFERENCE between the two types of awareness.

2. Another memorization question which can only be answered by either knowing Adams's theory or by knowing that the other theorists listed did not present that theory. Anywhere from 10-15% of the questions on the certification tests are based on knowledge of the theorists and key terms associated with their theories.

3. This question involves the test taker's knowing that in reading the term "oddity task" involves identification of an odd sound within a series of like sounds. Choice A dealing with mathematics plays on that discipline's definition of odd which would not be tested on a foundations of reading exam. The other choices are "common sense definitions" of oddity which are not appropriate answers for a test in reading.

4. The key word here is EXCEPT which will be highlighted in upper case on the test as well. All of the options are correct aspects of phonological awareness except the first one, A, because phonological awareness DOES NOT involve print.

5. This question requires knowledge of running records and familiarity with error recording and miscues. The test taker has to know that this is the standard format for a running record of reading behaviors and that choices "C" and "D" deal with attitudes and feelings which are not part of the running records used as part of the balanced literacy approach.

6. Choice A is not correct. All children are capable of becoming good readers and the other choices, given Ms. James's dedication, are not the most likely reason these three children (a minority of the class) are struggling.

7. The answer is "B" because all of the other options are essential for record keeping. The key word here is "EXCEPT."

8. The answer is "B" because the teacher does not want the room to appear more spacious, but wants parents to have a feel for the book bags which indicate the primacy of reading.

9. The answer is "C" and this is a memorization question.

10. All the answers are correct.

11. Given the fact this is a kindergarten in a public housing project, she will be most successful with wordless picture books, since there is no guarantee the children have had prior exposure to the other types of books listed. The answer "D" will allow them to construct a story from the pictures.

12. The answer is "B" because the question details that the adults are seated two by two holding copies of the same book. This is the buddy reading style.

13. The answer is "C" and this is a memorization question.

14. The answer is "D", Marie Clay, and this is a name you "have to know" from this guide or your courses.

15. This is a classic manifestation of "C", the logographic phrase of phonics learning.

16. The answer is "B", and again this answer would grow out of teaching experience and familiarity with manipulatives or reading this guide.

17. The answer is "C" because in today's balanced literacy classroom, a wall is a word wall.

18. The answer is "B" and this is a familiar device in today's reading classroom.

19. The answer is "D" and this is a key definition which should be memorized.

20. The answer is "C" by definition; also a teacher would never get into the other personal comments which are offered as choices with a second grader.

21. This is a question that any English literature or Reading major can answer. The answer is "B."

22. This is another question using current terminology. While all the other choices make sense, "C" is correct because a book that is used to teach reading and writing is called an Anchor book.

23. "C" is the only correct answer choice because small refers to group size.

24. The answer is "B" and this term is in the Glossary.

25. This IS a deliberately tricky question. Each of the choices has merit. The best choice is "B" because that one is confirmed by current research.

26. This one is "B" because Gracie is a neighborhood child and shouldn't be having these difficulties with pronunciation.

27. This is one you can work out. The answer is "B" because obviously Ronald's parents will not be singing with him and doing lots of read alouds.

28. All of these choices have an element of truth in them, but go with "B" which reflects research results.

29. The answer is "C" because all logs need to have dates and standards.

30. The answer is "C" and it is a definition question.
If you missed it, re-read through the Glossary.

31. The behavior described here only matches one reading activity, "B."

32. This is another deliberately tricky question. All of the answers may appeal to you, but, choice "B" is the theoretical way to describe what the teacher is doing when he or she writes down what the children are saying.

33. This is a standard part of "book holding", so that the answer is "C."

34. The key word here is "EXCEPT" and environmental print is not defined as print in a library book, so choice "B" is the right one.

35. Ironically "A" is correct because book handling as defined in reading, does not include putting covers on books.

36. Key word in this question is "best" and the answer is "C" because this type of a book is best for teaching and display.

37. This is another deliberately tricky question, since all of the answers make sense, but only "B" is correct because that is the definition of "WHOLE" in balanced literacy.

38. The answer is "D" and is another definition question.

39. The answer is "D." All of the above is the correct answer because captions, glossaries and diagrams are but three of the text features that students need to be able to identify in a text. Other text features include headings, charts, maps, indexes, and tables

40. This is a question, you can reason out. The most complex task described here is "B.".

41. This is a definition question and the answer is "C."

42. This too is a definition question and the answer is "C."

43. The answer is "A." The fact that Mr. Gentry wants his class to use this for both reading and writing, should help you pick the right choice even if you don't know the answer.

44. The answer is "D." Flesch was a proponent of the phonics approach to reading in his book "Why Johnny Can't Read" which was essentially a critique of the American educational system. Neither of the other three choices propose explicit teaching of phonics to help children master reading.

45. The answer is "B" and a definition question.

46. The answer is "B" and is a definition question. If you are missing many definitions, perhaps make flash cards of the Glossary words and study them intensively.

47. The answer is "C," Expository and Narrative. Fiction and non-fiction are genres, Primary and pre-K are grade levels, and Wordless and text rich are types of books for young children.

48. This is a tricky question because all of the choices have an element of truth in them. But the best choice is "D" because it includes the special approaches Barbara will have to take with her ELL and special needs students.

49. Functional literacy refers to knowing things that students have to do on a day to day basis. Reading a recipe is classified as functional literacy because students learn how to read directions to perform a task. The answer is "C."

50. Coupons, like want ads are functional the families can fill in or act on. The answer is "B."

51. The answer is "A" because the BIG BOOK is a good visual display tool, ' .

52. This is a deliberately misleading question; all the test taker can know for certain is that Margaret's first language is NOT English. You know she is an ELL student because the question talks about her "first language." The answer is "D."
53. The focus on letters and sounds is "C" a phonics approach.

54. This is another definition question; read the definition section carefully before the exam. The answer has to be "B."

55. The term is "B" recognition vocabulary. This is a definition you have to know.

56. Obviously, "B" can not be right. Generally, a caring teacher would not say "D," but "C" is the preferred wording in use now in reading classrooms.

57. Semantic cues are the hints that students can discern from the reading to help them make sense of the text. In some cases, the message of the text depends on the other words around them, so students learn how to determine the meaning from context clues. The answer must be "C."

58. This is another one of those answers using the language of linguistics in reading. The answer has to be "B," syntactic clues.

59. This question can actually only have a single correct answer. It is "C" because by definition a child from an ELL background does not have a strong accurate sense of what "sounds right" in English.

60. There is only one correct answer here and it is "B." This is a key principle of the running record.

61. While all of the choices are possibilities, the concept of the highly proficient reader tutoring leads to answer "C."

62. The answer is "D" and this has to be memorized and known.

63. Again the test taker has to find the choice which is incorrect and it is choice "B" when the teacher puts up a mandated word list.

64. By definition, a discussion group can convene only "A" after the children have read a work.

65. All of the answers will promote vocabulary, so the answer is "D."

66. The answer is "D" because all of the responses are correct.

67. There is only one correct answer here and it is logical, "B."

68. The correct answer is "C," 2-3 words. Teachers should select a small number of words for pre-teaching to allow the students time to comprehend the text and achieve the objectives related to the reading. For example, in a non-fiction text, these words could be key terms related to the main topic. Even students with an extensive oral vocabulary may not be able to recognize words in print because they are not words that they normally encounter in their reading. The activities the teacher plans in relation to the words will help the students internalize the strategies more readily when only a few words are selected each time.

69. This is another one where the correct answer is "B" and only "D" is an unlikely choice.

70. This is one you can reason through and choose "D" easily.

71. This is one you can reason through, if you know that generally during READ ALOUD you do not stop to explain many words. You would not want to give material for independent or shared reading where so many words had to be explained. Hence the correct choice is "C," guided reading.

72. The answer is "D" because those are the "just right percentages."

73. The answer by definition is "A" because if "just right." is synonymous with the independent reading level.

74. The answer is "D" and related to taking a child's running record.

75. This is choice "A" which is the definition of decodable.

76. Students learn at different rates, therefore students in any class will be at varying levels of learning. By differentiating instruction and incorporating assessment **for** learning rather than assessment **of** learning, teachers can help students succeed. When teachers assess student growth over time and monitor the areas in which they are experiencing difficulty, they can alter the instruction and the activities to match student needs. The answer is "C."

77. This is a definition question and the answer is "C."

78. While this is also a definition question, choice "B" is one that a linguist would choose.

79. "D" is the answer here and it also makes good sense to the test taker.

80. This is a question the literate test taker should be able to "reason" through. Vocabulary introduced by children and a good text with opportunities to expand vocabulary are needed. Answer "D" which includes both "A" and "B" is the right choice.

81. The astute test taker should get this right whether he or she actually knows these materials or not. "Hierarchical" appears in both the question and in the correct choice "C."

82. The answer is "C" and this is a definition question.

83. The answer is "C."

84. Answer "B."

85. The answer can only be "C" and should be part of the test taker's theoretical background.

86. The answer is "D" and historically these have been used to teach Greek and Latin roots.

87. This is related to phonics and the answer is "C."

88. The answer here is "D" and all of these graphic organizers would work with the topic of apples.

89. The answer is "C" and the trick is to notice the "better use of context" in the question and match it up with "C," contextual redefinition training.

90. The answer is "B" and it is one that is confirmed in theory and is referenced in this guide.

91. The answer is "C," a definition question.

92. This is easy to see that it is "D", scaffolded by the teacher. The child has been assisted by the teacher as he prepared the book review.

93. The answer is "D" since all the options are good ones.

94. The answer is again "D" since all the options work.

95. This is a tricky question and requires that the test taker know the very specific definition of the STOP and THINK strategy to know that the only correct answer is "B."

96. Again this has to do with the way "responsibility for your own learning" is now defined and the answer is "D."

97. This is a truism of ELL education and the answer is "B."

98. This is one where the correct answer of "D" is also the commonsense response that a literate test taker would select.

99. There is only a correct answer here by definition and "B" is it.

100. Again these are all definitions which the test taker should memorize before the test (see the Glossary in this guide). The correct answer is "A."

101. Again this is a definition answer and the correct choice is "D."

102. This is all about what a standardized test means and answer is "D."

103. The answer is "d," but this is a question anyone who has gotten through the coursework or taught, should have no problem with.

104. This is a question someone who has taught or gone through course work should ace to get "D." Remember going online with children and using approved search engines is fine.

105. The best answer is "B" and involves knowing about the "author's chair" concept.

106. This a question where the correct answer "D" makes good common and educational sense.

107. This is a question where you can reason your way to the correct answer, "C." "A" sounds chauvinistic and unrealistic and "B" is limiting and teaching only 2-3 words is not a good use of instructional time.

108. This is a question where the correct choice is "D" and makes good teaching and learning sense.

109. This is a question where choice "D" makes good sense to a teacher who knows the value of having newspapers for class projects.

110. The word "punishment" in the question should alert the test taker to the answer that the only choice "C" can be right.

111. This is a question that any literate test taker who has been in a children's book section recently can answer. Choice "D" is correct.

112. This question is tricky in that only choice "A", which deals with a student product, is correct. The others are all adult centered.

113. The only answer here is "C" which emphasizes "constructing meaning," the current phrase for "reading."

114. This is a definition question that a literate test taker can answer based on the general definition of inferences. The answer is "A."

115. Answer "D" is correct. Retelling and paraphrasing can be in oral form whereas the other choices all involve writing or the use of pencil and paper. By asking students to retell a story, the teacher can determine the level of comprehension. Of course, this has to be modeled for the student, especially paraphrasing, so that the student relates the important facts or events and does not include any information that is not necessary.

116. Although the question appears to be a very technical one, it actually can be easily and correctly answered by seeing how choice "B" echoes the fact that most children would have schemata based on family oral traditions.

117. This is a question which a caring and literate test taker could correctly answer and get "D" as a response. Everyone has prior knowledge of some sort.

118. Again this is a common sense question and "D" is the correct choice.

119. This is a question that a literate test taker could answer and the best choice is "A" because in their predictions, children evidence prior knowledge.

120. The answer is "C. "Online encyclopedias meet the information technology outcomes that align with language arts outcomes. When students are taught to avail of the online encyclopedias, it can save enormous amounts of space in the classroom as well as trips to the library. Students can complete all their work on the computer without having to stop and thumb through a regular encyclopedia to find the information they need.

121. This is a question where the correct choice "B" is the only one that mentions an author.

122. The only answer here is "B" because this is a technique children are taught and Ms. Clark is modeling it. "C" is insulting to Ms. Clark and "A" is insulting as well.

123. The only obvious choice after 7 minutes of talk is "A."

124. Choice "A" is the best theory answer here.

125. This is one where all the options are right. The answer is "D."

TEACHER CERTIFICATION STUDY GUIDE

Constructed Response Questions

Constructed Response Question One

Jean is a first year teacher who is taking over the classroom of a thirty-year veteran teacher who is retiring. Jean goes in to meet with the teacher. The teacher, Ms. Banks, talks about the importance of teaching the young first graders the concepts of print.

She gives Jean a list of these concepts and suggests that Jean create some assessment format so that she can be certain that all of her first graders learn these concepts. She also tells Jean that she will be volunteering her time in a neighborhood preschool program close to her home and so she will be taking her private books and materials with her. She suggests that Jean go over the list of concepts of print and consider the needs of her class as she prepares for teaching this crucial set of skills. Before Jean leaves the classroom, Ms. Banks tells her that the kindergarten teacher has let her know that three children who will be in her class next year are from ELL backgrounds where their families are not involved in oral story telling or reading from native language texts.

Ms. Banks' concepts of print list:

- STARTS ON LEFT
- GOES FROM LEFT TO RIGHT
- RETURN SWEEP
- MATCHES WORDS BY POINTING
- POINTS TO JUST ONE WORD
- POINTS TO FIRST AND LAST WORD
- POINTS TO 1 LETTER
- POINTS TO FIRST AND LAST LETTER
- PARTS of the BOOK: Cover, Title Page, Dedication page, Author and Illustrator

Jean thanks Ms. Banks for all of this help and asks if she can send Ms. Banks some of her teaching ideas for Concepts of Print and the ways she plans to differentiate instruction for her ELL students before the end of the year. Ms. Banks smiles and says she feels good to know that her classroom will be taken over by Jean. She promises to review Jean's response.

Constructed Response Answer One

First, as far as assessment for the key skills of concepts of print, I have decided that it is very important that I have a record of when and how well each of my students masters these concepts. After much thought, I realized that I will be keeping assessment notebooks for all of my students as part of my general reading and teaching. Therefore, I plan to print out all the key concepts of print on an 8" x 11" piece of paper in a grid format. This sheet will be included with other assessment grids for each individual child.

After conferencing with the child and I determine the child has demonstrated mastery of a particular concept, I will check it off on the grid and date that mastery. If I have other comments to make about the child's level of mastery or fluency, I will make an anecdotal notation about the child as well. I think that this will guarantee that I have a detailed checklist record and anecdotal record of all my children's individual progress on concepts of print.

I plan to use big books and many of the latest picture books, including Caldecott award winners in demonstrating and sharing with children many of the concepts of print. I will do much of my instruction mini-lessons. In fact I intend to use some of my own favorite alphabet books to introduce these conventions. With a book like Clare Beaton's, *Zoe and her Zebra*, I can easily and naturally cover the title page, cover, illustrator, and also manage to engage the children in the use of repetitive language.

Once I have shared that delightful book with the children as a read-aloud, we will be able to return to it again and use the repetitive language of it in its big book format to demonstrate for the children how they can point under each word as if there is a button to push. I can also demonstrate for the children how they should start at the top of the text and move from left to right. I will model going back to the left and under the previous line in a return weep.

After modeling this as part of the mini-lesson, the children can be divided in small groups or pairs and take other big book and practice the "point under each word" and the "return sweep" as part of "shared reading" or buddy reading. I should be able to identify some highly proficient readers who will be happy to serve as 'buddy" reader/tutors for the ELL children. I will ask that these "buddies" take time in small groups to work on another book from the alphabet book collection to share with the class as a whole. The use of the alphabet books also helps me to get some time in on the alphabetic principle.

I will also do a classroom writing workshop using the original alphabet book I use for the read-aloud, say *Zoe and Her Zebra* as a model for creating our own story. Perhaps we will call it *Barry and his Boxer*. In this way we will have a concrete literary product that demonstrates the children's mastery of and fluency in the concepts of print as they create an "in style of" story about a peer using illustrations, title page, dedication page, numbering of pages, back and front cover and other concepts of print.

I think that using individualized assessments, a group/class collaborative writing project, and an anchor alphabet book will help me successfully teach the concepts of print and address the needs of my ELL learners as well.

Constructed Response Question Two

Marianne has been selected as one of a team of teachers who will start teaching in a brand new school building that has been under construction for several years. While Marianne, a grade three teacher, is thrilled to be moving into new facilities, she is a bit overwhelmed to have to "set up her room" all over again at the new site. Her administrator, Mr. Adams, tells her that there are five new teachers with no previous experience teaching primary school age children who will be on staff. He tells her that these educators could really use help setting up their classrooms.

Marianne smiles and decides that she would very much like to use her set-up of her own grade three classroom as a workshop and demonstration for setting up a literacy teaching environment for these new staff members. Mr. Adams thinks that is a great idea and asks Marianne for an agenda and for a general description of what she will cover in her three hour workshop so that he can give it to the district office.

Marianne is happy to comply because she realizes that she will be assisting new colleagues and getting ten helping hands to help her set up all the materials she has accumulated over a twenty-year career.

Constructed Response Answer Two

The concept of sharing with new colleagues how to set up a classroom is very exciting to me. I know, based on my experiences, how crucial a well-planned and conceptualized space is for young learners' literacy learning. Therefore this is an agenda for what I will cover in my three hour in service session for my new colleagues.

First, I will discuss how whatever the size of the classroom space, it must be sectioned off into the following areas: a meeting area, with a sofa or "soft" setting; a chair, easel and basket to store book bags; a conference table; children's tables; and bin/basket main area for trade books; and another space for computers.

I may even give out a diagram of my classroom from my old school and some pictures. We will discuss collaboratively how I will set up my own new space as well as how they will want to set up their own spaces to allow for different uses of space within their own classrooms.

I will get into the issue of whether or not they want to have a traditional desk or use smaller tables for everyone. I think that they will need time to consider their own teaching styles in this regard. All teachers need to set up a space where they can easily confer with children and have access to individual assessment notebooks, reading folders (plus poetry/spelling, reading response, and handwriting notebooks) for all their students. I intend to show them how to prepare these folders for each child and how to store them so they can get to them when they need to make additional annotations for each child. Given the fact that I am working with new colleagues, I suspect that this will take at least an hour and a half of our time. I am also going to model for them a weekly reading log.

Most important of all, I am going to spend the major amount of time talking to them about the book bins as I place mine around the classroom. I will show them how to label the books using the Fountas and Pinnell levels and how to arrange the book bins with the spines out so that the children can see the books. Together we will examine how the bookcases should be close to the walls and the expository books should be separated from the narrative texts. I will also get together my audio-cassettes and book sets so that they can see how I set up my read-along center for all my children. I will share some dual language tapes I use with ELL students as well. I have some extra "author's hats" and author's chair slipcovers I will share with them.

I also intend to show them how to select big books for the easel display and anchor books to be shown there as well. By the way, I will also coach them how to write away for supplies and how to store supplies in common areas so that some children are not missing necessary materials for class activities.

Even though we are focusing on literacy, I am going to show them where to store mathematics materials, other texts, and art supplies. I will end the session by making sure that they know where to place their chart wall and the word wall. If I have time, I will sit down with each of them and start them on the word wall and some key charts for their first day. They will leave my room with an actual experience of setting up a literacy environment, plus viable teaching and reading suggestions for the first day. Most importantly, I will be available for an in-school classroom consultation, if necessary.

Tips and Reflections for tackling the Constructed Response Questions:

- Use as many phrases and words from the question as possible in your response.

- Be specific. Mention specific books, authors, theorists, and strategies you have studied. Even though this is a test about the teaching of reading, make specific use of children's trade books and literature if appropriate.

- Use as many details as you are given in the question to make your response. Write no more than 5-7 moderately brief paragraphs. The more you write, the larger the margin for error. Check your spelling, grammar and check to see that you answered everything that was asked, but no more than what was asked. Be positive and proactive about your ability to respond to whichever situation is presented.

- Stick with strategies, teaching ideas, and methods that are tried and true.

- Reread your writing at least twice for spelling and grammatical errors.

Additional Professional Citations

Block, Cathy Collins. (2002). *Comprehension Instruction: Research Based Practices.* New York: The Guilford Press.

Calkins, Lucy McCormick. (2001). *The Art of Teaching Reading.* New York: Longman.

Cambourne, Briane. (2002). "Conditions for Literacy Learning." *The Reading Teacher*, 55, (8): 758-62.

Cambourne, Briane. (1993). *The Whole Story: Natural Learning and the Acquisition of Literacy in the Classroom.* Auckland, NZ: Ashton, Scholastic.

Cunningham, Patricia M. (2000). *Phonics They Use: Words for Reading and Writing.* 3rd Edition. New York: Addison Wesley Longman.

Evidence Based Reading Instruction. (2002) Articles from International Reading Association. Newark, Delaware: *International Reading Association.*

Hoyt, Linda. (2002). *Make it Real-Strategies for Success with Informational Texts.* Portsmouth, NH: Heinemann.

Kimball-Lopez, Kimberley. (1999). *Connecting with Traditional Literature.* Boston: Allyn and Bacon.

Moustafa, Margaret. (1997). *Beyond Traditional Phonics.* Portsmouth, NH: Heinemann.

Owocki, Gretchen. (2003). *Strategic Instructions for K-3 Students.* Portsmouth, NH: Heinemann.

Owacki, G, and Y. Goodman. (2002*). Kidwatching-Documenting Children's Literacy Development.* Portsmouth, NH: Heinemann.

Quindlen, Anna. (1998). *How Reading Changed My Life.* New York: Ballantine Books, 1998.

Routman, Regie. (2000). *Conversations.* Portsmouth, NH: Heinemann.

Schultz, C. (2000). *How Partner Reading Fosters Literacy Development in First Grade Students.* Action Research project, Saginaw Valley State University, University Center, Michigan.

Short, K., J. Harste and C. Burke. (1996). *Creating Classrooms for Authors and Inquirers.* Portsmouth, NH: Heinemann.
Trelease, Jim. (2001). *The Read-Aloud Handbook.* 4th Ed. New York: Penguin.

Wilde, Sandra. (2000). *Miscue Analysis Made Easy: Building on Student Strengths.* Portsmouth, NH: Heinemann.

Wilde, Sandra. (2000). *Reading Made Easy*. Portsmouth, NH: Heinemann.

XAMonline, INC. 21 Orient Ave. Melrose, MA 02176
Toll Free number 800-509-4128
TO ORDER Fax 781-662-9268 OR www.XAMonline.com
NEW MEXICO TEACHER ASSESSMENT - NMTA - 2007

PO# Store/School:

Address 1:

Address 2 (Ship to other):
City, State Zip

Credit card number_____-_____-_____-_____ expiration_____
EMAIL _____
PHONE FAX

13# ISBN 2007	TITLE	Qty	Retail	Total
978-1-58197-750-9	NMTA New Mexico Assessment of Teacher Basic Skills 01		$34.95	
978-1-58197-751-6	NMTA New Mexico Assessment of Teacher Competency 03, 04, 05		$34.95	
978-1-58197-752-3	NMTA Elementary Education 11		$28.95	
978-1-58197-754-7	NMTA Language Arts 12		$59.95	
978-1-58197-760-8	NMTA Reading 13		$59.95	
978-1-58197-755-4	NMTA Mathematics 14		$59.95	
978-1-58197-761-5	NMTA Science 15		$59.95	
978-1-58197-762-2	NMTA History, Geography, Civics, and Government 16		$59.95	
978-1-58197-753-0	NMTA French Sample Test 18		$15.00	
978-1-58197-763-9	NMTA Spanish 20		$59.95	
978-1-58197-764-6	NMTA Visual Arts Sample Test 22		$15.00	
978-1-58197-756-1	NMTA Middle Level Language Arts 23		$59.95	
978-1-58197-757-8	NMTA Middle Level Mathematics 24		$59.95	
978-1-58197-758-5	NMTA Middle Level Science 25		$59.95	
978-1-58197-759-2	NMTA Middle Level Social Studies 26		$59.95	
			SUBTOTAL	
			Ship	$8.25
			TOTAL	

www.ingramcontent.com/pod-product-compliance
Lightning Source LLC
Chambersburg PA
CBHW080537300426
44111CB00017B/2774